TOXIC SPIRITUALITY

"*Anti-Semitism, fundamentalism, triumphalism, and moralism—these are the four horsemen of the church's apocalypse, according to Eric Gritsch. Time and again they pervert the gospel for their own ends, and Gritsch is compelling in his call for honest historical diagnosis and theological cure. He renews your wonder at how powerful the gospel can be in its purity.*"

Jane E. Strohl
Pacific Lutheran Theological Seminary, Berkeley

"*Eric Gritsch provides a guidebook for confronting the seductions of fundamentalism, triumphalism, moralism, and anti-Semitism. Here is a message of hope and encouragement for a church focused on and committed to the essential mission of proclaiming the gospel.*"

Robert G. Moore
Senior Pastor, Christ the King Lutheran Church, Houston

TOXIC SPIRITUALITY

FOUR ENDURING TEMPTATIONS
OF CHRISTIAN FAITH

Eric W. Gritsch

Fortress Press
Minneapolis

For Bonnie

TOXIC SPIRITUALITY
Four Enduring Temptations of Christian Faith

Cover design: Paul Boehnke
Book design: PerfecType, Nashville, TN

Library of Congress Cataloging-in-Publication Data
  Gritsch, Eric W.
    Toxic spirituality : four enduring temptations of Christian faith / Eric W. Gritsch.
        p. cm.
    Includes bibliographical references and index.
    ISBN 978-0-8006-6441-1 (alk. paper)
    1. Religious fanaticism—Christianity. 2. Religious addiction—Christianity. 3. Enthusiasm—Religious aspects—Christianity. I. Title.
    BR114.G75 2009
    230—dc22
                                                    2009012044

The paper used in this publication meets the minimum requirements of American National Standard for Information Sciences — Permanence of Paper for Printed Library Materials, ANSI Z329.48-1984.

Manufactured in the U.S.A.

13 12 11 10 09   2 3 4 5 6 7 8 9 10

*We are dwarfs who stand on the shoulders
of giants. That is why we can see more
and further than they did.*[1]
—John Salisbury, 1159

∽

*Those who do not remember the past
are condemned to repeat it.*[2]
—George Santayana, 1905

∽

*Tradition is the living faith of the dead,
traditionalism is the dead faith of the living.*[3]
—Jaroslav Pelikan, 1984

Contents

Introduction

Religious attitudes, be they Christian or non-Christian, need frequent reality checks because they disclose a tendency to align original teachings with spiritual convenience, or to ignore them altogether. During my half-century as a Lutheran church historian, teacher, and pastor, many Lutherans have told me that they are "justified by faith" in the literal inspiration of the Bible—a far cry from the original teachings of sixteenth-century Lutheranism. Roman Catholics declared that the apostle Peter was the first pope—without a shred of evidence from the first century. Pentecostals insisted that "speaking in tongues" was necessary for salvation—ignoring eight other spiritual gifts of the same, indeed higher, authority (1 Cor 12:8-11). Popular theological assertions range from ecumenical cacophonies to naive, indeed ridiculous, opinions without any link to historical sources. Even formal ecumenical dialogues, teaching events, or interdenominational gatherings have to work hard to align agreements or disagreements with reliable historical evidence. Such work often creates "neuralgia—intensive intermittent pain along the course of a nerve, especially the head and face"[1] of "the body of Christ," the church. It evokes the need for the application of the old adage that "the church must always be reformed" (*ecclesia semper reformanda est*).

Convenience, ignorance, and apathy, especially when combined, are good reasons for temptation among religious zealots who look for new recruits in their crusades to make the world ready for the kingdom of God as they imagine it: a realm of selfish spiritual security embodied in specific doctrines, rules of behavior, and institutional structures. Exciting rhetoric, cunning maneuvers, and attractive strategies are employed to ignore, indeed abandon, the ancient Christian mandate for selfless, suffering discipleship as the penultimate mark of the "gospel," the good news about an ultimate, never-ending future with God in Christ, beyond sin, evil, and death. "Converts" to citizenship in an earthly, triumphant kingdom are victims of an enduring temptation to substitute selfless cruciformity with selfish spiritual security. It is a temptation to be self-righteous, the chief symptom of spiritual poisoning resulting in a toxic spirituality.

The four spiritual toxicities we explore in this volume are essentially idolatry, the violation of the First Commandment of the Decalogue, "You shall have no other gods." It is the original or "inherited sin," the most dangerous poison for humankind, namely, to "be like God," thus able to know good and evil and never die (Gen. 3:4-5). Such high goals are accompanied by the lure of physical, aesthetic, and rational pleasures.

> When the woman saw that the tree was *good for food*, and that it was *a delight to the eyes*, and that the tree was to be desired *to make one wise*, she took of its fruit and ate; and she also gave some to her husband, who was with her, and he ate. (Gen 3:6; italics added)

Legend has it, and Christian paintings show, that the fruit was an apple poisoned with the desire to possess divine power. The Brothers Grimm's fairy tale *Snow White and the Seven Dwarfs* can be told as a counterpart to the biblical story of the Fall, a caveat for children of all ages against self-righteousness embodied in vanity. Vanity leads to deceit and violence (the wicked step-mother). Its target is childlike faith, linked to love and joy (Snow White and the seven dwarfs) and its happy end is a new life beyond death (the wedding to a prince—in the American film version the prince kisses Snow White back to life). Adam and Eve no longer wanted to be creatures but equal partners with the Creator. They desired a quick exchange of temporal earthly life for a timeless, eternal one. Like impatient, egocentric children, they wanted a quick fix, an easy life, to become "wise" as they saw fit. The cunning serpent makes the poison of idolatry very attractive by promising eternal satisfaction through the consumption of a forbidden fruit. The poison is hidden in an apple offered to Snow White by the wicked stepmother. It could also be in attractive mushrooms used for cooking a delicious meal, in mind-altering drugs, or in powerful ideologies promising a secure and easy life.

Yielding to the serpent's temptation confuses divinity and humanity. To be confused is synonymous with being "diabolical" (from the Greek *diaballein*, "to set things apart by throwing them, to confuse"). But God has the last word. "The eyes of both were opened and they knew that they were naked, and they sewed fig leaves together and made loincloths for themselves" (Gen 3:7). Instead of seeing God face to face, they only saw each other, became ashamed, and could stand each other only under a cover of clothes. They ended up "east of Eden" and were forever prevented from returning home, to their garden. A cherubim with a flaming sword enforced the divine mandate (Gen 3:24). God always remains in charge. Great expectations, but only self-deception! Or, as an ancient Roman proverb put it (based on Aesop's Fables from the sixth century B.C.E.), "The mountains were in labor but delivered only a mouse."

The antidote to the poison of original sin is the encounter with the biblical history of salvation, the call for a pilgrimage with God in Christ who promises the only real happy ending through the good news, the Gospel, that sin, evil, and death will be "swallowed up forever" (Isa 25:7; 1 Cor 15:54). Antidotes require stamina and courage; the encounter with the biblical history of salvation is not easy. The Old Testament describes life with God as a difficult journey from slavery to freedom, symbolized by the exodus from captivity in Egypt to a "holy land," and beyond it to a heavenly future with God through a Messiah. The New Testament depicts Christian life as a mean meantime, an interim between the first and second advents of Christ. Christians are people of "the Way" (Acts 24:14), moving to a future "where righteousness is at home" (2 Pet 3:13). They are "strangers and foreigners on earth," a pilgrim people longing for the "city of God" (Heb 11:13, 16).

The poison of idolatry has remained an enduring temptation of Christian faith. Despite the graphic biblical description of the danger of playing God, Christians continue the dangerous game like many of their contemporaries who have become attracted to drugs as means to avoid harsh realities. The spread of toxic spirituality illustrates how hazardous it is to "hand on" (*tradere* in Latin) the gospel in a climate threatened by sin, evil, and death. Church history discloses how the "handing on" becomes a sleight of hand, as it were, a skillful deception of the original "good news": the gospel.

There are four main toxic Christian traditions that above all others— in my opinion—ignore, indeed reject, the biblical view of Christian life as shaped by the sin of idolatry and as an interim between the first and second advent of Christ. They reinterpret the historic structure of Christianity: its beginnings in Israel, the home of Jesus; its authoritative guides, its Scripture and tradition; its relation to the world; and its moral expression. I am listing them as "isms."

1. *Anti-Semitism.* It is the toxic, enduring attitude of "hostility or prejudice against Jews."[2] In the course of history, two issues began to dominate Christian attitudes toward Israel: a theological anti-Judaism and a racist anti-Semitism. Theological anti-Judaism was driven by an ideology claiming that Jews lost their status as God's "chosen people" by rejecting Christ as the Messiah. Consequently, the divine favors were transferred to Christians as the "new Israel." A Christian mission to the Jews tried to convert them and, whenever it failed, became a crusade of contempt. A racist anti-Semitism in the twentieth century secularized the Christian ideology. advocating a myth of a super-race called "Aryans" destined to rid the world of inferior people best embodied by "Semites," identified as Jews. The result was the Holocaust in Germany during World War II.

2. *Fundamentalism.* It is the toxic, enduring attitude toward Scripture and tradition—"a form of Protestant Christianity that upholds belief in the strict and literal interpretation of the Bible, including its narratives, doctrines, prophecies, and moral laws,"[3] and a form of Roman Catholic "traditionalism—the theory that all moral and religious truth comes from divine revelation passed on by tradition, human reason being incapable of attaining it."[4] At stake is the issue of authority derived from the Bible and the Christian tradition. Protestants adopted the ideology of an inerrant, divinely inspired "Scripture." Catholics developed a theory of "apostolic succession" from the apostle Peter to the bishops of Rome. The centerpiece of the theory and its historical realization is an infallible ecclesiastical office, the papacy. Using an alliteration, it can be said that Fundamentalism affirms a combination: either a "pope," representing an infallible office or a biblical "paper pope," representing an infallible book.

3. *Triumphalism.* It is the toxic, enduring attitude of an "excessive exultation over one's success or achievements (used especially in a political context)."[5] At stake is the issue of the relationship between spiritual and secular power. Triumphalism either fuses or separates these powers. A fusion is driven by the attempt to create the heavenly "church triumphant" already on earth as a forerunner of the "kingdom of God" ushered in by Christ at the end of time. The "exultation" evokes a sense of triumph over the struggling "church militant" still mired in evil, sin, and death. This triumph is historically manifested in a theocratic, often violent, dominance of the world, usually in a political fusion of church and state: the medieval combination of imperial and papal power; eighteenth-century Puritan theocracy in New England; the zeal of "Evangelicals" who want to create a "Christian America." Or the triumph is manifested in the reverse, namely, a utopian separation from the world, usually in an abstention from politics, the realm of the" secular," in favor of a concentration on the inner life, the realm of the "spiritual": the monastic isolation of the "desert fathers" (followers of Anthony of Egypt in the fourth century); the "Franciscan spiritualists," addicted to speculations about the end-time (exemplified by Joachim of Fiore and his disciples in the twelfth century); a life in farm communes, without private property, separated from the outside world (exemplified by Hutterites in the sixteenth century); exuberant, charismatic Protestant sectarians (exemplified by Pentecostal churches at the beginning of the twentieth century in the United States).

4. *Moralism.* It is the toxic, enduring attitude in ethics, "the practice of moralizing, especially showing a tendency to make judgments about others' morality."[6] At stake is the issue of absolute moral control, be it by rational or physical means; the medieval Inquisition used both. The spiritual poison is the assumption of knowing divine moral mandates and how they are to be obeyed. Some moralists develop a "moral theology" of unchanging rules for Christian life and impose them by demanding ethical uniformity. In order to achieve and maintain such uniformity, they advocate fear of divine punishment and engage in clever reasoning, resulting in casuistic rules for a confession of sins designed to scare and to dominate believers (exemplified by Roman Catholic canon law and manuals for conducting private, or auricular, confession). Or, moralists do the reverse by developing moral rules for specific situations, trying to

determine a desired ethical action (exemplified by a Protestant situation ethics).

There are other expressions of Christian toxic spirituality, spreading at specific times and related to particular issues (such as racism and sexism). But they all proceed from the cesspool of the four poisons that threaten historic Christianity. Using a biblical paradigm, these toxic traditions could be called the "four horsemen of the Apocalypse" in ecclesiastical history (Rev 6:1-7) that trample through the "vineyard of the Lord" (Matt 20:1) and threaten the followers of the Lamb, but they will encounter the "wrath of the Lamb" (Rev 6:16). They embody prejudice (Anti-Semitism), ignorance (Fundamentalism), violence (Triumphalism), and fear (Moralism).

A scrutinizing Christian hindsight knows that life without sin begins only after the Last Day. "For now we see in a mirror darkly, but then we will see face to face" (1 Cor 13:12). That is why all earthly life is penultimate and offers no final solutions. But faith in the Last Day envisages earthly Christian life as a "triumphant procession" led by Christ, albeit with the smell of death. This procession spreads in every place the fragrance that comes from knowing him. For we are the *aroma of Christ* to God among those who are being saved and among those who are perishing; to the one *a fragrance from death to death*, to the other *a fragrance from life to life*. Who is sufficient for these things? "For we are not peddlers of God's word like so many, but in Christ we speak as persons of sincerity, as persons sent from God and standing in his presence" (2 Cor 2:15-17; italics added).

The two types of fragrance, one smelling of death and the other of life, have spread throughout the history of the church, and their roots can be discerned by critical hindsight.

But the results of sharp critical hindsight rarely, if ever, find their way into pulpits, pews, and Christian education resources. Inherited traditions, no matter how true or fallacious, are communicated for the sake of keeping a convenient status quo that can become as poisonous as the waste dumps that surround the polluted concentrations of human life. Many parishioners are tempted to believe arbitrary interpretations that consign them to an anachronistic pattern of Christian life. Some church members are so afflicted by a toxic spirituality that they defend a stance of status quo and perceive any change as a threat, indeed as a satanic attack, on their faith. As a frustrated pastor put it: "When Christ comes at the end of the world to usher in a 'new heaven and a new earth,' I will hear the seven last words from my parishioners, 'We never did it like this before.'"

The church has a bad record of diagnosing the evil of toxic spirituality. It does not obey well the missionary mandate of Jesus for an evil world: "be wise as serpents and innocent as doves" (Matt 10:16). The image of the serpent has an interesting history. First, it is a symbol of evil, exposing the spiritual megalomania of Adam and Eve, trying to be like God (Gen 3:5). Then, as a bronze serpent, it is a symbol of healing, protecting the people of Israel from poisonous snakes (Num 21:9). Finally, the bronze serpent symbolizes "the son of Man," Jesus, who gives eternal life to all who believe in him (John 3:14). The serpent is also a logo of healing and medicine in classical antiquity and today—a serpent curled around a staff, depicted in statues of the Greek demi-god of healing, Asclepius (c. 420 B.C.E.), the son of Apollo.

Using the medical paradigm of healing, Christians need to live in the world like well-trained physicians, cold-blooded and with a sharp mind, discerning the cunning temptations to be ego-centered rather than Gospel-centered. Since not everyone can become a medical specialist, some are to be called, educated, and employed as "doctors of theology," so to speak, who work against evil and, when necessary, like neurosurgeons, perform delicate theological surgeries to save Christian minds from becoming victims of the power of evil. On the other hand, Christians also must nurture a childlike faith which, like innocent doves, praises God from the rooftops of earthly life. But as any hunter of fowl knows, cooing doves can be shot at close range while making love. That is why serpenthood is needed to stay alert against evil, especially its devastating, terrorist features, as Jesus' missionary mandate warns.

> Brother will betray brother to death, and a father his child, and children will rise against parents and have them put to death, and you will be hated by all because of my name. But the one who endures to the end will be saved. (Matt 10:21-22)

The most important work of healing is diagnosis which, if correct, is followed by a prognosis and treatment. Discerning the poison of sins, be they doctrinal, moral, or institutional, opens up ways of containing, indeed overcoming them. But diagnosis must be scrutinizing and, at times, be secured by a second opinion. An example in an old anecdote:

> A teacher was unable to teach because of fear. He consulted a psychiatrist who, after a lengthy analysis, offered the diagnosis, "You have an inferiority complex that paralyzes you in the classroom. Find another vocation." The teacher was advised by a good friend to get a second opinion. So he went to another psychiatrist who, after a lengthy analysis, offered the diagnosis, "You do not have an inferiority complex. *You are inferior.*" Now the teacher could teach again, though not as well as many others, but well enough to make a living.

Critical Christian hindsight based on the scrutinizing study of church history is relatively young. It began after 1400 years of Christian history with a movement called "Humanism." Humanists became known through their slogan "back to the sources" (*ad fontes*) as the best way to establish sound authority (from the Latin *auctoritas*, "origination"). The Italian humanist Lorenzo Valla (c. 1405–1457) was the pioneer of a literary criticism which exposed revered documents as spurious, like the Apostles' Creed, which originated in the fourth century and thus could not have been composed by the apostles in the first century. Erasmus of Rotterdam (1469–1536) published a Greek text of the New Testament in 1516 based on Valla's numerous proposals for corrections in the sanctioned Latin Bible, the Vulgate. Martin Luther used the Greek text for his famous German translation of the New Testament, the "September Bible" of 1522. The Bible and the records of church history guided his reform movement. In his view, they constituted an antidote to a toxic spirituality that dominated a millennium of Christianity (500-1500). On July 4, 1519, Luther defended his stance in the famous Leipzig Disputation, using historical evidence against abusive ecclesiastical claims of authority.

While sin prevails until the end of time, the power of specific sins in the interim can be detected, diagnosed, and exposed, indeed neutralized, like some poisons in a household. This is the work of church historians who must find ever new means and ways to prevent the spread of toxic Christian teachings. Such work needs to be guided by the wise, serpentine strategy of humanists like Valla: focusing on a critical historical analysis of sources, and showing how they deviated from the core of the Christian tradition, indeed poisoned it, often by clever manipulation, fraudulent revisions of sources, and self-righteous ideologies.

I have followed this strategy. First, I present the historical analysis by way of narrating the trajectories of the four toxic Christian attitudes. Then, I show how they have poisoned the core of the Christian tradition by using it as a means to justify their own ends, the most enduring temptation. Finally, I offer a way of detoxifying, as it were, the four embodiments of toxic spirituality in church history by transfusing the original healthy lifeblood of Christian faith into the infected "body of Christ," the church. For the return to Christian origins, to the "good news" of the Gospel, opens the door to healing and a reform of Christian faith and life.

My study involves the Eastern Orthodox tradition only minimally, especially after the schism of 1054 when eastern and western Christianity went their own ways. Toxic spirituality seems to have found a better home in Roman Catholicism and in Protestantism—although aspects of "triumphalism" can also be discerned in Eastern Orthodoxy.

I deliberately used widely available publications as sources; some of them reflect "party lines," at times with attempts to retain a poisonous status quo. But I also used the best collection of sources and their critical analysis in a few important works available only in German. When published translations were unavailable, I used my own. Biblical quotations are from the New Revised Standard Version.

CHAPTER 1

Anti-Semitism

"The sun has never shown on a more bloodthirsty and vengeful people than they [the Jews] are who imagine that they are God's people."[1]

The term "anti-Semitism" was coined by the German journalist Wilhelm Marr in 1879.[2] In the same year, he also founded "The League of Anti-Semites" (*Antisemiten-Liga*), designed to protect Germany from the alleged threat of Jewish commercialism. This anti-Jewish stance was quickly linked with the racist theory of French philosopher Joseph A. de Gobineau, who distinguished between a strong Nordic race, the Aryans, and a weak race, the Semites.[3] The designation Semite is derived from the name of Noah's son, Shem (Gen 9:19). Aryan is a Sanskrit word meaning "noble." It became a designation for people who populated a large region in the Far East, now India. German National Socialists ("Nazis") and Adolf Hitler linked the Indo-Germanic languages to this mythical race. They defined Aryan as a white, Caucasian super-race, destined to create a new millennial world order. Today, a distinction is made between anti-Semitism (a prejudice against a biological heritage that includes both

Jews and Arabs) and anti-Judaism (a prejudice that specifically targets the Jewish faithful for their beliefs, often based on misunderstandings and false assumptions). Older literature was less careful in making this distinction.[4]

A History of Contempt

Anti-Judaism is as old as Judaism itself.[5] It has peculiar roots in the Hebrew Scriptures, the Christian Old Testament. Rabbinic interpreters blame Judaism itself for its conflict with the non-Jewish world. They see this conflict already foreshadowed in the story of Esau and Jacob (Gen 25:21—35:29).[6] It is a dramatic story whose details could easily become the libretto of an opera filled with intrigue, deceit, and a happy ending. Attention to these details is necessary in order to comprehend the birth pangs of Israel as God's chosen people in the midst of other nations.

The twins represent two nations (Jacob the Jew and Esau the non-Jew) already struggling with each other in the womb of their mother Rebekah (Gen 25:22). She did not want to live with the situation and asked God about for guidance.

> The Lord said to her, "Two nations are in your womb, and two peoples born of you shall be divided; the one shall be stronger than the other, the elder shall serve the younger." (Gen 25:23)

Esau was born first, a hairy man, a skillful hunter, and an outdoorsman. Jacob had smooth skin, was contemplative, and lived in tents. Their father Isaac loved Esau; their mother loved Jacob. The fraternal differences increased when Esau, famished after hard labor in the field, asked his brother Jacob to share a meal consisting of "red stuff" (*adom* in Hebrew for "red," and Esau's later name, Gen 25:30). Jacob agreed, but under the condition that Esau would trade his birthright as the older son for the meal. This transaction discloses the differences as well as the lack of trust between the two brothers.

> Esau said, "I am about to die; of what use is a birthright to me?" Jacob said, "Swear to me first." So he swore to him, and sold his birthright to Jacob. Then Jacob gave Esau bread and lentil stew, and he ate and drank, and rose and went his way. Thus Esau despised his birthright. (Gen 25:32-34)

The moral pressure of the story increases when Rebekah compels Jacob, her favorite son, to pose as Esau after her old and almost blind husband Isaac had asked Esau to prepare a savory last meal before death as the ritual step of blessing the firstborn son. Although Esau hunts for the meal, Rebekah prepares it. She tells Jacob to wear Esau's clothes, and she covers his smooth skin with the skins of a kid so that Isaac would identify him as Esau. When Isaac asks him who he is, Jacob responds that he is Esau. Isaac feels the hairy skin, but wonders why the meal is ready so soon. Jacob shifts his trickery into high gear. He tells his father that the meal was prepared quickly "because the Lord our God granted me success" (Gen 27:20). Isaac is satisfied and blesses Jacob, assuming that he is Esau. Immediately after Jacob leaves his dying father, Esau returns with his meal, asking to be blessed. Isaac admits to having been fooled by Jacob, but cannot give a second blessing to Esau who begged for it. He solemnly utters a prophecy to Esau, who cries out and weeps.

> See, away from the fatness of the earth shall your home be, and away from the dew of heaven on high. By your sword you shall live, and you shall serve your brother; but when you break loose, you shall break his yoke from your neck. (Gen 27:39-40)

Esau vows to kill his brother Jacob (Gen 27:41). When Rebekah hears of the threat, she tells Jacob to hide with members of her family far away. Then she persuades her old husband to bless a marriage between Jacob and one of the daughters of Laban, the brother of Rebekah. Isaac agrees and blesses Jacob as the future leader of Israel (Gen 27:42—28:5). Jacob marries Rachel and Leah, daughters of Laban (Gen 29:1-30) and is told by God in a dream that he was chosen to be the leader of "Israel," a name God gave him. (Gen 35:10). The twins reconcile (Gen 33:1-17). Esau becomes the "father" of the Edomites, and Jacob heads the people of Israel.

Rabbinical interpreters of this complex story of Jacob's immoral behavior (deceiving his father to receive the blessing of the first-born) see this deception as a cause for divine punishment by "other nations." But God is not consistent in dealing with Israel. God "hardens" the heart of Pharaoh (Exod 4:21) to keep the Jews in slavery, but also uses Moses to liberate them for the exodus to the "promised land." Again, God hardens the hearts of Joshua's enemies so that Joshua can utterly destroy them in battle (Josh 11:20). Such mysterious divine logic is woven into the Old Testament asserting the unique power of the God of Israel who controls the destinies of friend and foe. In this sense, anti-Judaism becomes a mystical, seemingly paradoxical device of God's to purify and uplift "the chosen people."

Just as the Jewish god has manipulated the Other Nations to punish his people, so Gentile hatred of Jews is to be understood most fundamentally as a divinely inspired device to prevent Jews from disappearing, from becoming ordinary and blending into Other Nations. The separatism of the Jews and their inability to forget their origins generate Gentile hostility, while that very hostility contributes to a lasting sense among Jews of unalterable separateness and difference from non-Jews. In short, eternal Jewishness and eternal anti-Semitism are somehow in the nature of things, part of a divine plan. Human efforts to mitigate the mutual hostility, seemingly effective in the short run, are in the long run futile.[7]

This mysterious link of Jewishness and anti-Semitism has generated assertions that Jewish suffering and punishment are deserved. As a Jewish chronicler [no name available] of the first Christian crusade put it in 1096, filled with vengeance and guilt: "The fault is ours! . . . Our sins permitted the enemy to triumph; the hand of the Lord weighed heavily upon his people."[8] Some modern Jewish thinkers favor exile, not life in a Promised Land, because Jews should not become like "other nations," corrupted by power. "It became clear to me," wrote Isaac Bashevis Singer, the Polish Jewish writer and Nobel Prize winner in literature in 1978, "that only in exile did Jews grow up spiritually."[9]

Deicide and Blood Libel

The attitudes of "other nations" to Jews in the pre-Christian era disclose reasonable toleration. Neither the Egyptians who enslaved the Israelites, nor the Greeks and Romans who rejected Jewish religion, persecuted Jews for racial reasons. There were occasional outbreaks of violence over religion. In 167 B.C.E., the Jewish leader Mattathias and his son Judas Maccabaeus revolted against the Hellenistic regime of Antiochus Epiphanes, which then permitted the establishment of a Jewish kingdom that lasted for a century until Rome destroyed it (65 B.C.E. to 63 C.E.). During the rule of the Maccabees, named after Judas Maccabaeus, Jews began celebrating their freedom from Hellenism in the annual festival of Hanukkah (which coincides more or less with Christmas). When Alexander the Great (352–323 B.C.E.) ruled the Eastern Mediterranean, Jews were part of the intellectual elite in the city of Alexandria. There were occasional clashes between Roman officials and Jews; but Rome opposed Jewish nationalism, rather than the religion of Israel. Jews in Rome were safe while Roman legions destroyed Jerusalem in 70 C.E. Without a land, Jews became dispersed and their numbers dwindled.

The first Christians were viewed by the Romans as a Jewish sect. But soon this Jewish sect developed a negative attitude toward the Jews. This attitude immediately focused on the Jewish rejection of Jesus as the Messiah. In the Gospel of Matthew, his death is demanded by an angry, bloodthirsty crowd. When Pontius Pilate refused to crucify Jesus, saying, "See to it yourselves," they responded, "His blood be on us and on our children" (Matt 27:25).[10]

The demand for the execution of Jesus and the prophecy about his blood became the two roots for the massive growth of Christian anti-Judaism: the charge of deicide and the "blood libel." Both roots grew out of the soil of irrational contempt. The charge of deicide falsely assumes that Jews knew Jesus as the second person of the Trinity, that is, as God. It is recorded that some passersby mocked Jesus on the cross for claiming to be "the son of God" (Matt 27:40). But it is unlikely that this was said by Jews. The medieval charge known as the "blood libel" communicates the notion that Jews advocate the continual shedding of Christian blood, exemplified by rumors of stealing a consecrated Christian host (the "real presence" of Christ in the Eucharist) and stabbing it with a knife. The continual killing of Jesus as the eucharistic Christ was linked to the equally senseless rumors that Jews killed Christian children as a blood sacrifice. The difference between fact and fiction is illustrated by one of the many reports of Jewish infanticide, appearing in 1235 in Fulda, Germany.[11] A fire in a home killed five young sons while their parents attended Mass on Christmas Eve. The Jews in town were accused of murdering the sons for ritual reasons, siphoning off the blood of the children into waxed bags. An enraged mob murdered thirty-four Jews in revenge. When authorities investigated the report about the Jewish blood libel, they could not produce any evidence in support of the charge of infanticide. Although other such rumors continued to multiply, they could never be supported by facts. But Christian fanaticism continued to demonize the Jews as murderers of God and of Christian children.

In the Gospel of John, Jesus tells the Jews, "You are from your father the devil, and you choose to do your father's desires" (John 8:44). This passage was used to demonize the Jews as part of a "fifth column" of the Antichrist, infiltrating the church to hasten the end of the world by persecuting Christians. The Acts of the Apostles, written by Luke, condemned the Jews for rejecting Jesus as the Messiah: "You stiff-necked people, uncircumcised in heart and ears, you are forever opposing the Holy Spirit, just as your ancestors used to do" (Acts 7:51). Research has shown that some anti-Judaic polemics have been interpolated into the New Testament. The classic example is 1 Thessalonians 2:13-16, where Paul allegedly advocates the "blood libel": The Jews killed Jesus and "they have constantly been filling up the measure of their sins; but God's wrath has overtaken them at last" (v. 16).[12]

Legal Restrictions and Forced Conversions

The legal restriction of Jews began with the Code of Theodosius II in 438 C.E., which established Roman Catholicism as the only legal religion in the Roman Empire. Justinian I (527–565) stripped Jews of their basic rights and encouraged ecclesiastical laws forcing the conversion of Jews. The "church fathers" Chrysostom (c. 345) in the East and St. Augustine (354–430) in the West created the first influential theological rationale for Christian anti-Judaism. Chrysostom (Greek for "golden mouth," referring to his effective preaching) called Jews idol worshippers who kill their enemies. They represent ultimate evil in their killing of Jesus, and they are like obstinate animals who "are fit for killing."[13] Augustine contended that the Jews represented the fratricide of Cain (Gen 4:1-16) in their killing of Jesus, and are punished by being homeless unless they are converted—a rationale for enslavement and expulsion. A decisive reason for the growth of anti-Judaism was the rumor, propagated since the eleventh century in some French, German, and British areas, that Jews plotted physical harm to Christians.

The First Crusade (1095–1096) attracted a variety of anti-Semites, ranging from noblemen who wanted to rid the "Holy Land" of Jews, to pilgrims and bloodthirsty mobs stirred up by itinerant preachers to join the adventure. Characters such as Peter the Hermit and the poor knight Walter the Penniless joined the French aristocrats called by the pope to lead the crusade. When Jerusalem was conquered in 1099, most of its inhabitants were slaughtered.[14] Subsequent crusades disclose little, if anything, humane. Only St. Bernard of Clairvaux (1090–1155) raised his voice against the fanatic crusaders, calling for patience and mercy because Jews were the "forefathers" of Christians.

> Jews must not be persecuted . . . Ask those who know the Sacred Scriptures . . . [They] are for us living words, for they remind us always of the divine passion. They are dispersed into all areas so that, while they suffer the appropriate punishment for such a crime [deicide], they are everywhere the witnesses of our redemption . . . from whom we have our forefathers, and from whom we have Christ of the flesh.[15]

This is an exceptional statement in the midst of a history of contempt for the Jews. Bernard regarded the dispersion of the Jews as the "appropriate" punishment for the crime of deicide, rather than death, as all other medieval Christian voices demanded; he did not call the church "the new Israel" and acknowledged Jews as Christian "forefathers." Thus, he is a mild breeze in contrast to the wild gusts of medieval anti-Judaism.

Church officials ordered Jews to gather for sermons designed for converting them and for refuting the Talmud as a heretical distortion of the Old Testament. The missionary campaign was led by monks and included occasional kidnappings of children for baptism. The well-known Franciscan theologian Duns Scotus (c. 1265–1308), known for his subtle argumentation, defended such actions.

> I believe that it would be a pious deed to coerce the parents themselves with threats and terror to receive baptism and cling to it thereafter. For even though they would not be true believers in their hearts, it would still be less harmful for them to be unable to keep safely their illicit religion than to be able to keep it freely. Their descendants, if properly brought up, would become true believers by the third or fourth generation.[16]

Here, cruelty is disguised in subtlety! Scotus approves the option that "the end justifies the means." Thus, it is better for Jews to be hypocritical Christians (without faith in their hearts) than to be free to exercise their religion. In the end, there would be a new generation of brainwashed Jewish converts ("properly brought up"). This kind of Christian mission reminds one of similar tactics employed by twentieth-century Fascist and Communist dictators. This is a very unsavory lesson of church history.

In Spain, where Jews had become an integrated part of society—indeed, members of the elite—they were ordered to convert. Many did so by public baptism, but secretly remained committed Jews, known as *conversos*, nicknamed *marranos* (a derogatory term meaning "swine," also used in Germany as *Judensau*, "Jewish sow"). The inquisition of the church relentlessly pressured the state to issue "edicts of expulsion." Spain issued one in 1492, resulting in a mass expulsion.[17] Consequently, European Judaism continued to exist only in dispersion or in various ghettos, sometimes tolerated by Islamic authorities. Cruel expulsion and irrational demonizing, linked to fantasies and ethnic myths, made Christian Jew-hatred unique.[18] The church tolerated the scandal of vicious anti-Judaism as a defense of the Christian truth. As Pope Gregory the Great (540–604) put it at the beginning of the Middle Ages: "Though scandal be taken as truth, it is better to permit the scandal than to abandon the truth."[19]

The Theology of Supersessionism

This climate of suspicion, prejudice, and violence dominated the Middle Ages (1100–1500 C.E.) and the sixteenth-century Protestant Reformation. The theological core of medieval anti-Judaism was a "theology of supersession" that taught that God's Old Testament covenant with Israel had been abrogated, or superseded, by a new covenant grounded in Jesus, the head of the Christian Church, the "new Israel." Accordingly, all the divine blessings linked to a glorious future through a Messiah had been transferred to Christians who had accepted Jesus as the Messiah. This view made Jews non-persons within the medieval society in which Christianity was the only acceptable religion. That is why Pope Innocent III decreed at the Twelfth (Fourth Lateran) Ecumenical Council of 1215 that Jews had to wear a visible yellow patch on their clothes in order to be marked as outcasts living in ghettos.[20] Popular preachers propagated the "blood libel," warning their listeners that the Jews continued to kill Jesus by stabbing consecrated hosts with a knife. As a medieval proverb put it, "Jews cannot exist or live without Christian blood."[21] By the thirteenth century, Jews had been thoroughly demonized and dehumanized. The core of Jewish religious literature, the Talmud (a commentary on the Mosaic law, augmented by a collection of rabbinic wisdom), was "Christianized." Fanatic revisionists even claimed that the plural Hebrew word for God, *Elohim,* indicates Jewish belief in the divine Trinity![22] Jews became the scapegoats for every disaster in nature or history, part of the trials and tribulations of the final age of the world. In 1348, Jews were attacked by Christian mobs for causing the Black Death, or plague. Black magic, sorcery, and usury became known as Jewish habits. Anti-Judaic handbooks were published by the church, among them the popular *Hammer against the Jews,* which appeared in Germany in 1513 as a companion to the equally popular *Hammer against Witches,* of 1487.[23]

The Renaissance and Humanism, usually portrayed as tolerant and enlightened movements dedicated to artistic imagination and the study of the past based on reliable sources, continued to see Jews as unwelcome outsiders. Erasmus of Rotterdam, an otherwise tolerant Humanist, viewed hatred of the Jews as proof of genuine Christian faith.[24] Martin Luther (1483–1546) moves from initial toleration to vicious hatred of the Jew—a radical transition! They are blood relatives of Christ, he wrote in 1521, closer to him than are the Christians—"we [Christians] are aliens and in-laws."[25] They should be received cordially in Christian love and be able to do business with Christians—"if some of them should prove stiff-necked, what of it? After all, we ourselves are not all good Christians either."[26]

When, in 1538, Luther heard rumors about Jews trying to convert Christians, he became angry and agreed with the verdict of medieval anti-Judaism that God had abandoned the Jews. He offered a theological conclusion about the intention of God concerning "his people."

Since fifteen hundred years of exile, of which there is no end in sight, nor can there be, do not humble the Jews or bring them to awareness [make them Christians], you may with good conscience despair of them. For it is impossible that God would let his people be without comfort and prophecy so long.[27]

Luther violated his own theological method, namely, not to specu-
late about the "hidden" God. Only the "revealed" God is the subject
of theology. Here Luther's sharp mind became dull because he lost his
temper. So he imposed a logical conclusion on God regarding the fate
of the Jews: God deserted them because they did not convert. To make
it worse, Luther's frustration over Jewish resistance to conversion drove
him to read the worst anti-Jewish slander spread by a Jewish convert,
Anthony Margaritha's *The Whole Jewish Faith (Der Ganze Jüdische
Glaube)*, published in Augsburg in 1530. It was a collection of the worst
items of medieval anti-Judaism. The author had left his prominent Jewish family in 1522 to become a "Lutheran." A leading part in the collection was the story that Jesus was the third child of a Jewish whore
named Mary and a blacksmith without a name. Margaritha's literary
filth provoked Christian and Jewish authorities in Augsburg to have him
jailed and then expelled. It seems unbelievable that a scholar like Luther
would fall for such nonsense, hook, line, and sinker. He even published
his fury in 1543 in the famous treatise, "On the Jews and their Lies."
There, he advocated severe punishment of unrepentant Jews, ranging
from the loss of their possessions to forced labor in camps. "We are at
fault in not slaying them," he fumed.[28] As it turned out, his views were
largely ignored because most Jews had left Germany and public attention had shifted to the religious schism caused by Luther's reform movement. Centuries later, the racist regime of Adolf Hitler used Luther's
treatise in support of its "final solution" of the Jewish problem, the
Holocaust of the Jews.

John Calvin (1509–1564), the most influential reformer of the sixteenth century, viewed Judaism as part of a salvation history that begins
with the Fall in the Old Testament and extends beyond the Bible into a
new era of the people of God. In this sense, the Old Testament is already
a "Christian" book because the Jews are already divinely predestined to
be saved. Thus, he did not write against the Jews, but used Jewish law
as part of a spiritual, "Puritan" foundation for Protestantism in Geneva.
Calvin taught "the harmony of promises of the Law and the Gospel."[29]
"Calvin, and more generally Reformed Protestantism, reacted against
Christian anti-Judaism whose intellectual emptiness they themselves
demonstrated."[30]

Toward the Final Solution

Protestant history after the Reformation discloses some toleration of Judaism, especially in the seventeenth and eighteenth centuries under the influence of the Enlightenment.[31] Some elitist intellectuals became known as "philosemites" because they called for an end to the persecution of the Jews.[32] This trend continued into the nineteenth century, when liberal Protestants focused on the historical Jesus as the defining moment of Christianity. This meant that Judaism and Christianity could no longer be antagonists as they were in medieval anti-Judaism. A host of controversies arose among biblical scholars and church historians in Germany about the quest for the historical Jesus.[33] But although the irrational aspects of medieval anti-Judaism no longer played a role (there is no more talk about Jews as demons and host snatchers), anti-Judaism in general became part of a xenophobia that distinguished between superior and inferior cultures. Western Europeans, especially in Germany, France, and England, viewed Eastern Europeans as "primitive" and in need of civilization. On the other hand, Russian Jews accused Jews in France and Germany of having adapted to non-Jewish ways, thus becoming inferior Jews. German Jews retorted that they spoke the sophisticated language of famous philosophers and poets, such as Immanuel Kant (1724–1804) and Johann Wolfgang Goethe (1749–1832); they considered Yiddish (the dialect of "Eastern Jews"—*Ostjuden*) "as a nasal whining and crippled ghetto jargon."[34]

A combination of Gobineau's vision of the origin of races and Charles Darwin's theory of evolution (in his work *On the Origin of Species*, 1859) created a widespread "scientific racism" as the principal ideological source for a growing global xenophobia. Christian anti-Semitism linked this racism with the biblical account of the world's nations as generations of descendants from Noah's three sons, Shem, Ham, and Japheth (Gen 9:18—10:32): Semites descended from Shem, African Hamites descended from Ham, and the Europeans descended from Japheth. Black Africans were singled out as the most inferior. Geographic distance created peculiar aspects of racism: The Chinese regarded Europeans as descendants of monkeys who never ascended to humanity, Arabs viewed Africans as stuck in animal existence, and Jews were seen as cunning.[35] Since Jews were forced into an itinerant style of life ("the wandering Jew")[36] and could only have liquid assets, they were rumored to be hard-hearted usurers—an accusation also spread by Christian anti-Semites during periods of economic depression and war. Moreover, the myth about the usurious "wandering Jew" was expanded to the myth about the Jew as shirker and war profiteer. After the great depressions caused by the crash of the stockmarkets in 1873 in Europe and in 1929 in the United States, bankrupt businessmen and politicians in Germany began to speak of an international Jewish conspiracy. Positive attitudes toward Jews had become rare. But Philosemitism persisted.[37]

Anti-Semitism blended well with the thriving, irrational racist mania in European society during the decades between the turn of the century and the rise of Russian Bolshevism and German Fascism. International congresses made the critique of Jews part of their agenda. This mania is well illustrated by the appearance of *The Protocols of the Elders of Zion* at the turn of the century, a forgery posing as a report of a secret meeting of Jewish elders in the Jewish cemetery of Prague plotting the take-over of the world.[38] Published in Russia, the unknown author claimed to be in the service of the Tsarist secret police that sought to justify Russian anti-Judaic policies. The publication quickly became an international best seller and part of the agenda of international congresses. German congresses were dominated by *The Protocols*, even though they were proven to be a forgery in 1921 and labeled "ridiculous nonsense" by a Swiss court.

In Germany, the anti-Judaic mania spread like a contagious disease, accompanied by a glorification of Germanic mythology, powerfully expressed in political propaganda and the music of Richard Wagner (1813–1883). Adolf Hitler called his regime the "Third Great German Empire" (*Drittes grossdeutsches Reich*), and predicted that it would last for a millennium and would subject the world to his rule. In fact, it lasted only about twelve years (1933–1945).[39] Satanic Judaism and godless Bolshevik Communism were targeted as the enemies that must be eradicated; they represented the inferior, impure non-Aryan races. Hitler went so far as to adopt the ancient Christian theology of supersessionism as the basis for his racism, dominated by anti-Semitism. "There cannot be two Chosen People," he declared. "We are God's people. Two worlds face one another—the men of God and the men of Satan."[40] Statistically speaking, there was only a ten percent chance that the Jews could dominate

Germany and the world, since only half a million Jews lived among fifty million Germans, and only eleven million in a world population of three hundred million.

When the National Socialists (Nazis) established their regime in 1933, the Roman Catholic Church negotiated a "concordat" that guaranteed mutual nonintervention.[41] Hitler agreed not to draft priests into the armed forces, though Protestant pastors were drafted. Bishops and priests had to obey German laws and abstain from political activities. Bishops had to take an oath of allegiance to the German government, and

> on Sundays and on authorized holidays in all Episcopal [headed by a bishop] as well as parish churches, their associated churches, and in the monastery churches of the German Reich as part of the service, in accordance with the precepts of the church liturgy, *a prayer [was] to be included for the well-being of the German Reich and folk.*[42]

It is one of the ironies of church history that the Roman Catholic Church agreed to offer its spiritual support to the openly racist, anti-Judaic ideology of the Nazis. Politically, the Concordat was a victory for Hitler since it eliminated any notion of resistance against him and his regime. Some Catholic bishops confessed at the end of World War II "that the Concordat had deceived the German Catholics and the whole world."[43] It could also be said that Christians in Germany and Austria (Hitler's native land) had been part of the solid, if not enthusiastic, support for the Nazi movement.

The Concordat made no reference to Jews. German violations of the Concordat, especially in regard to religious freedom, prompted Pope Pius XI in 1937 to issue an encyclical that could be understood as a critique of anti-Semitism. He rejected the myths of race and blood as contrary to revealed truth, and he declared that Christians were "spiritually Semites" as spiritual descendants from Abraham.[44] His successor, Pope Pius XII (1938–1958), hid behind a wall of diplomacy, unable or unwilling to condemn the killing of the Jews. Even when pressured by American and British envoys to the Vatican in 1942 to denounce the Holocaust, the pope continued to be silent about it. When pressured by his advisors, Pius XII did mention the Holocaust in his 1942 Christmas radio address—in twenty-seven words out of twenty-six pages of text—but the Jews were not mentioned.[45] The Holy See also refused to share information about the Holocaust with Catholic resistance movements that were trying to save Jews. The reason for the papal silence, it has sometimes been suggested, might have been fear of a Nazi bombardment of the Vatican. But, since the days of the 1933 Concordat, Vatican policy was explicitly premised on seeking to maintain Catholic privileges for witnessing marriages, recognition of ordained persons, and celebrating sacraments in areas controlled by the Nazis.

The mainline German Protestant churches (Lutheran and Reformed) were divided in their reaction to the Nazi regime. "Cultural Protestantism," combined with patriotism, blinded many church leaders and prevented them from making a clear, critical assessment of the regime. Leaders of a majority formed an alliance with Hitler in 1932, called "German Christians" (*Deutsche Christen*);[46] a minority, led by Martin Niemoeller (a heroic submarine commander in World War I who had become a Lutheran pastor in Berlin) organized an opposition to the regime in 1934 called "the Confessing Church" (*bekennende Kirche*).[47] The "German Christians," led by Bishop Ludwig Müller, supported Hitler's racist anti-Semitism: Jews represent "the danger of racial deterioration and bastardization. . . . Marriage between Germans and Jews is especially to be forbidden."[48] Two famous theologians, Paul Althaus in Erlangen and Emanuel Hirsch in Göttingen, supported the rule of Hitler without, however, affirming racial anti-Semitism. But neither of them opposed the "Aryan Paragraph" in the new Nazi Constitution of 1933, which ordered the dismissal of all "non-Aryan" state employees—including the clergy who served in state churches. Hirsch even contended that Jesus was not Jewish, but Aryan.[49] Only the New Testament scholar Rudolf Bultmann and the theological faculty in Marburg opposed any application of the Aryan Paragraph to the church. The Confessing Church openly opposed the tyranny of Hitler, but was silent regarding the fate of the Jews in its "Barmen Declaration" of 1934.[50] Only one of their theologians, Dietrich Bonhoeffer, denounced Christian anti-Judaism. "An expulsion of the Jews from the west," he declared, "must necessarily bring with it the expulsion of Christ. For Jesus Christ was a Jew."[51] He assisted in the smuggling of Jews to Switzerland in 1941, and he was executed in 1945 for his participation in the 1944 attempt to assassinate Hitler. But, on the whole, most German Protestants either cooperated, or if not, were removed from office or drafted into the armed forces. When the churches were reconstituted in 1945, church leaders issued a statement of guilt and penance, The Stuttgart Declaration of 1945. "We accuse ourselves," the signatories declared, "that we did not witness more courageously, pray more faithfully, believe more joyously, love more ardently."[52]

The large national Lutheran churches in Scandinavia rejected anti-Judaism. In an open Pastoral Letter in 1943, the Danish bishops protested against the planned deportation of the Jews. The people of Denmark saved the Jews from the Holocaust by various means, ranging from masquerading as Jews themselves by wearing the yellow patch on their clothes, to underground transportation to neutral Sweden.[53] The national Lutheran church of Norway, led by Bishop Eivind Berggrav, openly opposed a Nazi puppet government and supported organized armed resistance in 1941. But Hitler did not opt for a Norwegian bloodbath. He once again looked to the east, focusing on his invasion of Russia.[54]

Post-Holocaust Attempts at Reparation

The Holocaust subsequently engendered penance and commitments to oppose any and all ways of anti-Judaism. "We ask all Christians to renounce anti-Semitism," stated a resolution of the Evangelical Church in Germany (EKD) in 1950, "and where it rises anew, to resist it vigorously, and to encounter Jews and Christians in the spirit of brotherhood."[55] The Second Vatican Council composed a lengthy declaration on Jewish-Christian relations: Jews and Christians have a "common spiritual heritage," the church deplores all displays of anti-Judaism, and it strives for better understanding of Judaism. There was a long debate over the continual Roman Catholic tradition of accusing Jews of deicide. In the end, the Council offered a cautious denial.

> Even though the Jewish authorities and those who followed their lead pressed for the death of Jesus, neither all the Jews indiscriminately at the time, nor Jews today, can be charged with crimes committed during the passion [of Jesus]. It is true that the church is the new people of God, yet the Jews should not be spoken of as rejected or accursed *as if this followed from Holy Scripture.*[56]

Pope John XXIII declared that "the Jews will remain most dear to God."[57] But the present pope, Benedict XVI, did not act in a spirit of toleration when he agreed to revive the Latin Mass which, unlike other versions after Vatican II, offers a prayer for the conversion of the Jews in the Good Friday liturgy.

> Let us pray: Almighty and everlasting God, You do not refuse Your mercy even to the Jews; hear the prayers which we offer for *the blindness of that people* so that they may acknowledge the light of your truth, which is in Christ, and *be delivered from their darkness.*[58]

Intensive Jewish and ecumenical protests moved the pope to reformulate the prayer, omitting the reference to Jewish "blindness" in the context of praying for all people to convert to Christ.

Hindsight suggests that Christian attitudes to Jews are characterized by a trajectory of contempt, ranging from demonizing rhetoric to physical persecution. But even after the Holocaust, anti-Judaism is still part of the agenda of some churches and groups. They still teach the "theology of supersessionism," being active in a mission to the Jews. Some Jewish converts to Christianity, organized as "Jews for Jesus," are the most zealous missionaries to the Jews. In 1972, Moshe Rosen, a born Jew who converted at age seventeen to become a Baptist minister, founded the group. According to their mission statement (distributed in pamphlets), they want "to make the messiahship of Jesus an unavoidable issue to our Jewish people worldwide." They try to fulfill their mission in street rallies in many countries around the globe. While their zealous activities are opposed by Jewish organizations, they have some support from mainline churches that desire the conversion of the Jews.

Apostolic Refutation

The contemptible, dangerous historical trajectory of Christian anti-Judaism could have been avoided if the biblical testimony about Judaism had been heard and accepted. Although the New Testament contains anti-Jewish polemics, there is no decisive biblical evidence for any Christian anti-Judaism. Rather, the evidence supports the conclusion that there need not be a Christian mission for the Jews since they are and remain the chosen people of God, even after Christ. The evidence is summarized and persuasively argued by the apostle Paul, the most significant voice of the first Christian generation. Using laser-like logic, he supports his stance by using texts from the Hebrew Scriptures, the only "Bible" that Jesus and his followers would have recognized. When one looks at all the passages cited, one becomes convinced that the detailed biblical evidence is the irrefutable basis for the conclusion that Christian anti-Judaism is a contradiction in terms—an oxymoron.

Paul's life and work are portrayed in the first history of the Christian movement recorded by a Greek convert, Luke, a physician (Col 4:14), in two parts: the events from the birth of Jesus to his ascension (The Gospel According to Luke), and the growth of the Christian mission, focusing on Paul and ending with his stay in Rome (The Acts of the Apostles).

Paul was the son of a Pharisee who spoke Greek and was a Roman citizen. Paul, too, was such a citizen by birth and, named Saul, was educated in Jerusalem to be a Pharisee. Quite zealous, he hunted down Christians and committed them to prison; he approved of the killing of Stephen, the first Christian martyr (Acts 8:1-3). After a sudden conversion on the road to Damascus, Saul became Paul the apostle (Acts 9:1-19, 13:9). Thus the relationship between Judaism and Christianity became quite personal.

When Paul began preaching the gospel in Damascus, the Jewish residents felt betrayed and plotted to kill him; he escaped under the cover of darkness (Acts 9:23-25). Barnabas, a converted Jewish priest, introduced him to the young church in Jerusalem (Acts 9:27) and to its leaders, Peter and James, the latter being one of the brothers of Jesus (Matt 13:55). Paul quickly became involved in lively debates with the Greek residents (called "Hellenists") about the gospel. Soon, they were attempting to kill him (Acts 9:29). Paul escaped and, after some traveling, ended up in Antioch with the largest Christian community other than the one in Jerusalem. There, he and Barnabas were commissioned to undertake a longer missionary journey to Greece (Acts 13:2-3).

After their return to Antioch, some Jewish Christians appeared and told the Gentile Christians, "Unless you are circumcised according to the custom of Moses, you cannot be saved" (Acts 15:1). Luke records that Paul and Barnabas "had no small dissension and debate with them" (Acts 15:2). Paul rejected the requirement of circumcision, though he would encounter it again later in his missionary journeys. He told the Galatians, "In Christ Jesus neither circumcision nor uncircumcision count for anything; the only thing that counts is faith working through love" (Gal 5:6). They were "called to freedom" *from* self-righteousness *to* mutual love, summed up in the single commandment, "You shall love your neighbor as yourself" (Gal 5:13-14). In this sense, "there is no longer Jew or Greek" or any other distinction (Gal 3:28). Here Paul invites the Galatians to focus on the notion of sin. Circumcision had its own value, of course (Rom 3:2). It marks Jews as God's chosen people. But they, like the rest of humankind, did not remain righteous, because righteousness cannot be obtained by law alone; it is obtained by faith. "Both Jews and Greeks are under the power of sin" (Rom 3:9). God reckoned faith, not the works of law, to Abraham as righteousness—before he was circumcised (Rom 4:9-10). He is the prime example of faithfulness.

> The purpose was to make him the ancestor of all who believe without being circumcised and who thus have righteousness reckoned to them, and likewise the ancestor of the circumcised who are not only circumcised but who also follow the example of the faith that our ancestor Abraham had before he was circumcised. (Rom 4:11-12)

After Christ, Paul declared, there is the "circumcision of Christ" in baptism. Through it, one "is dead in trespasses and the uncircumcision of the flesh" and made alive by God who erases the record of unfulfilled legal demands (Col 2:11-14). Paul himself felt free enough in Christ to "become all things to all people" to save some, "a Jew to the Jews and a Gentile to Gentiles" (1 Cor 9:20, 22). He even had Timothy ("my loyal child in the faith," 1 Tim 1:2) circumcised when he took his mission to Jewish towns. Timothy, whose mother had converted from Judaism, was to pose as a Jew "because of the Jews who were in those places" (Acts 16:3).

But Paul's stance created sharp debates between Jewish and Gentile Christians. Christian Jews contended that Gentiles must adopt Jewish customs, such as circumcision. Gentile Christians adopted the theology of supersessionism and argued that Jews had forfeited their divine election through the rejection of the Messiah, Jesus. Consequently, the divine promise of salvation had been transferred to Christians, and Jews must convert in order to be saved.

The Council of Jerusalem

Two decades after the ascension of Christ, the lively young Christian church was threatened by schism. To avoid it, Paul and Barnabas were sent to Jerusalem to discuss the matter with the leaders there, especially the Christian stance regarding Mosaic law. After a brief welcome and a report about the successful Pauline mission to the Gentiles, conservative Jewish Christians in the assembly, identified as members of the sect of the Pharisees, declared: "It is necessary for them [the Gentiles] to be circumcised and ordered to keep the law of Moses" (Acts 15:5). The leaders—the apostles and elders—called a formal meeting to deal with the issue, later known as the first of many church councils, "the Apostles' Council of Jerusalem," in c. 50 C.E. (Acts 15).[59]

Peter spoke first. He reminded his audience that he had been chosen to bring the gospel to the Gentiles and that God gave them the Holy Spirit, just as it had been given to Peter. "In cleansing their hearts by faith he [God] made no distinction between them and us" (Acts 15:9). Peter referred to the spectacular conversion of the Roman military leader, the centurion Cornelius: "The circumcised believers who had come with Peter were astounded that the gift of the Holy Spirit had been poured out even among the Gentiles" (Acts 10:45). "Why are you putting God to the test," Peter asked the hard-line Jewish Christians in the assembly, "by placing on the neck of the disciples a yoke that neither our ancestors nor we have been able to bear?" (Acts 15:10-11). As experts in the Mosaic law, Peter surmised, Pharisees should know that circumcision was only required of infants on the eighth day after their birth (Lev 12:3). Occasional circumcision of adults is reported as a sign of solidarity between feuding families united by marriage (Gen 34:21-24). Such solidarity may have been deemed a sufficient condition for outsiders to live with Jews without a pledge to live like one born Jewish, who had to obey all the laws and rituals. Jewish law required circumcision as the proper initiation into the covenant, but for Jewish Christians the requirement seemed unnecessary. That is why Peter concluded his speech by contrasting faith in the law, i.e., legalism, with faith in spiritual freedom: "On the contrary, we believe that we will be saved through the grace of the Lord Jesus, just as they [the Gentiles] will" (Acts 15:11).

The assembly listened to the reports of Barnabas and Paul about their successful mission to the Gentiles. James responded, praising Peter's joyful experience with the Gentiles whom God has made "a people for his name" (Acts 15:14), and he quoted Scripture in support of a church consisting of both Jews and Gentiles. "It is written, 'I will rebuild the dwelling of David . . . so that all other peoples may seek the Lord—even all the Gentiles over whom my name has been called" (Acts 15:16-17; Isa 45:21; Jer 12:15; Amos 9:11). James concluded with a decision recommended to the council for adoption: "We should not trouble these Gentiles who are turning to God, but we should write to them to *abstain from things polluted by idols and from fornication and from whatever has been strangled and from blood*" (Acts 15:19-20; italics added). The four recommendations are parts of the ancient Law of Moses (the Torah) for the tribes of Israel (Lev 17–18) and for "aliens who reside among them" (Lev 17:13).

James may have intended to remind his listeners of specific laws regarding aliens and strangers. Resident aliens should not be oppressed, but loved because Jews were strangers in Egypt (Exod 23:9; Deut 10:19); "cursed be anyone who deprives the alien, the orphan, and the widow of justice" (Deut 27:19); and "the Lord watches over the strangers" (Ps 146:9). This was a way to define converted Gentiles, as well as the young international Christian church, as being an integral part of the "chosen people" of Israel. James rejected any demand to make the Mosaic law a condition for salvation.[60] But he asked Gentile Christians not to offend Jewish Christians by adopting four abstentions and by showing respect for obvious ethnic differences. They are visible signs that non-Jewish Christians are joined to the ancient covenant with God, "a light to the nations" for the glory of God (Isa 42:6).[61] Although the glory of God is revealed in the Torah, it is fully manifested in Jesus Christ who "is the end of the law so that there may be righteousness for everyone who believes" (Rom 10:4).

The first recommendation—abstention from things contaminated by being sacrificed to idols—deals with the Jewish sacrifice of animals to "goat-demons" outside the camp, defaming the tabernacle of God (Lev 17:3-4, 7). Paul encountered similar sacrifices that Gentiles made to demons (1 Cor 10:19-21). James asked Gentiles to abandon such dangerous rituals to show solidarity with Jewish Christians.

The second recommendation—abstention from fornication—protects the stability of communal life from widespread practices, such as incest, adultery, and bestiality (Lev 18:16-23). This applies also to aliens residing within the Jewish community (Lev 18:26).

The third recommendation—abstention from eating animals that have been strangled, that is, died naturally or having been killed by wild animals (Lev. 17:15)—prohibits the eating of blood. Blood must be properly drained from the carcass; otherwise, in eating the meat, one becomes "unclean" (Lev 22:8).

The fourth recommendation—abstention from eating blood—explains why it is "unclean." Blood signifies life, and drinking it would mean to feed on live bodies. "For the blood is the life, and you shall not eat the life with the meat" (Deut 12:23). Humans are not to be like animals that suck blood from living creatures.

James seems to have chosen these four aspects of Jewish law to make it possible for Jews to feel more comfortable with Gentiles. Obedience to some rules regarding food and sex might make them more welcome as "aliens" in the Jewish communities. James hoped that synagogue attendance by Gentiles (Paul usually took Gentiles there, Acts 13:13-14) might even make them appreciate the Mosaic law more. After all, it "has been read aloud every Sabbath in the synagogues" (Acts 15:21). James disagreed with the Pharisees that the admission of Gentile "aliens" to the Jewish community required the circumcision of male adults. He judged the four recommendations as sufficient. He also could have listed other Mosaic laws shared by the non-Jewish world and contained in the Decalogue, such as the prohibition of murder, theft, and other uncivilized actions. But he opted for a reasonable compromise.

The assembly decided ("with the consent of the whole church," Acts 15:22) to send Judas and Silas along with Paul and Barnabas to Antioch, carrying a letter with the recommendations of James as the decision of the assembly. The letter also addressed the mission of Barnabas and Paul "who have risked their lives for the sake of our Lord Jesus Christ" (Acts 15:26). Then the decision was cited.

> It has seemed good to the Holy Spirit and us to impose on you no further burden than these essentials; that you abstain from what has been sacrificed to idols and from blood and from what is strangled and from fornication. If you keep yourselves from these, you will do well. Farewell. (Acts 15:28-29)

The "essentials" are actually "non-essentials" because they are based on the uncompromising conviction, expressed by Peter, that salvation comes only through the grace of Christ: "We believe that we will be saved through the grace of the Lord Jesus" (Acts 15:11). This is *essential*.

Anything else is *non-essential* for salvation. Consequently, Christians should tolerate, indeed honor, some ethnic religious customs and rituals, as long as they are not viewed as necessary for salvation, be they circumcision or regulations regarding food and sex.

Jews and Christians Together

Paul presented his systematic reflections on the role of Judaism in the history of salvation in his Letter to the Romans (9–11), probably written shortly after the council in Jerusalem in 57 c.e., perhaps in Corinth.[62] Many converted Gentiles had concluded that the Jews' "No" to the gospel also implied God's "No" to the Jews—a view later known as a supersessionism, that is, the notion that all the ancient divine Jewish blessings had been transferred to Christians. That is why Christians no longer viewed Jews as the chosen people of God. They must choose Christ in order to be saved.

Paul begins his reflections with the recognition of the power of evil that is subject to divine judgment. No one can earn salvation from this judgment by trying to appease God through efforts to obey the law. God promises salvation to everyone who has faith, to the Jew first and also to the Greek. This is the "gospel." "For in it the righteousness of God is revealed through faith for faith; as it is written, 'The one who is righteous will live by faith'" [Hab 2:4] (Rom 1:16-17). "Abraham believed God, and it was reckoned to him as righteousness" (Rom 4:2-3). Reliance on laws alone only creates an endless struggle between good and evil.

> I do not understand my own actions. For I do not do what I want, but I do the very thing I hate. Now if I do what I do not want, I agree that the law is good. But in fact it is no longer I that do it, but sin that dwells within me. For I know that nothing good dwells within me, that is, in my flesh. I can will what is right, but I cannot do it. For I do not do the good I want, but the evil I do not want is what I do. . . . Wretched man that I am! Who will rescue me from this body of death? Thanks be to God through Jesus Christ our. Lord! (Rom 7:15-19, 24-25)

Paul regrets that his own people did not extend their faith to Christ as the Messiah and Savior, as he did. He even would be willing to be "cut off from Christ" if thereby his own people would gain salvation (Rom 9:3). They have a long tradition of being the people of God from whom emerged the Messiah, Jesus, "according to the flesh" (Rom 9:4-5). But, Paul argues, they also were not always faithful, be it in their obedience to divine laws or in their attitude to God. The Old Testament testifies that the true Israelites are the descendants of Abraham, Isaac, and Jacob, "the children of the promise," not "the children of the flesh" (Rom 9:8-9). God remains faithful to them, as God assured Moses when he interceded for his stiff-necked people: "I will have mercy on whom I have mercy, and I will have compassion on whom I have compassion" (Exod 33:19; Rom 9:15). The issue, therefore, is not whether the *Israelites have earned God's salvation* by their works of the law, but whether *God remains faithful* to them, be it in wrath or mercy. God is free to choose any people, as Hosea was told: "Those who were not my people I will call my 'my people'" (Rom 9:25; Hos 1:9, 2:23). In short, God "justifies the ungodly" even if they do not do the works of the law (Rom 4:5). As a result, Gentiles attain righteousness through faith, not through the law, as Jews advocate (Rom 9:30-31). The law has become their "stumbling stone"—the notion that zealous obedience of the law would earn righteousness.[63] Righteousness is a gift of God through faith. The prophet Joel linked it to the Last Day, when God calls those chosen to survive for a never-ending future without sin, death, and evil. Christians believe that Christ has already promised such a future; he "is the end of the law so that there may be righteousness for everyone who believes" (Rom 10:4). Jews do not yet have such a faith and continue to rely on the law as the link to a future, the Last Day, when the law is no longer needed. But in the end, "there is no distinction between Jew and Greek; the same Lord is Lord of all and is generous to all who call on him. 'Everyone who calls on the name of the Lord shall be saved'" (Rom 10:12-13, quoting Joel 2:32).

Paul wants the non-Jewish Christians in Rome to know that God has not rejected Israel, even though God "foreknew" that they would become unfaithful, indeed would kill divine prophets and demolish divine altars. They had to be disciplined by Elijah who was told by God to gather a remnant of seven thousand who remained faithful (1 Kgs 19:14, 18; Rom 11:4). Paul sees a remnant also in his own day, different from the Jews to whom "God gave a sluggish spirit, eyes that would not see and ears that would not hear down to this very day" (Isa 6:10; Rom 11:8). David's prophecy is similar when he sang of "darkened eyes and their backs forever bent" (Ps 69:23; Rom 11:9). Paul even offers the theological speculation that through the sins of the Jews, salvation came to the Gentiles.

> So I ask, have they stumbled so as to fall? By no means! But through their stumbling salvation has come to the Gentiles, so as to make Israel jealous. Now if their stumbling means riches for the world, and if their defeat means riches for Gentiles, how much more will their full inclusion mean! (Rom 11:11-12)

Root and Branch

Turning his attention to the Gentiles, Paul tells them that his own mission to them is related to God's way with Israel. Gentile Christians are rooted in the election of Israel. They are not like the branches broken off an olive tree, "a wild olive shoot." On the contrary, they are grafted into it to share the rich root of the olive tree. "Do not boast over the branches," Paul tells the Gentile Christians. "Remember that it is not you that support the root, but the root that supports you" (Rom 11:18). That is why Jews and Gentile Christians belong together.

> Note then the kindness and the severity of God: severity toward those who have fallen, but God's kindness toward you, provided you continue in his kindness; otherwise you will also be cut off. And even those of Israel, if they do not persist in unbelief, will be grafted in, for *God has the power to graft them in again.* For if you have been cut from what is by nature a wild olive tree and grafted, contrary to nature, into a cultivated olive tree, how much more will these natural branches *be grafted back into their own olive tree.* (Rom 11:22-24; italics added)

But how will the "natural branches," the Jews, be "grafted back," that is, become once again the "people of God?" Paul's answer is that it is a "mystery," but with some clues pointing to a conclusion.

> I want you to understand this mystery: *a hardening of heart has come upon the part of Israel, until the full number of the Gentiles has come in.* And so all Israel will be saved; as it is written [Isa 59:20-22], "Out of Zion will come the Deliverer; he will banish

ungodliness from Jacob. And this is my covenant with them, when I take away their sins." As regards to the gospel they are enemies of God for your sake; but as regards election they are beloved, for the sake of their ancestors; for the gifts and the calling of God are irrevocable. Just as *you were once disobedient to God but have now received mercy* because of their disobedience, so they have now been disobedient in order that, *by the mercy shown to you, they too may now receive mercy.* For God has imprisoned all in disobedience so that he may be merciful to all. (Rom. 11:25-32; italics added)

Paul offers some clues or "interconnected elements" that, though controversial, shed some light on the mystery.[64] First, many Jewish hearts have been "hardened" against the covenant that promises delivery from sin; presumably it is God's hardening, just as God hardened the heart of Pharaoh and of everyone he chooses (Exod 4:21; Rom 11:7). Second, the hardening may last until all Gentiles have joined the Jews, as Jewish prophets had proclaimed (Isa 2:3), perhaps even until the end-time. Third, since both Jews and Gentiles have been "imprisoned in disobedience," there is no distinction between them; punishment and salvation are the same for both.

Paul's theological reflections clearly exclude any notion of a "conversion," a "proselytizing," or a "mission to the Jews" as the conditions for Jewish membership in a predominantly Gentile church. As Paul sees it, Gentiles abandon their religion when they accept the gospel (1 Thess 1:9-10), but observant Jews who accept it do not change religions but reconfigure the religion they already have. Together, both groups constitute something new, a new 'people' united by a shared conviction about the Christ-event as God's eschatological act.[65]

These clues enlighten part of the mystery that, however, should be solemnly respected, indeed praised, as "the depth of the riches and wisdom and knowledge of God" whose judgments and ways are "unsearchable" and "inscrutable" (Rom 11:33). Such God-talk—theology—sees the role of Judaism in the history of salvation from the viewpoint of biblical Wisdom theology.[66] Accordingly, God is to be worshiped rather than explained. Paul also employs Greek Stoic rhetoric at the end of his theological reflections, a poetic praise of a mysterious God, a liturgy of reverence, as it were, recalling Jewish prophecy and Greek philosophy.[67]

For who knows the mind of the Lord? Or who has been his counselor? For from him and through him and to him are all things.[68] To him be glory forever. Amen. (Rom 11:34-36)

Paul offers a clear, well evidenced, and persuasive argument for a common bond between Jews and Christians. They are bound together in the history of salvation. There is no need for a "mission to the Jews." They are, and they remain, the chosen people of God. Christians are engrafted in them through Christ, the incarnate will of God. Self-righteousness, attributed to the Jews by Christians, always comes home to roost and contaminates the nest.

From Penance to Justice

The wise counsel of the apostles' assembly in Jerusalem and its strong support through the reflections of the apostle Paul should evoke a powerful repentance among Christians around the world, a true "change of mind" (from the Greek *metanoia*, "conversion")—the mandate of Jesus (Mark 1:15). There must be penance about Christian anti-Judaism, the product of prejudice, slander, and hatred. Like poisonous gas from the chimney of a chemical plant whose owner is unconcerned about ecological damage, anti-Judaism has polluted the faith of Christians throughout centuries of church history. When medieval Christian, dehumanizing, and demonizing anti-Judaism was secularized in Adolf Hitler's cruel, cunning "final solution," the church was finally pushed to do some penance in the face of the dangerous contamination of its heads and members.

The French Jewish scholar Jules Isaac has called the core of Christian anti-Judaism theology the "teaching of contempt."[69] He identifies and analyzes three aspects of this teaching: (1) that the dispersion of the Jews is a punishment for crucifying Jesus; (2) that because of the degenerate state of Judaism at the time of Jesus, Christianity inherits the divine promise of salvation originally made to the Jews—"supersessionism"; and (3) that the Jews committed the crime of deicide. Although much official ecclesiastical penance has been done in varying degrees after World War II and the Holocaust, such anti-Jewish doctrines can still be heard in some Christian quarters as reasons for any arrogant "mission to the Jews." A critical analysis of them, based on scrutinizing hindsight, refutes the three "teachings of contempt," and an exposure of their historical roots eliminates such theological causes. "It is not history that must come to terms with theology; on the contrary, it is theology that must come to terms with history."[70]

Dispersion

Jews were already dispersed before the Common Era, beginning with the continuing destruction of the Jewish kingdoms: the northern kingdom of Israel by the Assyrians in 722 B.C.E., and the southern kingdom of Judah by the Babylonians in 586 B.C.E. On the other hand, Jews were not dispersed when they were punished by the Romans who destroyed their temple in 70 C.E. Again, they were a united, settled community when they began a bloody revolt against Rome in 132 C.E. (the second Judean war) and were defeated by Emperor Hadrian a few years later. A sizable Jewish community lived in Jerusalem during the first Christian crusade in 1099; Crusaders reported that they had trapped many Jews in the synagogue after setting fire to it.[71] The continual dispersion of the Jews began in the Middle Ages and extended into the twentieth century, when arrogant churches and tyrannical rulers tried to rid the world of Jews. To view such dispersion as an action of God is blasphemy.

Critical hindsight also discloses solid evidence that the early Christian tradition regarded dispersion as a way of life. Based on the example of Abraham, first-century Christians "confessed that they were strangers and foreigners on the earth seeking a homeland" (Heb 11:13). Just as Abraham was residing as a stranger and alien in foreign territory, looking for a home (Gen 23:4), so do Christians, longing for the heavenly city that God has prepared for them (Heb 11:16). The Christian "promised land" is a never-ending life with God beginning at the end of time; the Jewish "promised land" is a state in Israel, as modern Zionists have demanded and still defend it as a homeland for dispersed Jews. Thus, the notion of dispersion identifies Christians better than Jews.

Supersessionism

Supersessionism claims that a new divine covenant was established in Christ, replacing the old one because of self-righteous Jewish legalism. What has been called "the charm of supersession" became popular in the middle and late second century when Gentile Christians dominated the church.[72] They saw the replacement of the old covenant with a new one through Jesus in the biblical prophecies about the Messiah, in the prediction of the destruction of the temple, and in the announcement of the trials and tribulations of the end-time (Mark 13:1-8; Heb 10:9). They concluded that the gospel was meant for the Gentiles (Luke 2:32) and they assigned the embarrassing messianic prophecy of a triumphant rule over Israel's enemies to the second coming of Jesus. This view had become official doctrine in the western, medieval Roman Catholic Church. It is again one of the ironies of church history that Roman Catholicism reaffirmed its medieval stance, even during the time of the Holocaust. Pius XII declared, in his Encyclical Letter of June 29, 1943, that the New Testament took the place of the Old Law [Old Testament] that had been abolished.[73] In 1943, Nazi death camps for the Jews were no longer a secret.[74] After the Holocaust, the Second Vatican Council rejected its theology of supersessionism in 1965: "The Church acknowledges that in God's plan of salvation the beginning of her faith and election is to be found in the patriarchs, Moses and the prophets."[75]

It is inaccurate to view Judaism as driven by messianic expectations. Such expectations do not dominate the Jewish theological perspectives. Even in the first two centuries of the Common Era, when messianic speculations flourished, Diaspora Judaism was hardly affected by it. Community patterns focused on the commandments of God, not on messianic expectations; those expectations were generated by Christians who related them to Jesus and his second advent. "Whatever conclusions Christian theologians reached, they assumed that their historical victory gave them the right to define Judaism in Christian terms."[76] The theology of supersessionism has no solid biblical evidence to stand on. It is refuted by the principal apostolic testimony on Jewish-Christian relations, provided by the leaders in Jerusalem, Peter and James (Acts 15) and, above all, by Paul (Rom 9–11). Accordingly, the relationship between the church and Israel is to be viewed in an eschatological context: God "hardened the hearts" of the Jews toward the Christian gospel to make them negative witnesses, as it were, to God's unsearchable ways that will be revealed at the end of time. This is God's "eschatological reservation." The final divine judgment on Christian-Jewish relations is reserved until the endtime. Both church and synagogue are called to tell the world that God, not anyone else, will finish the work of salvation. That is why Christians cannot claim to be the "new Israel" in the sense of having received all the blessings of the "old Israel." According to Paul, the Jews are and remain the people of God, even though they do not accept Jesus Christ as their messiah. Why this is so, only God knows.

Some theological rethinking has been done after the Holocaust.[77] A variety of theologians in the United States issued "A Statement to our Fellow Christians" in 1974. They were assisted by the Commission on Faith and Order of the National Council of Churches and by the Secretariat for Catholic-Jewish Relations of the National Conference of Catholic Bishops. The theologians listed fourteen propositions for study and discussion in Christian communities: 1. The church is rooted in the life of the people of Israel. 2. Christians and Jews depend on each other for mutual enrichment in the light of the western world's far-reaching crisis of values. 3. Faith in Christ does not abrogate the covenant relationship of God with Israel. 4. The quest for Christian unity and the tragic reality of the Holocaust, together with the conflict in the Middle East, make urgent a reconsideration of the relationship between Christians and Jews. 5. The rampant anti-Judaism of the past must be faced with penance in the present. 6. Christian churches must confront the problems associated with the state of Israel, the question of the Palestinians, and the problems of Arabs, especially the refugees in the Middle East. 7–9. Christians must support the state of Israel as a nation that has a moral and legal right to exist as an alternative to dispersion. 10–14. The lessons of history must be used for a ministry of reconciliation and as a guard against the virus of anti-Judaism.[78]

Deicide

The very idea of "killing God," or deicide, is unintelligible to both Christians and Jews who respect history and common sense. Nevertheless, Christians accused Jews of crucifying Jesus and, since he is the second person of the Trinity ("true God from true God"),[79] they killed God. The idea of deicide has been traced to Christian theological speculations about the relationship between the story of the divine command to Abraham to sacrifice his son Isaac (Gen 22:1-19), and the story of the "sacrifice" of the Son of God incarnate in Jesus who was crucified. The "old covenant" between God and Israel is grounded in Abraham's unconditional faith, involving infanticide; and the "new covenant" between God and Christianity is grounded in God's willingness to sacrifice "His Son." Moreover, the new covenant, established in Christ, ends all human sacrifice and makes unconditional faith in Christ the means of salvation from sin. Again, this "teaching of contempt" becomes invalid in the face of critical hindsight. Jewish authorities lacked the political power to execute Jesus. The Roman governor, Pontius Pilate, reluctantly consented to it when an angry Jewish mob agreed to blame themselves for any charges of injustice ("his blood be on us and our children," Matt 27:25). Accordingly, not *all* Jews demanded the execution, and Jesus was known only to a minority of Jews as "the Son of God."

The apostles accused the Jews of having Jesus killed "in ignorance" (Peter, in Acts 3:17). Thus, it was homicide through ignorance rather than premeditated deicide, a charge made popular in the second century when Greek syllogistic speculations invaded the church (the killing of the "Son" implies the killing of the "Father"). They were suppressed by the dogma of the Trinity (defined in the Nicene Creed of 325 C.E.), which calls for doxological praise rather than theological speculation. God is to be praised rather than explained. One can only conclude that, on the basis of historical evidence and normative ecumenical tradition, the crime of deicide and its link to Judaism makes no sense at all. Such claims ignore historical reality and violate common sense. That is why the persistent charge of Jewish deicide in formal Roman Catholic teaching was removed from magisterial doctrine. The Second Vatican Council declared in 1965 that "what happened in His [Christ's] passion cannot be charged against all Jews, without distinction, then alive, nor against the Jews of today . . . The Jews should not be presented as rejected or accursed by God, as if it followed from the Holy Scriptures."[80]

True change of mind, or repentance, involves a thorough historical "reality check"—i.e., viewing things as they really are. From such a perspective, Christian anti-Judaism is an arrogant construction of spiritual superiority based on prejudice and fear, making unconverted Jews the scapegoats for the evils in the world, in the same way that the medieval western church blamed Jews for everything that went wrong. After the Holocaust, there needs to be a sustained Christian-Jewish dialogue about evil.[81]

The Hebrew Scriptures define evil as idolatry, that is, as the most serious violation of the First Commandment of the Decalogue ("I am the Lord your God . . . You shall have no other gods besides me"). This definition appears in the biblical account of the Fall when the serpent tempts Eve "to be like God" (Gen 3:5). Although Christians and Jews may radically disagree on what their faiths affirm, they can unite on what constitutes evil according to the story of the Fall: the desire to be like God. Following the example of the Jewish Christian Paul, they should stop speculating about the reasons, the means, and the timing of each other's salvation from the "original sin" of playing God. Rather, in the mean (and sometimes "mean") time of earthly existence, they should converge in the common task of standing guard against the evil of idolatry—be it in the realms of politics, or morals, or even of religion. Adolf Hitler was neither the first nor the last to view himself as a god who could challenge the Jewish Christian Lord of history. Hitler and his followers created the Holocaust, which has become part of common history. That is the most obvious reason why Christians and Jews must now, more than ever before, share sentry duty against evil, even though they remain divided in their religious affirmations. After all, they share a common obligation for life in a world of sin, evil, and death.

> God has told you, O mortal, what is good; and what does the Lord require of you but to *do justice, and* to love kindness, and to walk humbly with your God. (Mic 6:8; italics added)

> "You shall love the Lord your God with all your heart and with all your soul, and with all your mind." This is the greatest and first commandment. And the second is like it: "You shall love your neighbor as yourself." On these two commandments hang all the law and the prophets. (Matt 22:37-40; italics added)

Detoxing Anti-Judaism

Post-Holocaust theologians admitted that the church had misread Paul for centuries, thus allowing anti-Judaism to contaminate Christian minds.[82] But theological reflection on the relationship between the gospel and Israel has to move beyond Paul and take up the question of Jewish-Christian co-existence. Paul had a vision of Jews and Christians as one community before God at the end of time. But what should this relationship be before the Last Day? Paul lays the theological groundwork for an answer when he speaks of the power of faith.

For we hold that a person is justified by faith apart from works prescribed by the law. Or is God the God of Jews only? Is he not the God of Gentiles also? Yes, of Gentiles also, since God is one; and he will justify the circumcised on the ground of faith and the uncircumcised through that same faith. (Rom 3:28-30)

Since both Jews and Christians are made right with God, or "justified," by the unsearchable and inscrutable ways of divine love, they can work on being right with each other as earthly creatures sharing a common destiny of salvation. Here they can use their minds, or reason, to be as creative as possible without worrying whether or not God approves, for they are liberated from the speculation, doubts, and anxieties of having to please God by what they do, by "works of law." Human reason can be fully employed to develop ways in which faith is active in love of others. Such love is the antidote, as it were, against a toxic spirituality of self-help which, when zealous, spreads the poison of a dangerous egotism and self-righteousness. Seen from this perspective, reason has a greater *ethical* function than a *theological* one—namely, to facilitate the best possible love of neighbor without any speculations about motives and merit. Social ethics discerns and develops the means achieved between different groups bonded by history. Post-Holocaust Jews and Christians know better than anyone else how hard it is to create rules for finding "just," balanced ways for a common life in a penultimate yet still evil world. Ethicists speak of a "golden rule," or an "ethics of reciprocity," summarized in the saying, "Do unto others as you wish to be treated." The rule exists, in one form or another, in all major religions and cultures.

Jews and Christians can accept the religiously neutral notion of justice as "order" through obedience to laws for the common good. These laws facilitate interpersonal communication and a balance of rights as well as a fair distribution of goods, and when the balance is threatened and rights are violated, there must be restitution, including punishment for violations of laws by common consent.

Justice creates the best possible balance for life in a penultimate world. The results of just deeds are the same regardless of religion, culture, or any other differences. Consider the following situation:

> Someone is drowning and is pulled out of the water by three swimmers: a Christian, a Communist, and a Hindu. They proudly proclaim that their religious convictions motivated their good deed. The action was the same, though the confession of faith made it a Christian, a Communist, or a Hindustani deed. "It makes no difference who saved me," said the survivor. "I just wanted to be pulled from the water."

When specific ethical efforts are exhausted, new and different attempts must be made, knowing that final solutions are only possible when all penultimate ways have run their course prior to the Last Day. All attempts should at least include realistic programs for the common good.[83] In a world plagued by myriad ways of injustice, then creative, stubborn, and enduring struggles for justice must become part of life in a world marked by unspeakable crimes against humanity.

Anti-Judaism represents a toxic spirituality in its view and interpretation of the Old Testament. Fear, prejudice, and superstition have overruled clear thinking and critical scholarship. It is incredible how Christian biblical scholars like St. Augustine, Martin Luther, and others could ignore the authority of Scripture represented by the apostle Paul! After all, he, unlike almost anyone else, could have used his conversion to reject his Jewish past. Yet he thought through the problem of Jewish-Christian relations, concluding that one should live with the mystery of God's ways rather than with a syllogistic theology of supersession. Consequently, Paul advocates a reconciled diversity between Jews and Christians as the people of God in Christ on the way to a common future with the spiritual heirs of Abraham, Isaac, and Jacob. A denial of such apostolic wisdom inevitably leads to blasphemy with all its terrorizing consequences.

CHAPTER 2

Fundamentalism

The character of the [Bible's] contents, the unity of its parts, the fulfillment of its prophecies, the miracles wrought in its attestation, the effects it has accomplished in the lives of nations and of men, all these go to show that it is divine, and if so, that it may be believed in what it says about itself.[1]

Bibliolatry is "an excessive adherence to the literal interpretation of the Bible," also known as "Fundamentalism."[2] The term "fundamentalist" was coined in 1920 by a journalist and Baptist layman, Curtis Lee Laws, as a designation for a popular movement based on periodicals entitled *The Fundamentals*. These were published by two natives of Pennsylvania, the brothers Lyman and Milton Stewart, who had made a fortune in oil and were the chief stockholders in the Union Oil Company in Los Angeles and Chicago. They were Presbyterians who lamented the growing laxity in faith and morals. To combat this situation, Milton supported a mission to China; Lyman supported the revivalist Moody Church in Chicago.

The Path of Bibliolatry

Dwight L. Moody (1837–1988), a native of Massachusetts, had been a shoe salesman bent on making money through the stock market. He used a portion of his profits to begin a Sunday school in a neglected area of Chicago. When hundreds of children attended and adults showed interest, Moody founded the Moody Memorial Church and decided to use his money to work as a lay preacher. After the devastating Chicago fire of 1871, he moved to England where he staged successful revival meetings in most of the major cities; he also extended his preaching to the urban centers in Scotland and Ireland. Quite famous by the time he returned to America in 1876, he spent the rest of his life trying to unify disenchanted church members through Bible study at his Bible Institute in Chicago. Enthusiastic students flocked to his meetings in Northfield, Massachusetts, and motivated him to create The Student Volunteer Movement for Mission in 1886, followed by other similar organizations focused on "the evangelization of the world in this generation" (the slogan of the movement).

The Bible Institute in Chicago attracted large numbers of conservative Christians who rejected "secularism"—the invasion of new, scientific ways of interpreting the Bible and of understanding human nature. These new ways of studying the Bible concentrated on a critical literary analysis of the text and on the historical Jesus. When radical foreign (German) liberals such as David F. Strauss declared in his *Life of Jesus* (1835) that the divinity of Jesus was a "myth," American Fundamentalists rallied against the onslaught of modernist fallacies. New ways of understanding human nature were associated with Charles Darwin (1809–1882) and his theory of evolution linking humans to animals (*On the Origins of Species by Means of Natural Selection,* 1859 and *The Descent of Man,* 1871). The plan to unite Christian minds against such liberal teachings through unconditional loyalty to *The Fundamentals* came from a pastor at the Moody Memorial Church in Chicago, Amzi Clarence Dixon. Lyman Stewart gave him $300,000 and persuaded his brother Milton to help finance the project. Dixon established an editorial committee consisting of three clergymen and three laymen who were millenarians; they believed that the final millennium had arrived. The fundamentalist periodicals were to be a unique effort to evangelize the English-speaking world before the end-time. Sixty-four authors were chosen to write articles for the periodical, most of them British and American millenarians.]. Lyman Stewart organized the Testimony Publishing Company. It published ninety articles between 1910 and 1915: twenty-nine defended biblical literalism; thirty-one defended the five "fundamentals" derived from the Bible; and the rest were personal testimonies, attacks on science, and proposals for mission. The five fundamentals constituted a "creed" that had to be unconditionally affirmed: (1) an inerrant Bible, (2) the virgin birth of Jesus, (3) the substitutionary atonement of sins through Jesus, (4) a resurrection with the same body, and (5) the second coming of Jesus. The first "fundamental," an inerrant Bible, is the foundation for the other fundamentals. After World War I, The World's Christian Fundamentals Association was founded in 1919 in Philadelphia, and it remained the key advocate for Fundamentalism over the next decade.

The notion of an inspired, inerrant Bible can be traced to the first Greek Jewish converts, known as "Hellenists."[3] This view became prominent by way of the Hellenistic Jewish philosopher Philo of Alexandria (25 B.C.E.–45 C.E.). Philo contended that the Old Testament authors wrote in a state of "ecstasy" (from the Greek *ekstasis,* "standing outside"). Significant ancient Christian writers adopted this view, imagining that biblical authors heard divine messages, indeed single words, transmitted by the Holy Spirit and accompanied by flute-like tunes. The influential theologian Irenaeus (c. 130–200) spoke of a "dictation"; the famous Greek Bible scholar Origen (185–254) regarded the Bible inspired as a whole. But Origen no longer thought that inspiration occurred through ecstasy but through concentrated listening to what the Holy Spirit revealed in the text. Eventually, a distinction was made between "verbal" (word for word) and "plenary" (as a whole) inspiration. This latter view of biblical inspiration soon raised the question of to what extent Christian doctrine and life should be judged by the inspired Bible as "the Word of God." The medieval, western (Roman Catholic) church taught that whatever was handed on in history—i.e., tradition—should not go beyond the written Word of God. The most influential medieval theologian, Thomas Aquinas (1225–1274), asserted that even though the Bible can be interpreted in several ways, the literal meaning prevails. "All meanings are based on one sense, namely the literal sense."[4] But as long as there were no major controversies, the distinction between the authority of the Bible and the authority of the church remained fluid.

The Reformation Turn

The Protestant Reformation of the sixteenth century, initiated by Martin Luther, criticized specific required ecclesiastical practices as violations of biblical authority. The most debated issue was the sale of "indulgences," that is, the selling of promissory notes offering salvation without a confession of sins. Luther attacked this abuse in his famous Ninety-Five Theses of 1517. The first thesis states that according to the Bible, Christ "willed the entire life of the believer to be one of repentance" (Matt 4:17).[5] But Luther did not identify the Bible with the Word of God. If this were done, Luther contended, then the Word of God would be just written law, not gospel. Both must be carefully distinguished. The power of the gospel is sensed best in "live" communication.

> The gospel should really be not something written, but a spoken word which brought forth the Scriptures, as Christ and the apostles have done. This is why Christ himself did not write anything but only spoke. He called his teaching not Scripture but gospel, meaning good news or proclamation that is spread by word of mouth.[6]

This view is a wedge against bibliolatry, even though some Lutherans and Protestants used the Reformation slogan "Scripture alone" (*sola scriptura*) to defend the inerrancy of the Bible. When second-generation Lutherans advocated "pure doctrine" over against impure teaching, they turned fundamentalist.[7] They used two of the classic fundamentalist proof texts: "All Scripture is inspired by God and is useful for teaching, for reproof, for correction, and for training in righteousness" (2 Tim 3:16). "No prophecy ever came by human will, but men and women moved by the Holy Spirit spoke from God" (2 Pet 1:21). The Lutheran theologian Abraham Calov (1612–1686) called the biblical authors "secretaries" of God (in Latin, *amanuenses*). They and their readers must accept the inerrant Bible "by faith alone" (*sola fide*), even if it meant an offense to the intellect. "If our mind and intellect are to be taken captive in obedience to faith, then it is necessary for us to believe even if we cannot assent with our mind, nay, even if we are persuaded in our mind that what we believe is false."

Moreover, the Bible does not contradict itself nor does it agree with history, geography, or science in general. When Matthew 27:9-10 quotes

Zechariah 11:12-13 as a quote from Jeremiah, "nothing is said in the text about Jeremiah's writing. And so what Jeremiah said, his disciple Zechariah wrote." The Bible's description of the moon as a great light (Gen 1:16) is God's way of accounting for the human views of it; God created the moon as it actually is. Desperate Lutheran apologists introduced a "doctrine of condescension": God adjusted the Bible to the speech and style of uneducated people, "as when it calls Joseph the father of Christ because this was what was thought by common people, or when it says that stars fell from heaven because uninformed people think comets are stars." It is amazing how these sophisticated German theologians depicted God as so condescending that he adjusts the verbal inspiration of the Bible to ignorant and uneducated people!

Millenarianism

British and American Fundamentalists combined biblical inerrancy with a strong revival of biblical millenarian hope during the late eighteenth and nineteenth centuries. Viewing the Bible as the literally inspired record of prophesies about the future, revival preachers offered historical speculations about the end of the world and advocated a drive for "holiness" as a condition for avoiding the trials and tribulations prophesied in Matthew 24–25. These end-time speculations also generated great interest in a worldwide Protestant mission to Roman Catholics and Jews. The rationale for such a mission was quite polemical: Catholics had betrayed Jesus through the papacy, and Jews had rejected Jesus as the Messiah. Needless to say, the mission hardly got off the ground since its two targets, Catholics and Jews, rejected such efforts as arrogant and self-righteous.

The most radical representative of millenarian revivalism was the Scottish preacher Edward Irving (1792–1834), who established his own congregations with members from all levels of society. Periodicals such as *The Morning Watch* and *The Christian Herald* created a fervent millenarian climate, marked by people "speaking in tongues" (1 Cor 12:10). After Irving's death, the Irish Anglican priest John N. Darby (1800–1882) founded the Plymouth Brethren as a millenarian movement loyal to what they perceived as the unchanging truth of the Bible. Darby taught the "secret rapture" of true believers from this life to the next; the rapture would be sudden and secret, based on the biblical saying, "Then two will be in the field; one will be taken and one will be left. Two women will be grinding meal together; one will be taken and one will be left" (Matt 24:40-41). The rapture would affect a special, chosen group (i.e., disciples of Irving) who would escape the trials and tribulations of the world near the end-time—a kind of "eschatological elite" with the special privilege of avoiding the persecution foretold by verbal inspiration (Matt 24:9-14).

Advocates of millenarianism and defenders of biblical inerrancy organized large Bible study conferences in Chicago, St. Louis, and Philadelphia. From 1882 until 1897, these conferences, lasting one or two weeks, were held during the summer at Niagara-On-the-Lake, Ontario. The summer meeting was known as The Niagara Conference. About 120 leaders directed the meetings. A "Niagara Creed" had been published in 1878 by leaders who later attended The Niagara Conference;[8] it became quite popular during and after the millenarian meetings. Fourteen articles summarized the millenarian views. Article One declared that the entire Bible is inspired by the Holy Spirit "to the smallest word and inflection of a word, provided that such a word is found in the original manuscripts." Article Fourteen asserted that the present age is marked by apostasy, and that "the Lord Jesus will come in person to introduce the millennial age, when Israel will be restored to her own land, and the earth shall be full of the knowledge of the Lord."

British millenarian speculations and the American dream were blended into the notion that America was destined to experience the final millennium. William Miller, a millenarian Baptist from Vermont, predicted the millennium for the year 1843. He had arrived at this conclusion on the basis of calculations deduced from Daniel 8–9. Anglican archbishop James Ussher had used the King James Version of the Bible to devise a day-equals-year analogy, from which he then deduced the date of 457 B.C.E. for the events predicted in Daniel 9. Accordingly, Miller calculated that Christ's second coming would occur in Vermont in 1843: the seventy weeks in Daniel 9:24 added up to 33 C.E., the year of Christ's death; and the 2300 years of Daniel 8:14 added up to 1843. This millenarian scheme was propagated through sermons, meetings, and the hymnal, *The Millennial Harp*. When the end did not come, the Millerites established an "adventist church," headquartered since 1855 in Battle Creek, and called themselves The Seventh-Day Adventists. Massive financial support came in 1868 from John H. Kellogg, the king of breakfast cereals.

Millenarianism flourished in the new American urban centers of New York, Boston, Chicago, and St. Louis. A monthly periodical, *Prophetic Times*, was edited by Lutheran, Episcopalian, Dutch Reformed, and Baptist theologians. The movement became quite popular with the publication of *The Scofield Reference Bible* in 1909 (amplified and amended in 1919). It was the King James Version with commentaries composed by Cyrus Ingerson Scofield, a Confederate Civil War veteran and lawyer from Dallas, Texas, where he had organized a correspondence school for studying the Bible. Scofield identified seven ages, or "dispensations," in the Bible: (1) The age of innocence, being the covenant between God and Adam in the garden; (2) the age of conscience, being the covenant between God and Adam after the Fall; (3) the age of human government, being the covenant between God and Noah after the Flood; (4) the age of promise, being the covenant between God and Abraham in which Israel was chosen; (5) the age of the law, being the covenant between God and Moses, ending with the crucifixion of Jesus by Jews and Gentiles; (6) the age of grace, being the covenant in and through Jesus for humankind until the second coming of Christ; and (7) the age of the fullness of time, being the millennium of Christ.

Pentecostalism

Millenarians perceived the Civil War and World War I as the principal trials and tribulations before the end-time predicted by the Bible (Matt 24:3-8). But they also continued to stress the need for "conversion" to become "holy." Methodism, founded by John Wesley, defined Christian discipline as guided by "justification" through the atonement of Christ and by "sanctification" through the gift of the Holy Spirit. Wesley himself spoke of "perfection" as "purity of intention,"[9] and as "having the mind of Christ" (Phil 2:5). Although a residue of sin remains, there is a growth in grace that affects human motives and desires to become "perfect" in the end. Wesley envisaged a special role for Methodists in the history of salvation. There is a "grand disposition which God has lodged with the people called Methodists."[10] Methodist "holiness camp meetings" and the periodical *Banner of Holiness* flooded the cities in the North and the farms in the South, denouncing institutional Christianity as a breeding ground for sinful worldliness. "Holiness associations" created a "come-outism" movement that would provide the link to the final millennium. In 1894, dissident revivalists were ousted by The General Conference of the Methodist Episcopal Church. But the dissidents viewed the clash with church authorities as a sign that Methodism had succumbed to worldliness and apostasy.

Usually called the "Church of God," this "Pentecostal" movement was united by "dispensational pre-millennialism," the conviction that there is an age of tribulation before the "millennium of righteousness" initiated at the second advent of Christ. The final spiritual struggle would take place in America, where one can discern biblical prophesies of doom in modern clues such as the devastation of the Civil War (1861–1865), agnostic natural sciences, and a lack of Protestant consensus as a shield against Roman Catholicism and whatever was deemed unpatriotic.

The Princeton Theology

The intellectual center of this Bible-centered, millenarian, and Pentecostal Fundamentalism was Princeton Theological Seminary. Two professors, Charles Hodge and Benjamin B. Warfield, developed a "Princeton theology," propagated for four decades in the journals *Biblical Repertory* and *Princeton Review*, edited by Hodge. He also summarized his views in a three-volume *Systematic Theology* (1872–1873). It was grounded in the literal inspiration of the Bible, advocating the stance that natural science and biblical theology are two equally significant scholarly enterprises: natural science arranges and systematizes the general facts of the world to ascertain the laws by which the facts are determined; biblical theology systematizes the facts of the Bible in order to ascertain the principles, or general truths, involved in those facts. But both science and theology are interrelated and guided by the infallible and divine authority of the Bible, the scientific foundation of all truth. God put the actual words into the mouths of biblical writers (Jer 1:9) and, despite some literary imperfections, the biblical texts are the original autographs of the Holy Spirit through the pens of authors who faithfully recorded what the Holy Spirit dictated.[11] This "Princeton theology" is reflected in the essays on biblical authority in *The Fundamentals*. One of the authors, James M. Gray, summarized the Princeton stance in no uncertain terms.

The character of [the Bible's] content, the unity of its parts, the fulfillment of its prophesies, the miracles wrought in its attestation, the effects it has accomplished in the lives of nations and of men, all these go to show that it is divine, and if so, that it may be believed in what it says about itself.[12]

Hodge also led the fight against Darwinism, especially after Darwin published *The Descent of Man* in 1871. Hodge countered with his book *What is Darwinism?* in 1874, arguing that Darwin's principles of natural selection could only lead to atheism. As the champion of the anti-Darwinists and of the biblical Fundamentalists, Hodge gained enough support to shape the doctrinal stance of the Presbyterian General Assembly in 1892, which declared the Hodge-Warfield doctrine of biblical inerrancy "essential and necessary." The five truths listed in *The Fundamentals* became a test for orthodoxy and the cornerstone of Presbyterian Christian education. In 1893, two Old Testament scholars who denied biblical inerrancy were dismissed from seminary faculties: C. A. Briggs at Union Seminary in New York City and Henry P. Smith at Lane Seminary in Cincinnati. In 1900, the well-known historian of New Testament literature A. C. McGiffert resigned from the ministry over the same issue.

The main targets of Fundamentalism were biblical "higher criticism" and the "theology of the social gospel." These two intellectual movements, unlike Darwinism, were seen as a threat from the inside. "Higher criticism" distinguished between spiritual and scientific truths in the Bible (for example, it claimed that the Bible discloses salvation in Christ but not the geological age of the world). The "social gospel" advocated socioeconomic justice through a balance between profit and poverty. The principal advocate of the "social gospel" was the Baptist pastor and theologian Walter Rauschenbusch (1861–1918), who began his ministry in one of the poorest sections of New York City known as "Hell's Kitchen" and taught at Rochester Theological Seminary. He envisaged a Christian alternative to agnostic socialism based on the teachings of Karl Marx (1818–1883). In defense of biblical inerrancy and millenarianism, *The Fundamentals* launched literary attacks against these enemies of a "Protestant consensus," based on the five "fundamentals." Fundamentalists argued that the collapse of such a consensus was precipitated by mainline denominations which, trying to be "in the world," fell prey to the satanic forces of Roman Catholicism and secularism.

The battle for or against biblical inerrancy as a wedge against science, whether literary criticism or Darwinism, was fought in some large denominations, including the Baptists, Presbyterians, and Disciples of Christ. In 1908, Fundamentalist Disciples founded the "Churches of Christ." In 1922, the famous Baptist preacher Harry E. Fosdick, who taught at Union Theological Seminary in New York and was a regular guest preacher at the large First Presbyterian Church, attacked fundamentalism in a sermon entitled "Shall Fundamentalism Win?" He had become angered by the increasing propagation of biblical inerrancy and millenarianism through the work of Protestant missionaries in China. The publication of his sermon in *The Christian Century* unleashed a Fundamentalist storm of protest. The General Presbyterian Assemblies of 1923 and 1924 requested that Fosdick become Presbyterian so that he could be disciplined for violating the "five truths" adopted by the denomination. But Fosdick declined and instead accepted a call to be pastor of the interdenominational Riverside Church in New York, built through the generosity of John D. Rockefeller.

The conflict continued when twelve hundred Presbyterians submitted the Auburn Affirmation to their General Assembly in 1924, protesting a fundamentalist stance as a threat to unity. It was the beginning of a schism between Fundamentalists and non-Fundamentalists. The leader of the ultra-conservatives, the Princeton New Testament professor J. Gresham Machen, called for a total separation of Fundamentalists and "liberals" in his book *Christianity and Liberalism*, published in 1923. Three successive Presbyterian assemblies (1925–1927) produced a compromise, declaring that the Presbyterian ecclesiastical system permitted different points of view; local presbyteries had the authority and license to ordain ministers even though they might not always conform to all decisions of the General Assemblies. Accordingly, Fundamentalism was no longer the norm of faith and life. A schism in the denomination was avoided; the Fundamentalist Machen faction seceded from Princeton Theological Seminary and organized its own training institution, the Westminster Seminary in Philadelphia. The Scofield millenarians, led by Pastor Carl McIntyre (Princeton class of 1929) and other radicals, formed the Bible Presbyterian Synod in 1937.

Baptist Fundamentalists created the Conference on Fundamentals of Our Baptist Faith in 1920. "Counter-seminaries," such as the Northern Baptist Seminary in Chicago (1913) and Eastern Seminary in Philadelphia

(1925), became the conservative ideological centers against liberalism. Fundamentalists were no longer united.

The Crusade against Darwinism

The most notorious aspect of American Fundamentalism was the crusade against Darwin's theory of evolution, tested in the famous "monkey trial" in 1925 in Clayton, Tennessee, a national media event manifesting the hostility between Southern conservatives and Northern liberals.[13] Fundamentalist organizations, led by the World's Christian Fundamentals Association, initiated legislative efforts to prohibit the teaching of evolution in public schools, especially in the South. The Bible Crusaders of America, founded in 1925, spearheaded the attack. A wealthy Florida businessman, George F. Washburn, donated $200,000 to the Crusaders; the governor of Florida and several state senators became officers in the organization. The magazine *The Crusaders' Champion* published articles calling for the salvation of America from the evils of modernism and Darwinism. The Crusaders' fusion of fundamentalism and politics was exhibited in the slogan, "Back to Christ, to the Bible, and to the Constitution." Three "remedies" were offered to cure the country of un-Christian diseases: (1) a boycott of all publications and educational institutions that supported modernism and evolution; (2) an attempt to find the ways and means to expel liberals and to elect conservatives to govern church and state; and (3) a drive for legislative action against un-Christian science, especially Darwinism. Washburn even proposed a constitutional amendment to make America Christian again—a utopian political oxymoron in the light of the First Amendment of the Constitution that prohibits any kind of fusion of church and state!

Washburn offered to finance public debates between prominent Fundamentalists and the famous liberal trial lawyer Clarence Darrow, or any other agnostic, modernist, evolutionist, or atheist. The Crusaders staged demonstrations and lobbied for legislation in favor of anti-evolution laws in Florida, Tennessee, Mississippi, Louisiana, and North Carolina. But they succeeded only in Tennessee, where the teaching of evolution became prohibited by law. However, people seemed not to be attracted to them, perhaps because of their blatant politics, the flaunting of large sums of money, and the attention focused on the "monkey trial."

The trial began when a young biology teacher and athletic instructor at Rhea County High School, John T. Scopes, was found guilty of violating the Tennessee anti-evolution law in the spring of 1925 and was fined $100. The American Civil Liberties Union persuaded Scopes to appeal and thus test the constitutionality of the law. The trial, conducted over the span of eleven hot summer days (July 10–21, 1925), became a worldwide news event. More than a hundred news reporters attended the trial, which climaxed in the confrontation between the liberal Chicago lawyer Clarence Darrow and the Fundamentalist jurist and politician William Jennings Bryan (three times an unsuccessful Democratic presidential candidate and Secretary of State under President Woodrow Wilson, 1913–1915). The presiding judge sat under a banner that bore the inscription "Read the Bible daily," and a massive outpouring of emotions marked the entire event.

Bryan charged that the theory of evolution corrupted young minds in schools, that it was an insidious attempt by a political minority to destroy Christianity under the guise of science, and that it was an assault on the divinely sanctioned nobility of human beings. Darrow, on the other hand, challenged Bryan's fundamentalism as being ignorant and prejudiced. "Were Adam and Eve real people?" he asked. "Did Joshua make the sun stand still?" (Josh 10:12). Bryan's "yes" to these and other questions made him appear naive and ignorant, threatening his reputation as a lawyer and politician. In his staunch defense of biblical inerrancy, he was forced to admit that he had not consulted ancient history, philosophy, and comparative religion. Frustrated and exhausted like a weak boxer in the ring, he could not endure the cruel cross-examination by Darrow, so the judge saved him from an embarrassing defeat by calling an end to the trial. Bryan died a few days later, a disappointed and beaten man. Scopes was the only person who benefited from the trial. He accepted a scholarship at the University of Chicago to study geology, a subject he researched and taught successfully through the remainder of his life.

The trial, labeled the "monkey trial" (referring to human evolution from monkeys), did nothing but "inherit the wind," as the title of the Hollywood movie version suggests. But it also disclosed a foundational characteristic of fundamentalism, exemplified in the tragic figure of William Jennings Bryan, an intelligent lawyer, potential president of the United States, and a loyal Christian—an anachronism that transports the biblical worldview of a three-story universe to a totally different, modern world that no longer envisages heaven above, hell below, and the earth in between. Decent, civilized Christians with a basic education about life, like Bryan, became showcases of ignorance and immaturity, asked to sacrifice their intellect for an alleged bulletproof spiritual security.

Evangelicalism

Although Fundamentalism began to wane in the 1930s, it reemerged after World War II in the context of a revival movement that understood itself as "evangelical" (from the Greek *euangelion*, "gospel," meaning "good news"). Sidney E. Ahlstrom described "evangelicals" in America as Protestants marked by six characteristics: (1) a refutation of Roman Catholicism; (2) an adoption and defense of biblical inerrancy; (3) use of the Bible as the only source for Christian morality; (4) a stress on experience and conversion more than on institution and sacraments; (5) a preference for a legalistic rather than situational ethic; and (6) resistance to communion with other groups who do not share their convictions.[14]

"Evangelicals" are moderate Fundamentalists. Eschewing a strict biblical inerrancy based on verbal inspiration, they prefer a more moderate theological truth, tolerating some considerations of historical facts not derived from the Bible. The Book of Genesis, for example, "has an artificial literary structure and is not concerned to provide a picture of chronological sequence but only to assert the fact that 'God made everything.'"[15] The "six days" of creation are not chronological days, "but days of dramatic vision, the story being presented to Moses in a series of revelations spread over six days," or perhaps "one day" is a "geological age." Similarly, the two different accounts of the ascension of Jesus—Luke 24:51 which implies that the ascension happened on the same day as the resurrection, and Acts 1:11 which postpones it for forty days (Acts 1:3)—are harmonized by giving priority to Luke: "The resurrection and ascension both occurred on Easter Sunday."

"Evangelical" theologians make a distinction between the "Word of God" and the Bible, affirming the inerrancy of the former but not of the latter. But the Lausanne Covenant, organized at a conference held in 1977 in Switzerland on the topic of "World Evangelization," still affirmed "the divine inspiration, truthfulness, and authority of both the

Old and the New Testaments in their entirety as the only written *Word of God* without error in all it affirms, and the only *infallible rule of faith and practice.*"[16] Some defenders of biblical inerrancy use naive analogies that seem to depict the Bible as one, though the most important, instrument of God's revelation. As Billy Graham put it:

> In God's classroom there are three textbooks—one called nature, one called conscience, and one called Scripture. The laws of God revealed in nature have never changed. In the written textbook of revelation, the Bible, God speaks through words. The Bible is the one book which reveals the Creator to the creature he created.[17]

Others used revival meetings to present their views, or to scold those who rejected fundamentalism. Billy Sunday (1862–1935), a native of Iowa who gave up playing professional baseball after a conversion, lost all restraint when he preached, even using foul language. His companion and musical director, Homer Rodeheaver, played a trombone and composed gospel songs for the campaigns. Sunday wanted to recruit Fundamentalist soldiers who were not "hog-jowled, weasel-eyed, sponge-columned, mushy-fisted, jelly-spined, pussy-footing, four-flushing, Charlotte-russe Christians."[18]

A Presbyterian from North Carolina, Billy Graham helped Evangelicals to organize The National Association of Evangelicals in 1942 as a united front against the liberal Federal Council of American Churches. But ultraconservatives had already founded The American Council of Christian Churches in 1941, led by Carl McIntyre. They propagated an American way of life grounded in the inerrant Bible, and they often draped the American flag over the cross to make their simple point. Graham, however, became the leader of the Evangelicals after his sensational tent meeting in Los Angeles in 1949. In 1956, he formed the Billy Graham Evangelistic Association, using mass meetings to promote Fundamentalism.

Carl F. H. Henry, a former professor of New Testament at Northern Baptist and Fuller seminaries, joined the movement with his periodical, *Christianity Today*. He wanted to overcome the Fundamentalist image of being anti-intellectual and anti-scientific by arguing that the fundamental Christian truths are in harmony with reason and patriotism. Fuller Theological Seminary in Pasadena, California, fostered an evangelical style of scholarship that attempted to establish a harmony between the intellect, the arts, and social concerns. But the most elaborate attempt to evangelize the world, The Campus Crusade for Christ initiated in the 1950s by Bill Bright (1921–2003), asserted biblical inerrancy without any compromise—the Bible is verbally inspired, inerrant, and infallible.[19] The National Association of Evangelicals, founded in 1942, has become the political arm of Fundamentalism; it consists of members from about forty-five denominations.

During and after the stormy political period of the 1960s in the United States, focusing on the "civil rights" of African-Americans and on the war in Vietnam, groups of "Evangelicals" began to unite for political action. They revived the traditional "evangelical" stance that America was corrupted by a massive violation of biblical morality, ranging from homosexuality to atheism. Three leaders exemplify and have put their stamp on contemporary "Evangelicalism."

Oral Roberts (1918–), a cradled Baptist with early exposure to the Pentecostal tradition, made himself known as a faith healer through massive tent meetings.[20] In 1963, he founded Oral Roberts University in Tulsa, Oklahoma, followed in 1981 by the City of Faith Medical and Research Center. Roberts claimed that Jesus had appeared to him in a vision to appoint him to find a cure for cancer. He resided in the exclusive St. Andrews Country Club in Boca Raton, Florida, using a private jet for transportation. Allegations of misappropriations of university funds made him resign as President of the University in Tulsa; he "semi-retired" in California with an income of less than $100,000 per year. His academic enterprises, combined with the Abundant Life Prayer Group which operates day and night, continue to focus on the morals of an inerrant Bible. But Roberts seemed convinced, in a vision in 2004, that the final divine judgment of the world was imminent.

Jerry Falwell (1933–2007) was the most "political" Evangelicals.[21] A Baptist minister, he became the founding pastor of a large church in Lynchburg, Virginia in 1956, and founded Liberty University in 1971 as the center of his activities. He became known for his radical Fundamentalist opinions, ranging from calling the "civil rights movement" the "civil wrongs movement" to labeling homosexuals "brute beasts." But his "Moral Majority" movement of 1979 organized millions in favor of a conservative Christian Coalition in politics; it is credited with giving

Ronald Reagan the presidency in 1980 and George W. Bush a second term in 2004. The main items in the campaign of the Moral Majority read like an attack against American constitutional rights, especially the First Amendment regarding the separation of church and state; opposition to the Equal Rights Amendment; enforcement of a traditional (Christian) vision of family life (no homosexuality); and censorship of media promoting "anti-family" agendas. In 1989, the Moral Majority became the Christian Coalition Network, linked to Pat Robertson.

Pat Robertson (1930–) is the most successful "evangelical" organizer and televangelist. He founded The Christian Broadcasting Network, Regent University in Virginia Beach, Operation Blessing International Relief and Development Corporation, the American Center for Law and Justice, and the International Family Entertainment, Inc. (since 2001, owned by the Disney Corporation as part of the ABC family). He has his finger in almost every political pie, as it were, whether as a candidate for President of the United States or in numerous annoying utterances (such as his recommendations to assassinate heads of state who are hostile to the United States).

These and other leaders of "the religious right" advocate political actions that they believe will preserve biblical faith and morals: heterosexual marriage (no homosexuality), the unconditional value of human life (no abortion), and (in the United States) a "Christian America."[22] The movement plays with high stakes—a new Constitution of the United States, without the guarantee of freedom of religion asserted in the First Amendment, and eliminating other basic liberties envisaged and legislated by the "founding fathers."

Among mainline denominations, only the Lutheran Church–Missouri Synod adopted "an untinctured Fundamentalism" in 1973,[23] ending frequent controversies about biblical inerrancy in its own ranks, but causing it to become isolated from other Lutheran church bodies.

Traditionalism

> Scripture and tradition must be accepted and honored with equal feelings of devotion and reverence.[24]

Protestant biblical Fundamentalism claimed to "hand on" (*tradere* in Latin) the Bible without any "tradition" added to its interpretation. As the verbally inspired Word of God, it needed only to be translated for readers who were unable to read the original text, Hebrew and Greek, dictated by the Holy Spirit to authors who knew these ancient biblical languages. But Fundamentalists had to concede the existence of human problems, such as faulty hearing, choices in translations, and contradictory texts. In this sense, there is at least a minimal tradition that is generated over the course of time. But the longer the time, the more difficult it is to transmit the content of the Bible to generations of readers who have lived in a different context than the first generation of Christians. That is why Roman Catholicism speaks of "Scripture" *and* "tradition" as necessary means to understand and communicate the full meaning of the Word of God. Already in the second century C.E. a cadre of church leaders was charged to oversee the process of tradition, especially the transmission of the gospel. They became known as "bishops" (*episcopoi* in Greek, "overseers"). They met in a council to discover the best possible ways to hand on the gospel for the sake of Christian unity. When strong disagreements threatened unity, they put the gospel tradition into the form of a creed, the Nicene Creed of 325 C.E. Its dogma of the Trinity was to guide all other traditions.

Soon, questions arose concerning the definition of tradition. Should it simply be a judgment by the council of bishops on the question of what is "orthodox," "heterodox," and "heretical?" The first, albeit unsatisfactory, attempt to define "tradition" was made by Vincent of Lerins (d. c. 450) during the fifth-century controversy on sin and grace between the revered bishop Augustine and the monk Pelagius. Vincent proposed a threefold test of catholicity: "What has been believed everywhere, always, by all" (*quod ubique, quod semper, quod ab omnibus creditum est*); the Bible is the ultimate authority as interpreted according to "the ecclesiastical and catholic sense."[25] But this definition raised more questions than it answered. How does one assess what is believed "everywhere, always, and by all?" Who interprets the Bible according to the "ecclesiastical and catholic [ecumenical] sense?" When different doctrines and liturgical rituals were developed in the eastern churches, the bishop of Rome in the west claimed to have the authority to preserve and maintain unity. Although he was honored and respected, ecclesiastical authority was still seen to be located in the council of bishops. So the eastern churches refused to accept the leadership of a Roman "pope" (*papa* in Latin, "father").

This disagreement led to a schism between east and west in 1054 C.E. Eastern Christianity became known as "Greek (Eastern) Orthodoxy," centered in Constantinople and led by "patriarchs" (*patriarches* in Greek, "male ruler of a family"). The West continued to approve new traditions through a council of bishops, chaired by the bishop of Rome. Such a council represented the ecclesiastical "teaching authority" (*magisterium* in Latin, "office of the master"), the final authority that decides what is needed in "faith and morals" for the Christian life. This is the beginning of a poisonous "traditionalism." It assumes that only the Western church, led by the bishop of Rome, has been endowed with the task of transmitting divine revelation through Scripture and tradition, both having equal authority as channels of divine revelation. When revelation needs to be clarified, the council of bishops, led by the bishop of Rome, establishes what is, or is not, revealed truth. If, for example, a biblical passage is unclear, the Episcopal Council functions as the teaching authority, the magisterium, and clarifies the passage.

The Authority of Rome

The full power of the magisterium was eventually ascribed to the bishop of Rome, due to his central geographic location and his political skills. When Rome was conquered by the Visigothic king Aalaric in 410, Pope Innocent I assisted in an unsuccessful negotiation for peace. He and other Roman bishops declared that the Roman bishop was not "first among equals" (*primus inter pares*), as is the case of Eastern Orthodox Patriarchs who have a primacy of honor but share the common episcopal power. In contrast, the bishop of Rome claimed that his sole primacy among bishops dated back to the first century, beginning with the apostle Peter. Here Catholic traditionalists operated like Protestant Fundamentalists. They used two biblical texts to prove that the papacy is rooted in the sayings of Jesus about the apostle Peter. After Peter confessed that he believed Jesus to be the Messiah and "the Son of the living God," Jesus said,

> Blessed are you Simon [Peter], son of Jonah! For flesh and blood has not revealed this to you, but my Father in heaven. And I tell you, you are Peter, and on this rock [*petros* in Greek] I will build my church, and the gates of Hades [hell] will not prevail against it. I will give you the keys of the kingdom of heaven, and whatever you bind

on earth will be bound in heaven, and whatever you loose on earth
will be loosed in heaven. (Matt. 16:17-19)

He [Jesus] said to him the third time, "Simon son of John, do you
love me?" ... And he [Peter] said to him, "Lord, you know everything; you know that I love you." Jesus said to him, "Feed my
sheep." (John 21:17-18)[26]

Meticulous ecumenical research has shown that although a privileged
"Petrine function" is disclosed in these texts, they do not reveal sufficient
evidence for the establishment of an apostolic succession leading to a
papacy. "The question whether Jesus appointed Peter the first pope has
shifted in modern scholarship to the question of the extent to which the
subsequent use of the images of Peter in reference to the papacy is consistent with the thrust of the New Testament."[27] Substituting later images of
Peter as pope for his role in the New Testament contaminates the original
text; favored notions are read into it, thus hiding its real meaning.

Various reformers appealed to the authority of the Bible over against
the alleged authority of the church's hierarchy as expressed in the decisions of the magisterium. The British priest and scholar, John Wycliffe (c.
1325–1384) used the authority of the Bible to show that the papacy was
the result of an illegitimate doctrinal development, combined with the
abuse of power. John Hus (c. 1369–1415), a priest and professor of Biblical Studies at the University of Prague in Bohemia (now the Czech Republic), adopted Wycliffe's proposals for reform. Moreover, Hus contended
that the Bible rejects the papacy. He was given safe-conduct to present
his views in 1414 at the Council of Constance in Germany. When he
arrived, he was imprisoned and interrogated for eight months; in 1415 he
was burned at the stake as a heretic. Wycliffe was given the same verdict
posthumously.[28] Pope Martin V gave orders in 1427 to seize Wycliffe's
bones from his tomb in St. Mary's Church in Lutterworth, England, to
burn them at the stake, and to throw the ashes into the wind. Disciples of
Hus organized a military revolt against the empire and, after fierce gue-
rilla battles, went underground and survived as "Hussites," later known
as The Moravian Church.

Martin Luther affirmed the authority of Scripture and tradition
as long as tradition did not violate the Word of God in Scripture, the
divine offer of salvation in Christ without human merit. Accordingly,

nonbiblical traditions are valid interpretations of Holy Scripture, such as the liturgy of the Mass, auricular confession, and holy days, in addition to other "human traditions" that do not violate biblical authority, such as the Trinitarian Creeds, infant baptism, and church councils (excluding bishops in apostolic succession led by the pope).[29]

The Council of Trent

The Protestant schism in the West, almost a millennium and a half after the schism with the East, led to a reformulation of Roman Catholic doctrine and life. One of the most debated issues was the relationship between Scripture and tradition. This was done at the fourth session of the Council of Trent (1545–1563) in 1546, "so that the purity of the gospel, purged from all errors, may be preserved in the church."[30] But the diplomatic language of the solemn declaration once again strengthened the role of the magisterium as the arbiter and supreme judge in matters of faith and morals. Consequently, the purity of the gospel is preserved through the chain of the apostolic succession of Catholic bishops led by the Roman bishop, the pope, as the special successor to Peter. This succession is viewed as being divinely inspired, as is the Bible, because God is the "author" of both channels of revelation. Jesus Christ "first proclaimed [the gospel] with his own lips" and "then bade it to be proclaimed to every creature through his apostles as the source of all truth and rule of conduct."[31]

> This truth and this rule are contained in written books and in *unwritten traditions* that were perceived by the apostles from the mouth of Christ himself, or have come down to us, handed on as it were from the apostles themselves at the inspiration of the Holy Spirit. . . . Following the example of the orthodox fathers, the Council accepts and venerates with a like feeling of piety and reverence all the books of the Old and New Testament, *since the one God is the author of both as well as the tradition* concerning both faith and conduct, *as either directly spoken by Christ or dictated by the Holy Spirit,* which have been preserved in unbroken sequence in the catholic church.[32]

Here, biblical and traditionalist Fundamentalism are united: both the canonical Bible and the tradition of the church are viewed as being verbally inspired. Such inspiration characterizes the apostolic succession of bishops begun by the apostle Peter and ending in the bishop of Rome, the pope.

Papal power continued to increase after the Council of Trent and reached its climax in the assertion of papal infallibility at the First Vatican Council in 1870. At that meeting, the pope became the guarantor of the truth of the gospel, even without the consent of the church.

> The Roman pontiff, when he speaks ex cathedra—that is, when in the exercise of his office as pastor and teacher of all Christians he defines, by virtue of his supreme apostolic authority, a doctrine of faith or morals to be held by the whole church—is by reason of the divine assistance promised to him in blessed Peter, possessed of that infallibility with which the divine redeemer wished his church to be endowed in defining doctrines of faith and morals and, consequently, that such definitions by the Roman Pontiff *are irreformable of their own nature (ex sese) and not by reason of the church's consent.*[33]

This part of traditionalism exhibits the most toxic form of Christian spirituality because the contamination of original sin is at its highest level in Christian history. One can virtually hear the echo of the serpent's tempting promise to Adam and Eve in the garden, "You will be like God" (Gen 3:5)—a sound reaching from Eden to Rome! When the church, represented in the apostolic succession of bishops, claims to have been guided by the Holy Spirit to grant inerrant and infallible power to one of its own members, whether the church approves or disapproves, then all theological bets are off. The penultimate has become the ultimate, time has become eternal, and one no longer sees "in a mirror dimly" (1 Cor 13:12). The end-time, the "eschaton," is realized in the papacy.

Marian Devotions

The dogma of papal infallibility caused a schism within Roman Catholicism. In 1869, several dioceses in the Netherlands, Switzerland, and Austria banded together in Utrecht, Holland, and declared themselves to be "Old Catholics." German bishop Joseph H. Reinkens was consecrated by the bishop of Utrecht to be the head of this new church body. Several theologians, among them the well-known German church historian Ignaz von Doellinger, rejected papal infallibility on historical grounds and was excommunicated. What puzzled some Catholics and angered many non-Catholics was the use of papal authority to strengthen and confirm Marian devotions that were nurtured by stories of visions, healing miracles, and pilgrimages. Ecumenical protesters pointed out that Mary does not have the appropriate significance in the Bible to be elevated to a mediator (*mediatrix*) of salvation through intercessions, for she is depicted as the virgin mother of Jesus only in one gospel (Luke 1:26-28). However, on December 8, 1854, Pope Pius IX secured her special role as an object of worship by extending Mary's virginity to her own birth by way of the dogma of the immaculate conception.[34] A liturgical feast celebrating such a conception had been introduced by Franciscan monks in 1263. Dominican monks, especially the revered theologian Thomas Aquinas and his disciples, strongly opposed such teaching. German Lutherans and other Protestants launched heavy theological attacks against the new dogma, contending that Mariology endangered Christology by making Mary a mediator of salvation. But Catholic popular support, nurtured by successive popes, propelled a minor liturgical feast into an infallible dogma.

Since the notion of an immaculate conception has been debated since the eleventh century, the dogma is protected by a hermeneutical firewall, as it were, consisting of anthropological presuppositions and proof texts from the Bible and the "church fathers." When combined with a history of the liturgical Feast of the Immaculate Conception, "explicit universal acceptance" was claimed in the end.

> The Blessed Virgin Mary in the first instance of her conception, by a singular privilege and grace granted by God, in view of the merits of Christ, the Savior of the human race, was preserved exempt from all stain of original sin.[35]

The anthropological presuppositions define "conception" as the union of the mortal body and an immortal soul. Here, views from classical antiquity are used, especially those of Aristotle (384–322 B.C.E.). Joseph plays a role in the conception, but the conception was completed when the immortal soul was infused. "The body was formed in the womb of the mother, and the father had the general share of formation."[36] While all others are conceived in sin (as the result of "original sin") and must be baptized in order to "remove" it, Mary was "excluded" from sin and was as pure as Eve before the Fall. That is why she is called "the second Eve." The chief proof text from the Bible is Genesis 3:15 (God said to the serpent, "I will put enmity between you and the woman, and between your offspring and hers; he will strike your head and you will strike his heel"). The "woman" is Mary, and the "offspring" is Christ. She received the gift, "sanctifying grace," of being immune to the serpentine poison of sin and thus did not just give birth to an ordinary child, but "the Redeemer." This text is supposedly supported by Luke 1:28, the greeting of the angel Gabriel, "Greetings, favored one!"—or in the Catholic translation, "Hail, full of grace!" Other peculiar texts were added, exalting the "wisdom of God," such as Song of Solomon 4:7, "You are altogether beautiful, my love." A peculiar caveat was offered: "These passages, applied to the Mother of God, may be readily understood by those who know the privilege of Mary, but do not avail to prove the doctrine dogmatically."[37]

The proof texts from the "church fathers" speak of Mary as "the second Eve" and of her "absolute purity." Some even ascribe a purity from sexual sin to her parents, who may have belonged to "an immaculate active generation" thus Mary was born of a virgin. *The Catholic Encyclopedia* grants that these texts are more prevalent in the Greek Orthodox Church.

The western medieval (Roman Catholic) church experienced much controversy about Mary's immaculate conception after the eleventh century. Its liturgical celebration was sporadically abolished in England. French monks contended that the Feast was foreign to church tradition. The most honored medieval theologian, Thomas Aquinas, rejected the doctrine. Biblical theologians cited Romans 5:12 as a proof text against the doctrine ("all have sinned")—no one is exempt from sin. But *The Catholic Encycopedia* defends the "party line" that this text only "insists on the need which all men have of the redemption by Christ," and is not applicable to the mother of Mary.[38]

After intensive academic debate between opponents (Dominicans) and proponents (Franciscans), the influential theologians at the University of Paris affirmed the doctrine in 1439, and the liturgical celebration became mandatory in 1476. But theological disputes continued. The Dominicans continued their opposition, but celebrated the "sanctification" of Mary, not her immaculate "conception." Rome prohibited further debate until the Holy See would decree a solution—the dogma of 1854. No voting in a council of bishops, but only the infallible papal fiat!

Mariology continued to preoccupy papal minds and Catholic devotional life, resulting in the promulgation, on November 1, 1950 by Pope Pius XII, of the infallible dogma of Mary's assumption into heaven. Linking this infallible dogma with that of the "immaculate conception," the dogma declares "that the immaculate Mother of God, ever virgin, having completed the course of her earthly life, was assumed body and soul into heavenly glory."[39] The word "immaculate" in the 1950 document also assures the infallibility of the dogma of the Immaculate Conception of 1854. Massive argumentation from the tradition and the threat of excommunication for denying this "truth" accompanied the dogma. But ecumenical opposition to such a dogma had already arisen before its promulgation. An official "opinion" (*Gutachten*) appeared in print in the name of the Protestant Heidelberg Theological Faculty in Germany. It spelled out "serious misgivings": there is no biblical evidence for Mary's assumption; if claimed, it would obscure the incarnation of Christ; and it would cause painful ecumenical estrangement. In short, Rome was promulgating "the dogmatization of a myth lacking historical foundation."[40]

After the promulgation of the new dogma, Protestant church leaders and prominent members of the ecumenical movement launched solemn protests. This polemical mood was summarized by a leading Protestant theologian, Gerhard Ebeling: "The mariological dogmas mean the dogmatization of the basic structure of Catholicism."[41] It is a point well made with reference to toxic traditionalism. A rather insignificant theological, indeed mythological, notion is used to elevate one of the many ecclesiastical structures, the papacy, to the level of an eternal truth, synonymous with the gospel.

This institutional arrogance was sealed by the Second Vatican Council when it fused Scripture and tradition as the

> single sacred deposit of the Word of God which is entrusted to the church. . . . The task of giving an authentic interpretation of the Word of God, *whether in its written* [biblical] *form or in the form of tradition, has been entrusted to the living teaching office of the church alone* . . . in the supremely wise arrangement of God. Tradition, sacred scripture and the magisterium of the church are so

connected and associated that one of them cannot stand without the others. Working together, each in its own way under the action of the Holy Spirit, *they all contribute effectively to the salvation of souls.*[42]

Here is an unholy Trinity, as it were, of Catholic traditionalist fundamentalism: tradition, Scripture, and the magisterium. Note that "tradition" and "magisterium" flank "Scripture"—the Word of God in the Bible is only fully revealed when approved or logically extended by the "teaching office of the church, the magisterium." If this office is the last resort for deciding what is and is not revealed truth, then the magisterium can neither be changed nor exchanged for another way of establishing teaching authority. Thus, it could be said that if Protestant biblical fundamentalism is marked by the slogan "Scripture alone" (*sola scriptura*), or "the Bible alone" (*sola biblia*), Catholic traditionalist fundamentalism could match it with the slogan "the church alone" (*sola ecclesia*), or more precisely, "the magisterium alone" (*solum magisterium*).

The Lesson of Origination

Fundamentalism, whether Protestant bibliolatry or Catholic traditionalism, represents a drive for intellectual security, for a "religion of the head" (over against a "religion of the heart" as exemplified by anti-intellectual revivalists). This drive has been decisively influenced and deliberately shaped by the ancient Greek metaphysical tradition associated with Plato (ca. 427–347 B.C.E.) and Aristotle (384–322 B.C.E.). Plato envisaged the essence of reality as "ideas" reflecting an incorporeal immortal world that is inaccessible to the human mind except via "shadows," an inferior copy of the world of ideas. An immortal soul connects the two worlds, the real world "above" and the shadowy world "below." But the soul is polluted by corporeal desires focused on the love of self (closer to *eros* in Greek), not on the true love of purity and truth (*agape* in Greek). Death liberates the soul from the sensuous, corporeal world and lets it be united again with the eternal, incorporeal world.

Aristotle developed a philosophy of life in the corporeal, temporal, and mortal world. This philosophy consisted of theoretical foundations for the practical rules of living that existed in the scientific, political, moral, and aesthetic (music and the arts) realms. "Theology" is the most important part of these theoretical functions because it deals with the mind (*nous* in Greek) as linked to the "prime mover," from which everything is derived and rationally organized. Aristotle makes basic distinctions between his definitions of reality. Everything in the world has an "essence" (*hypostasis* in Greek) or a "substance" (from the Latin *substantia*). Each substance is self-sufficient, but can be perceived as "form" that is contingent or "accidental" (from the Latin *accidens*). To illustrate: I am "substantially" a human being and "accidentally" a person with biological characteristics (male, tall, short, etc.). The "natural sciences" deal with the visible, corporeal, and temporal world; "metaphysics" deals with what comes "after nature" (*meta physis* in Greek), or is "above nature" (*supra naturam* in Latin). In the earthly, natural, material realm, the mind can "prove" by syllogism that something exists. Example: All human beings are rational; I am a human being; therefore I am rational. The mind can also discern specific connections to the metaphysical world.

The Eucharist and Metaphysics

The Roman Catholic doctrine of "transubstantiation" is a case in point.[43] The metaphysical substance of Christ is present in the physical "accidents" of bread and wine when the priest intones the "Words of Institution" ("This is my body . . . This is my blood.") Accordingly, the elements are "transubstantiated" in the Eucharist but not "transaccidented"—the biological realities of flesh and blood are absent. This complex philosophical argument became official doctrine at the Fourth Lateran Council in 1215, and was confirmed by the Second Vatican Council in 1967. It so happens that the phrase *hocus pocus* has been traced, though certainly not beyond the shadow of a doubt, to the recitation of the Latin Words of Institution, "*Hoc est meum corpus*" ("This is my body").[44] One could surmise that naive, illiterate, and obedient medieval worshippers in the pews, quite distant from the altar, observed the mysterious ritual of the officiating priest. At the precise moment when the priest had completed the consecration of the Eucharistic elements, bread and wine, an altar boy rang a handbell, announcing the miracle of "transubstantiating" the or consecrating the bread and wine into the body and blood of Christ. Thus, the most solemn part of the "sacrament of the altar" could convey a sense of magic. Worshippers did not hear well, or understand, the speedy recitation of the Latin words. They heard a strange intonation by a priest who had been given the sacrament of ordination that enabled him to offer the faithful laity a miraculous "communion" with Christ through the consecrated host. He alone consumed the wine, protecting it from being spilled by excited communicants. The misheard words became a popular phrase that was later used by magicians. It is ironic that the modern definition of *hocus pocus* conveys the exact opposite of the original meaning—"meaningless talk or activity, often designed to draw attention away from and disguise what is actually happening."[45]

The use of Greek metaphysics to "explicate" the mystery of the Eucharist is, in my opinion, counterproductive. Communicants tend to become spectators rather than participants, and the shrouding of Christ in a philosophical analysis may cause a needless spiritual paralysis. For, as psychiatry has demonstrated, too much analysis can cause paralysis. Other mainline churches also use Greek metaphysical categories to "prove" the authority of the Bible (as some fundamentalists do), or to position themselves in controversies. For example, authoritative Lutheran documents, known as "Confessions," use the distinction between "substance" and "accidents" in their explanation of original sin, confessed in worship with the phrase "We are by nature sinful and unclean."[46] "By nature" should not mean that nothing good remains in a human being after the Fall; that would eliminate faith in God's creation as "very good" (Gen 1:31). "Nature," therefore, is an "accident" in the divine creation which is the "substance" of life. That is why "original sin is not a substance (something that exists by, in and of itself) but an *accidens* (something that does not exist by, in and of itself)."[47] Sinners remain creatures of God's good creation. Seventeenth-century Lutheran theologians used the distinction between a divine, invisible, spiritual realm and a material one in their quest for "pure doctrine" derived from the Bible. They also used Aristotle's language about "first" and "second causes," God being the "first cause" working as the Holy Spirit, dictating the text of the Bible to the authors as the deposit of eternal truth.[48]

The Authority of the Biblical Text

The biblical way of talking about God is quite different from the Greek metaphysical argumentation. Biblical texts view God as disclosed in *historical events* rather than in *ontological speculation*. God declares solidarity with Israel in Egypt ("I will be your God," Exod 6:7). God is a warlord who helps defeat the Egyptians (Exod 15:3). God uses unbelievers like the Assyrians to teach Israel a lesson about the covenant (Isa 10:5). God is incarnate in the person of Jesus at a chosen time ("When the time had fully come, God sent his son," Gal 4:4). While the Greek metaphysical tradition tries, with dedicated philosophical sophistication, to keep God in the realm of timeless immortality, the biblical tradition attests to God's radical presence in time. That is why the apostle Paul called preaching Christ to the Gentiles, also known as Hellenists, "foolishness" (1 Cor 1:23). This is a radical change in God-talk, "theology." In the Bible, God "comes down," as it were, to care for a world of sin; in Greek philosophy a timeless God is reached by humans who "go up" through reason. But the God of the Bible is not the aloof resident of a metaphysical heaven, who loves to be pleased by human logic. Rather, God is disclosed in the risky relationship embodied in the Jesus of Israel. Divine revelation is embedded in *historical relationships*, not in ahistorical exercises of the mind.

The conscious experience of historical events involves change that cannot be predicted. I may encounter someone whom I come to love. So I find myself changing, opened up for a future I never anticipated because it has been disclosed only in the encounter with another. The new relationship will create its own authority, engendered by trust in someone else. I might even find my own identity in the way another human being assesses me. I experience the authority of relationships so prominent in the Bible. Accordingly, there is little, if any room for a Christian individualism that seeks security through either the head or the heart, that is, through dogmatic reasoning or emotional satisfaction. The language of relationship opposes the language of security, which discloses a demand for the control of self and of others. The language of relationship avoids the pitfalls of rationalism and pious sentimentality by the realistic biblical doctrine of sin: "You will [want to] be like God" (Gen 3:5). True sin, therefore, is the illusion of self-deification, that is, having no relationships and having the power over death.

If God is to be identified with the words, ideas, concepts, and worldviews disclosed in the Bible, then the Bible is literally the Word of God. But those who are aware of mortal existence in human space and time will not necessarily have ultimate trust in the Bible as a book. They will agree with the best ecumenical insight that one cannot draw unchanging teachings from it regarding faith and morals. The Word of God, which has become the code name for God's revelation, is a power disclosed in the certainty of faith, not in the security of philosophical speculations. The Word of God cannot be controlled by human reason; it is embodied in fullness only in Christ when he comes again at the end of time. In this sense, the Word of God is end-oriented, or eschatological. Believers live in the interim between Christ's ascension and his second advent.

The core of ecumenical Christianity has always affirmed the ancient distinction between the Bible as the written word, and the gospel, the good news of salvation, as the spoken word. "Faith comes from what is heard" (Rom 10:17). It needs to be summarized in doctrine and rules in times of crisis when the people of God, the church, are confused or paralyzed. But the Word of God is always a living voice that creates relationships, gathering people together by the speaking, hearing, and sacramental enactment of this Word. The Bible is a "first tradition," as it were; subsequent traditions can be tested by it. It was declared to be authoritative in the sense that it constitutes a "norm," a canon, for postbiblical generations. The church can formulate creeds and doctrines that reflect different linguistic and cultural contexts. So there is in church history a kind of hierarchy of truths and traditions, all of which are derived from and witness to God's revelation in Christ. Such a view locates the Bible properly as a literary embodiment of the witness of God's revelation in Christ, the "apostolic" witness of those who saw, heard, and spoke the gospel. This is the legal authority of the Bible, the norm being used to test teachings for their faithfulness to the gospel. The issue is not whether biblical studies are faithful to certain doctrines, such as inerrancy or infallibility, but whether biblical study liberates students from the drive for security, based on fear, and creates a certainty that points them to a never-ending future with God through Christ. The biblical notion of original sin, "to be like God" (Gen 3:5), encompasses the desire to control everything, including the way the Bible must be read, or how one must talk about God. Thus, the drive for security and control leads to idolatry.

The Bible does not speak of inerrancy based on verbal inspiration. The fundamentalist proof text for biblical inerrancy, 2 Timothy 3:16 ("all scripture is inspired by God"), refers to the Old Testament; otherwise, the author, Paul, would have had to be so inspired as to be inerrant. More-over, the Greek text says "wafted by God" (*theopneustos*), translated in Latin editions of the Bible as "divinely inspired" (*divina inspirata*). Paul makes a clear distinction between his own view and the Lord's command regarding marriage. He tells the Corinthians, known for their spiritual egotism, that his view is not based on a command from the Lord—even though he would like them to be like him. "I wish that all were as I am myself. But each has a particular gift from God, one having one kind and another a different kind" (1 Cor 7:7). Should Paul's personal views become enduring laws? Should women be silent in the churches (1 Cor 14:34), and thus never lead in teaching or never be ordained? Should women be ruled by their husbands? "Just as the church is subject to Christ, so also wives ought to be, in everything, to the husbands" (Eph 5:24). Should anyone who is unwilling to work not eat? (2 Thess 3:10). But the opinionated Paul does let God be God. "What then is Apollos? What is Paul? . . . Apollos watered, but God gave the growth. So neither the one who plants nor the one who waters is anything, but only God who gives the growth" (1 Cor 3:5-7). Paul and the other authors of pas-toral letters would be surprised, indeed angry, if they knew that many Christians in the past two millennia have made their letters into channels of unchanging divine revelation about Christian life.

Biblical inerrancy becomes true nonsense, that is, it makes no sense when Old Testament laws and regulations are applied to life in non-Jewish cultures. Fundamentalists choose specific issues dear to them, such as sexuality rather than food, two of the most basic aspects of life. Although there are many rules for sexual conduct, the Fundamentalists' focus is on the prohibition of homosexuality; the rule applies to men. "You shall not lie with a male as with a woman; it is an abomination" (Lev 18:22)—"a thing that causes disgust or hatred."[49] Violators are to be punished by being "cut off from their people" (18:29). But the Jewish "holiness code" lists many other moral rules that are on the same level as homosexuality, and violators are severely punished, indeed executed. Whoever works on the Sabbath "shall be put to death" (Exod 35:2). Since Fundamentalists substitute Sunday for the Sabbath, a literal appli-cation of the rule would be cruel in the light of contemporary attendance at worship. Slavery would be part of economic life, using outsiders or recent immigrants (Lev 25: 44-45). Blasphemers are to be stoned to death

(Lev. 24:10-16). Should handicapped people (blind, lame, hunchbacks, dwarfs, indeed anyone with a blemish) be prohibited from approaching an altar to worship God (Lev 21:18)? Should those who cut their hair and trim their beards be excluded from the body of the faithful (Lev 19:27)? Should playing football be prohibited in order to avoid the touching of unclean pigskin (Lev 11:7)? Should people who sleep with their in-laws be burned at the stake (Lev 20:14)? Why not endorse polygamy, since it is a common custom in the Old Testament? Should celibacy be the rule—"those who have wives be as those who had none" (1 Cor 7:29)? Should the morality of ancient Jewish culture be normative today? The biblical codes of ethics are too varied and too vast to be applied, even at the time of their origin. Fundamentalists ignore, indeed often do not even know, the whole text of the Bible. They select texts for specific moral issues they regard as important.

The Bible is not a holy book of timeless truths, but a record of God's dealing with people who, despite their divine origination, went astray and became idolatrous. The generation of the New Testament, who lived with the Old Testament as their Bible, left behind their own witness of how God invaded their time as the Christ who mediates a new creation. They read their Old Testament Bible in the light of this divine revelation and created a large collection of testimonies reflecting a great variety of experience.

The history of the collection, as well as the process of selecting some writings and regarding them more authoritative than others, their canonization, reads like a murder mystery. "The history of the development of the biblical canons is complex and at times uncertain."[50] Why so many other significant writings, the so-called non-canonical books, were not included in the biblical canon remains a mystery.[51] Modern editions of texts are readily available, including six gospels on the infancy of Jesus, gospels on his ministry and passion, and stories known as "the Pontius Pilate Cycle." In addition, there are "Apocryphal Acts" attributed to the apostles Peter, John, Paul and Thomas; a number of "Apocryphal Epistles"; and "Apocryphal Apocalypses." The authors of this massive collection of texts offer fascinating accounts of the life and deeds of Jesus. The Infancy Gospel of Thomas, for example, presents an angered boy Jesus who makes another boy fall down and die because he ran and knocked against his shoulders.[52] Miracle stories abound. Most popular were various fourth-century accounts of the assumption of Mary into heaven after she had been buried for three days. More significant than the apocryphal writings is a collection of texts from the first three centuries known as "the Apostolic Fathers."[53] They were used as authoritative sources to explicate the four gospels and the apostolic epistles of the New Testament. No single, formal decision was made regarding the number and authenticity of New Testament writings. The problem is exemplified in Paul's Corinthian correspondence: two letters are extant in the New Testament, but they indicate that the apostle may perhaps have sent two more letters (1 Cor 5:9; 2 Cor 2:4, 9).[54] If they were discovered, would they have the same authority as the first two, and should they be included in the biblical canon?

When the church was unified under the rule of Constantine I in 313 C.E., bishops agreed to select twenty-seven writings for the New Testament and add them to the thirty-nine writings of the Old Testament. The bishop of Rome, Damasus, asked the renowned Bible scholar Jerome to develop a standard Latin text, a translation of the Hebrew and Greek biblical writings. Jerome finished the gigantic project between 382 and 405 C.E. It was published and approved by the western church as the "Vulgate" (from the Latin *vulgata*, "common"), the commonly accepted text.[55] Later generations of scholars discovered more reliable manuscripts and translation errors. That is why editions of the Bible are constantly updated, since translations always involve interpretations reflecting the language and culture of a particular period. The popular English translation, the King James Version of 1611, is no exception. Much of its faults have been corrected in the latest English edition, The New Revised Standard Version of 1989.

The Importance of Hermeneutics

The Bible is the freezer, as it were, which preserves the original Christian witness of the Word of God regarding the destiny of the people of God. The postbiblical tradition shows how the Word of God is thawed and communicated throughout the centuries.[56] It is a history of incredible complexity, ranging from a contradictory variety of ecclesiastical teachings to the persecution, indeed slaughter, of many innocents in the world. The main reason for such a scandalous history of Christian immorality in the name of the Bible is a lack of "historical reason," that is, the lack of commitment to a discipline of historical scholarship that sorts out what is the genuine ancient witness and what needs to be added as faithful "tradition" to counter unsavory proliferations. When history is taken seriously as the arena of God's activity through human creatures, timeless uniformity, marked by the loss of freedom and justice, can never become a godly way of life on earth. Besides, how can one claim to love the Bible without encountering and appreciating all its details generated by the love of those who wrote it?

The American Academy of Arts and Sciences funded a massive project to study Fundamentalism, recruiting scholars from around the world.[57] They discovered that the phenomenon of Fundamentalism includes an uneasy blend of various components related to different cultures. Two scholars have tried to define Fundamentalism.[58] They concluded that Fundamentalism is an attempt to claim authority over a sacred tradition as an antidote for a society that has strayed from its cultural moorings. This fear factor seems to be significant because Fundamentalists are afraid of losing the "cultural moorings" they are familiar with. So Fundamentalism is marked by a continual drive for security among anxious believers who feel destined to preserve a certain way of life and thought, grounded in a preferred culture. One should add to this definition the glaring absence of eschatology: the recognition of the biblical notion of time as penultimate—that ultimate meaning, eternal truth, or any other claim "to know it all" is not possible before the end-time. Like Abraham, all people of God have to confess that they are "strangers" and "foreigners" on earth on the way to the "city of God" (Heb 11:13, 16).

Biblical inerrancy and ecclesiastical infallibility are the two pillars of Christian global Fundamentalism that is guided by a drive for spiritual security, backed up by a rationalistic and/or an emotional structure—orthodox, "pure" teaching, and/or revivalistic pacification. But Christian life ought to be grounded in hope, not fear. Faith is "the assurance of *things hoped for*, the conviction of things *not seen*" (Heb 11:1' italics added). The dogma of biblical inerrancy makes the Bible the "paper pope" of many prejudiced Protestants; and the dogma of papal infallibility makes the ancient Christian office of oversight, the episcopacy, an allegedly inerrant guardian of a schismatic tradition. Biblical Fundamentalists quickly insist that other Christians are lost to salvation, and ecclesiastical traditionalists do the same, or, if they pretend to be "pastoral," call them "defective" because they do not have all the benefits of the "true church." Such Fundamentalism, be it biblical or traditionalist, represents a toxic spirituality rather than the penultimate, ecumenical pilgrim church struggling through the interim between Christ's first and second advents. Moreover, Fundamentalists claims to possess unquestionable, indeed infallible, "truths" which, however, become irrelevant and unnecessary when examined through the lens of a hermeneutics of Christian doctrine and ecclesiastical institutions. For such a hermeneutics, the discipline of interpreting historical texts clearly shows that Scripture and tradition are complex channels of divine revelation, marked by human deformation and reformation under the ever present condition of original sin. To ignore this insight is unblessed ignorance.

Anti-Semitism

From *the medieval cathedral at Strasbourg, this statue,* The Synogogue, *portrays Judaism as a blind maiden.* Photo: Erich Lessing/Art Resource, NY

This depiction of a sixteenth-century burning of 38 Jews in Berlin for host desecration attests to the violent results of virulent Christian anti-Judaic propaganda. Photo: Bildarchiv Preussischer Kulturbesitz/ Art Resource, NY

The Synogogue of Eberswalde was among the thousands of Jewish structures destroyed in Kristallnacht, 1938. Photo: Bildarchiv Preussischer Kulturbesitz/Art Resource, NY

Fundamentalism

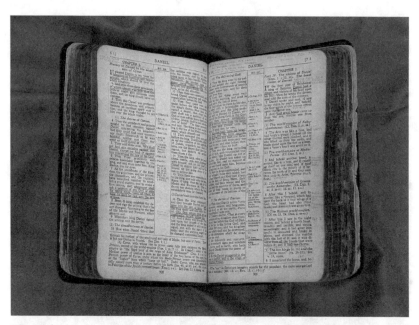

The Scofield Reference Bible, *published in 1909, became a pillar of American fundamentalism and its dispensationalist theology.* Photo: Copyright © 2009 Dallas Theological Seminary

Charles Hodge, Princeton Seminary professor whose Systematic Theology *(1872-1873) articulated a full-fledged fundamentalist theology and who also led American religious opposition to Charles Darwin.* Photo: Matthew Brady, Washington D.C.

Triumphalism

Although representing the height of the medieval worldly papacy, Pope Innocent III here meets St. Francis and approves the Franciscan rule of strict poverty. Photo: Alinari
Art Resource, NY

Triumphalism

New England minister and theologian Cotton Mather (1662-1728) embodied the theocratic ideal in early America. Image copyright © The Metropolitan Museum of Art/Art Resource, NY

Moralism

Typical of medieval understandings of virtue and vice, this fresco from the Castello de Masnago, in Varese, Italy, envisions Chastity between Lust and Vanity. Photo: Alinari/SEAT/Art Resource, NY

Moralism

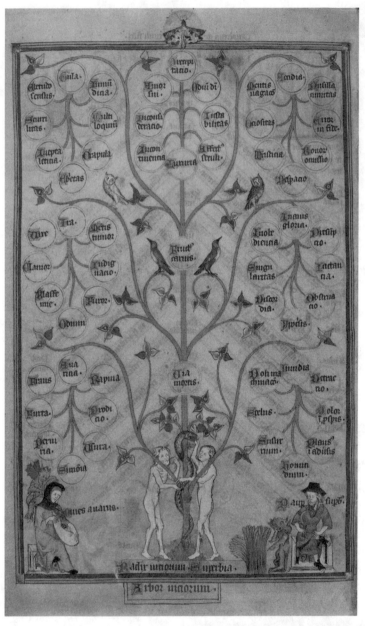

The elaborate typologies of medieval moral theology are shown in this fourteenth-century portrayal of "The Tree of Vices," growing from branches of the seven deadly sins. Photo: British Library, London, Great Britain/HIP/Art Resource, NY

CHAPTER 3

Triumphalism

Theocratic Dominance

> Now, therefore, we declare, say, determine and pronounce that for
> every human creature it is necessary for salvation to be subject to
> the authority of the Roman Pontiff.[1]

> Know this place where the Lord will create a new Heaven and new
> Earth, in new churches, and a new Commonwealth together.[2]

An unholy alliance began in 313 c.e. when Emperor Constantine I (also
called "the great") was converted and began legally to tolerate Christianity. In the new religion, the emperor saw the power that could make
him an autocrat, and the church wanted him to become its guardian. It
was the beginning of a theocratic domination of the world by way of
the fusion of church and state that subsequently dominated the political
landscape for centuries.

The story of this fusion is recorded by the well-known theologian Eusebius of Caesarea, who had survived the final phase of the persecution
of Christians by the Roman emperors, and, as an admirer of Constantine, was appointed bishop in 313.[3] He decided to write the history of

the church from its humble beginnings to its glory under Constantine. Known as the *Ecclesiastical History*, this multi-volume work contains a eulogistic *Life of Constantine* with a detailed account of how he attributed his political and military success to a miraculous conversion. The account discloses the work of a zealous, partisan "court historian" whose subject, Constantine, can do no wrong. Fact and fiction create the story of a "holy emperor" under the spiritual tutelage of the bishop of Rome. The dramatic beginning of the eulogistic "history" needs to be told in some detail in order to illustrate its triumphalist exultation over the bonding of spiritual and secular power.

Convinced that his military power and strategy needed supernatural help, Constantine had become a devotee of the Greek family god Apollo, son of Zeus. But when his enemies and their gods were defeated, he became doubtful.

Hearing of the great power of the "supreme God" of the Christians, Constantine decided to call on him before the decisive battle for the conquest of Rome in 312. While he was praying in his military headquarters near the gates of the city, he saw "a most marvelous sign" in the early afternoon: "A cross of light in the heaven, above the sun, and bearing the Greek inscription "Conquer by this sign [*touto nika*]." The whole army was said to have seen the sign. While Constantine pondered the experience, "night suddenly came on; then in his sleep the Christ of God appeared to him with the same sign and commanded him to make a likeness of that sign and to use it as a safeguard in all engagements with his enemies." Since this is such a "tall" story, Eusebius assures the reader that his account can be trusted.

> The account might have been hard to believe, had it been related by any other person. But since the victorious emperor himself long afterwards declared it to the writer of this history, when he was honored with his acquaintance and society, and confirmed his statement with an oath, who would hesitate to the relation, especially since the testimony of after-time has established its truth?

Constantine immediately had his miraculous vision transformed into an emblem, the like of which could not be found again:

> A long spear, overlaid with gold, formed the figure of the cross by a transverse bar laid over it. On the top of the whole was fixed a wreath

of gold and precious stones; and within this, the symbol of the Saviour's name, two letters indicating the name of Christ by means of the
initial characters, the letter P being intersected by X in its center; and
these letters the emperor was in the habit of wearing on his helmet
at a later period. From the cross-bar of the spear was suspended a
cloth, a royal piece, covered with a profuse embroidery of most bril-
liant precious stones; and which, being also richly interlaced with
gold, presented an indescribable degree of beauty to the beholder.
This banner was of a square form, and the upright staff, whose lower
section was of great length, bore a golden half-length portrait of the
pious emperor and his children on its upper part, beneath the trophy
of the cross, and immediately above the embroidered banner.

The emblem became known as a "labarum," depicting the "sign of
salvation." Similar emblems depicting this sign were to be carried at the
head of Constantine's military units. Constantine had himself instructed
about the theological meaning of the sign, and "he determined henceforth
to devote himself to the reading of the inspired writings [the Bible]."
According to Eusebius, priests became his counselors. But he postponed
baptism until his dying day in order to be assured that all his sins were
forgiven; converts were afraid that post-baptismal sins might go with
them to heaven.

Constantine's legislation favored Christianity without, however, formally prohibiting other religions. But Sunday became a legal holiday;
many new beautiful churches were built; and the capital of the Eastern
empire, Byzantium, was re-named Constantinople. When intensive theological controversies threatened to divide the young Christian church,
Constantine took it upon himself to restore unity. In 325, he summoned
318 bishops to come to a council in Nicaea, near Byzantium, to share
their views.[4] Most of them served in the East; the bishop of Rome, Sylvester I, was represented by two presbyters. Constantine paid all expenses
and chaired the council. He also had his court theologian and biogra-
pher, Eusebius of Caesarea, submit a compromise formula reflecting the
baptismal creed of the bishop's diocese. A majority of bishops favored
the compromise. But when the theological bickering reached an impasse
regarding the proper words depicting the relationship between God the
Father, and God the Son, Constantine introduced the Greek catchword
"of one being" (homousios). Accordingly, the first part of the Nicene

Creed would read "of one being with the Father."[5] All but two bishops signed the creed with this formulation, and unity was preserved.

The Donation of Constantine

Christian adoration honored Constantine like a saint, with a special feast day in the East (May 21) and with a document in the West, *The Donation of Constantine*, which, however, turned out to be a forgery produced in the ninth century.[6] The document is a classic example of the way in which ecclesiastical leaders claimed to have miraculous political powers. In a first part, the forgery relates how the emperor was instructed in the Christian faith by the bishop of Rome, Pope Sylvester I, who baptized Constantine and cured him of leprosy. But Constantine was baptized just before he died, and there is no evidence that he had leprosy. In a second part, the forgery relates how Constantine rewarded the pope with a testamentary "donation," consisting of primacy over all the bishops in the world and jurisdiction over Italy and "the western world," that is, all of Europe. Moreover, the pope was to have the privilege of appearing in public showing imperial insignia, such as a golden crown and a purple cloak. The document closes with the assurance that it was signed by the emperor and deposited in the tomb of St. Peter in Rome (for which there is no historical evidence). Any violation of the "Donation" would incur maledictions.

In the fifteenth century, Lorenzo Valla and other Humanists quickly identified the "Donation" as a primitive forgery disclosing the ninth-century language and culture of the era of Charlemagne. Moreover, the document was never used in the papal chancery until the middle of the eleventh century, during the reign of the Frankish emperor Otto III (983–1002). Although the author cannot be identified with certainty, he seems to have been a Roman ecclesiastic, eager to "prove" the miraculous power of the pope. The story of Pope Sylvester's cure of the emperor's leprosy has been found in another forgery depicting the apocalyptical "acts of Sylvester."

Pope and Emperor

Constantine had a mausoleum constructed in the Church of the Apostles where he would rest from his labors in the midst of the memorial plaques to the first twelve disciples of Christ. His mother, Helena, made pilgrimages to Palestine, where she designated "holy places," such as the Church of the Nativity in Bethlehem. She was made a saint, honored on August 18 in the West and on May 21 in the East. Her sainted son, however, was no saint: he fought brutal battles against rivals of the imperial throne, and in 326, he had his oldest son Crispus and his second wife Fausta put to death for an alleged conspiracy. Such details are not part of the biographical legend. It is an irony of history that the first political benefactor of Christianity used the title "Prince of Peace" (Isa 9:6) for his ambitious climb to autocracy.

Constantine's fusion of church and state was legally enforced by Emperor Theodosius I in 380. A new code of laws (*Codex Theodosius*) made Christianity, identified with the bishop of Rome, the exclusive religion of the empire. Christianity is claimed to be the successor of the Roman Empire in the guise of Roman Catholicism.

> We desire that all people under the rule of our clemency should *live by that religion which divine Peter the apostle is said to have given to the Romans,* and which it is evident that Pope Damasus and Peter, bishop of Alexandria, a man of apostolic sanctity, followed; that is that we should believe in the one deity of the Father, Son and Holy Spirit with equal majesty and in the Holy Trinity according to the apostolic teaching and the authority of the Gospel.[7]

This is a distortion of the "proof text" for the papacy (Matt 16:18) that, however, makes no reference to "the Romans." Hearsay becomes a solemnly promulgated divine truth, enforced by law.

Justinian I expanded the Theodosian Codex into a massive collection of laws governing every aspect of life in the new state church, the *Corpus Juris Civilis* of 534, later known and still in force in Roman Catholicism as "Canon Law" (*corpus juris canonici*). It had no tolerance for dissent, not even for differences in thinking. The famous academy of philosophy in Athens was closed in 529, thus ending all connections to classical antiquity and silencing any critics. But Justinian himself did not live by the standards he so zealously enforced. His private life revealed that he had married a dancing girl, Theodora, who belonged to a sect that did not acknowledge the dogma of the Trinity—a crime punishable by death. Although her sexual immoralities have not been fully substantiated, her anti-Trinitarian heresy seems to have been shared by Justinian.[8]

The unholy union of church and state was complete in the coronation of a "Holy Roman Emperor" in 800, the Frankish king Charles I, also known as Charlemagne. He became the protector of the Roman Catholic Church, the only church in the empire. Pope Leo III continued to advocate the notion that the state is to protect the church, albeit only if the pope approves the emperor. Charles I obliged by defeating papal enemies, some by execution. Thus he was ready to be acknowledged as the secular head of the imperial church headed by a pope. Pope and emperor defined the power of the imperial church. Historical records relate that Charles and Leo III met at the Church of St. Peter in Rome at the celebration of a pontifical Mass. After the Gospel had been sung, Charles knelt and Leo placed a crown on his head. The large crowd of worshippers shouted, "To Charles, the most pious Augustus, crowned by God, to our great and pacific emperor life and victory!"[9] This affirmation repeated the claim of the Code of Theodosius that both pope and emperor represented the continuation of the Roman Empire; "Augustus" (from the Latin *augustus*, "venerable," "holy") is the title given to Roman emperors. A Holy Roman Emperor was crowned by a Holy Roman Pope as the head of an imperial church.

In order to "prove" unlimited papal authority, a series of sensational literary forgeries appeared in the middle of the ninth century, known as the *The Decretals of Pseudo-Isidore*.[10] The collection consists of nearly one hundred pieces linked to an author whose pseudonym is Isidore Mercator (not to be confused with the Spanish theologian Isidore of Seville, c. 560–636). The forgery is clever, sophisticated, and plagiaristic. It begins with a chronicle, "The Book of Popes" (*Liber Pontificales*), listing real and fictitious popes beginning with St. Peter. The author cites invented decrees and papal letters, using parts from various works. Thus, the collection is made to look like a work based on historical evidence. As an analyst of the forgery put it:

> His work is a regular mosaic of phrases stolen from various works written either by clerics or laymen. This network of quotations is computed to number more than 10,000 borrowed phrases, and Isidore succeeded in stringing them together by that loose, easy style of his, in such a way that many forgeries perpetrated either by him or his assistants have an undeniable family resemblance. Without doubt, he was one of the most learned men of his day.[11]

Among the hundred documents of the collection, there are "papal letters" and a mixture of authentic and false "decretals," that is, legal pieces posing as canon law, favoring the broad power of popes over bishops. The forger used documents written long after the times of the popes to whom he attributes them. Thus, popes of the first three centuries are made to cite sources that did not appear until later, sometimes not even before the eighth century. Moreover, he interpolated his forgeries into a genuine Spanish collection of canon laws from 633, known as *Hispana*. But he made the mistake of using a French faulty edition, tampering with the text. The forgery was published between 847 and 852 in northern France, at a time when the papacy was weak and needed a lift. The "false decretals" provided just such a lift by claiming an earlier date for later papal claims that spiritual authority has supremacy over secular authority. This is spelled out in regard to episcopal authority: only the pope can authorize the calling of a council of bishops, and only the pope can make a final judgment in ecclesiastical trials. All this is presented in great detail with authentic and invented texts in legalese.

The forgeries were accepted as facts throughout the Middle Ages. One is reminded of the quip of a satirical journalist, "If you repeat a story often enough it becomes fact." When some church officials and secular scholars recognized the extensive fraud, church officials in Rome refused to believe them and retained the false decretals as part of the official collection of canon law, the Corpus Juris, until 1628, when the French Protestant (Reformed) church historian David Blondel proved conclusively that the decretals were the work of Pseudo-Isidore.[12] He also investigated a legend, popular between the thirteenth and seventeenth centuries, that there was a female pope in men's clothing from 855 until about 858—depicted as a very intelligent young woman from Mainz, Germany, named Joan (Johanna), who was elected as John Anglicus. Blondel proved that the legend was the product of the imagination of anti-papal polemicists rather than historical fact.[13]

Since 1059, popes have symbolized their power by a headdress, the tiara, with one crown, then expanded to three by 1314. It was an emblem of princely secular power, used in audiences, while the Episcopal emblem, the miter, was worn when the pope presided at the liturgy.

The dominance of the church was severely tested in the power struggle between Pope Gregory VII and the German emperor Henry IV in the eleventh century. Gregory tried to bolster the weakening power of the papacy by promulgating twenty-seven theses in 1075.[14] They disclose an irrational megalomania. Using the "False Decretals of Isidore," they affirm the absolute authority of the pope over the universal church, his position as the supreme lord of the world, and his complete legal authority over bishops. Princes must kiss his feet because they, like the moon, receive their light from the sun, the pope. Finally, the pope enjoys the special supernatural protection of St. Peter and thus is "holy" and can never err. The theses use a biblical proof text, Jeremiah 48:10 ("Accursed is the one who is slack in doing the work of the Lord; and accursed is the one who keeps back the sword from bloodshed") to "prove" that the pope has an obligation to fight the enemies of the papacy to preserve the liberty of the church.

So armed, Gregory launched the reform of the tenth-century church, which had been plagued by two enduring abuses ever since there was a privileged clergy: simony (buying ecclesiastical offices, a term derived from a magician, Simon Magus, who tried to buy the power of the Holy Spirit from the apostles; see Acts 8:18-24) and incontinence (unrestrained sexual sins). This general debasement of the church was described by the church historian, Vatican librarian, and cardinal, Caesar Baronius, in his twelve volume *Ecclesiastical Annals (Annales ecclesiastici)* of 1588. It was a time "that Christ was as if asleep in the vessel of the church."[15] St. Bruno, bishop of Engi, testified in his biography of Pope Leo IX (1049–1054) that "the whole world lay in wickedness, holiness had disappeared, justice had perished and truth had been buried: Simon Magus was lording over the church whose bishops and priests were given to luxury and fornication."[16] The Italian teacher, monk, and reformer, Peter Damian, described the sins of the clergy, married and unmarried, in lurid detail; he entitled his critique *Book of Gomorrah (Liber Gomorrhianus*, c. 1059). Gregory himself complained to his venerated friend, Abbot Hugh of Cluny, in a letter of 1075:

> The eastern church has fallen away from the Faith and is now assailed on every side by infidels. Wherever I turn my eyes to the west, to the north, or to the south—I find everywhere bishops who have obtained their office in an irregular way, whose lives and conversations are strangely at variance with their sacred calling: who go through their duties not for the love of Christ but from motives

of worldly gain. There are no longer princes who set God's honor before their own selfish ends, or who allow justice to stand in the way of their ambition. And among those I live—Romans, Lombards, and Normans—are, as I have often told them, worse than Jews and pagans.[17]

In his first Lenten Synod of 1074, Gregory moved against the abuse of clerical simony and incontinence. He decreed

That clerics who had obtained any grade of office of sacred orders by payment should cease to minister in the Church.

That no one who had purchased any church should retain it, and that no one for the future should be permitted to buy or sell ecclesiastical rights.

That all who were guilty of incontinence should cease to exercise their sacred ministry.

That the people should reject ministrations of clergy who failed to obey these injunctions.[18]

These rules created opposition in Germany, where the marriage of priests was quite common. The whole body of married clergy told the papal legate at a meeting in Nuremberg that they would rather renounce their priesthood than their wives. Their defense through biblical texts echoes contemporary arguments in favor of the institution of clerical marriage: "It is better to marry than to be aflame with passion" (1 Cor 7:9); "a bishop must be above reproach, married only once" (1 Tim 3:2); marriage is better than celibacy, which is for "those to whom it is given" (Matt 19:11).[19] In the face of such opposition, many bishops ignored the Gregorian decrees. One bishop almost lost his life, and an episcopal council in Paris condemned the Roman decrees as intolerable and irrational. The bitter disagreement demonstrates that clerical marriage was the rule rather than the exception, even though popes taught that clerical celibacy had been the rule since the time of the apostles. But St. Peter was married (Matt 8:14)!

The Arrogance of Papal Power

The German emperor, Henry IV, had promised Gregory to eradicate simony in his traditional role as protector of the church. But when he failed to fulfill the promise, the pope used his power as "the supreme lord of the world" to prohibit the appointment of any bishop by secular princes, as had been done in Germany. There was to be no "lay investiture," that is, the investing of ecclesiastical power by a layman. Gregory excommunicated bishops who had been so invested and threatened also to ban secular authorities for doing so. When Henry IV refused to obey, Gregory excommunicated him and released Henry's subjects from their oath of allegiance to the emperor. The stage was set for a test of how much the church could dominate the state.

The test revealed a pitiful drama of the arrogance of power on both sides. Henry did not receive sufficient support to stand up against the pope. So he fled with his wife and a single servant in the winter of 1076 to the Canossa castle in the foothills of Tuscany, the safe, fortified residence of an old friend, Countess Mathilda. But Gregory, afraid of treachery on his way from Germany to Rome, had also sought refuge there. Perhaps the countess arranged the "coincidental" meeting of the two feuding parties. In any case, Henry knew that he, like any ordinary Christian, could be released from excommunication by doing penance before a priest. But when he approached Gregory to receive priestly absolution, the pope refused. So Henry played the role of a miserable penitent; he put on simple clothes and was said to have stood for three days (January 25–27, 1077) in ice and snow outside the castle to beg for forgiveness. The pope had to offer it since priests cannot refuse the plea for forgiveness by a miserable, penitent sinner. Henry was restored as a legitimate member of the church.

The story is related in a letter by Gregory to the German princes, whom he may have tried to impress with the story of the emperor's humiliation at Canossa. But the German princes seem not to have been impressed and refused to support the pope, and the feud continued. Henry gathered disenchanted Lombard noblemen, and bishops guilty of simony, in 1080 in Brixen, where he had an anti-pope elected, Clement III. Then he marched on Rome and captured the city in 1084. Gregory fled to the isolated mountain monastery in Monte Cassino and spent his final days in Salerno. Three days before his death, he withdrew all the censures of excommunication and was reported to have died with the words, "I have loved justice and hated iniquity, therefore I die in exile."[20] In 1728 he was canonized as a saint! Henry crushed the Saxon rebellion in Germany in 1089, but his son revolted against him and became Henry V in 1106 when his father died.

The whole series of events reveals the drive for power by emperors and popes, spreading doubt about their alliance as a sign of divine wisdom. Playing God prevails. Instead of penance and reform, cruel Christian crusades were launched in 1096. For three centuries, they imposed Christian terror not only on non-Christians in the "holy land," but also on fellow Christians who advocated a variety of views. The Fourth Crusade, launched by the super-pope Innocent III, turned against eastern, Byzantine Christians, resulting in the barbaric sack of Constantinople in 1204. The Ottoman Turks finally stopped the tide of Christian crusades in 1369 when Muslims massacred 100,000 crusaders at Nicopolis in Bulgaria.

Innocent III continued the papal hunger for power. In his negotiations with German emperors he imposed his papal authority on secular rulers by way of the decree *Venerabilem* of 1202; it became part of canon law in the *Corpus Juris Canonici*. Its principal points are quite telling: 1. The right of German kings to elect an emperor was given to them by the pope because he anointed Charlemagne, thus transferring power from the Greeks and Romans to the Germans. Here Innocent employs and expands the notion of "apostolic succession": divine authority moves from the apostle Peter to the Romans (as Theodosius had contended), then via the Romans to the Greeks and via the Greeks to the Germans. The glory of ancient Rome is transferred to the Roman Pontiff. 2. The pope investigates and decides whether a king is worthy of imperial dignity and, if so, must be consecrated by the pope. If a king refuses to be the divinely appointed patron and defender of the church, then another king must be elected and approved by the pope. 3. In cases of doubt, or a double election, the pope must arbitrate, "failing which, he must of his own accord and by virtue of his office decide in favor of one of the claimants."[21] There would be no emperor without the approval of the pope!

Innocent practiced what he preached. With diplomatic finesse, he involved himself in almost all of the political power struggles in Europe. In Germany, he declared himself the arbiter in the struggle between two candidates for the imperial crown, Otto and Frederick. He crowned Otto as Otto IV, but when Otto opposed the decree on papal superpowers, he excommunicated him in 1210 and crowned Frederick as Frederick II.

In France, Innocent ordered King Philip Augustus to be reconciled with his lawful wife, Ingeburga of Denmark, and to leave his Italian second wife, Agnes, the daughter of the Duke of Meran. When the French king refused to obey, the pope put all of France under interdict. Since the king's subjects sided with the pope—probably because of their ruler's immoral conduct—Philip Augustus obeyed. In England, Innocent involved himself in the struggle between two candidates for the office of the Archbishop of Canterbury. King John offered the pope a large sum of money to accept the royal favorite, John de Grey. But Innocent refused the bribe and supported the election of a third candidate, Stephen Langton, favored by the monastic community. King John continued to lobby for John Grey after Langton had been consecrated by the pope. He drove the monks from their monasteries and confiscated their property. Innocent excommunicated him and formally deposed him in 1212, and he ordered King Philip of France to enforce the papal verdict. Threatened by a French invasion, King John succumbed and acknowledged the new Archbishop of Canterbury. He even surrendered the English empire to the pope, who returned it to him as a fief. Hence John was known in some annals of history as "King John without a land." Innocent lifted the ban of excommunication from the king in 1213. Many of the British barons used the weakness of King John to gain individual rights in the famous Magna Carta of 1215, which sowed the seeds for a constitutional government. The pope declared the Carta null and void, but could not prevent King John from signing it. "There was scarcely a country in Europe over which Innocent III did not in some way or other assert the supremacy which he claimed for the "papacy."

Innocent III celebrated his papal superpower in the Fourth Lateran Council of 1215.[22] Its atmosphere was drenched with pomp and circumstance, reflecting the absolute supremacy of the Roman Pontiff. He chaired the council for three weeks and his decisions were accepted without opposition by seventy-one patriarchs and metropolitans from the East, including by the patriarchs of Constantinople and Jerusalem, by 412 bishops from the West, and by 900 abbots and priors. In addition to about 2000 participants (and their entourages), there were envoys from almost every European nation. Innocent III had prepared seventy-nine canons or decrees that defined dogma, decided controversial issues, condemned heretics, and announced another crusade to the Holy Land.

Here are the important canons that illustrate the might of a single Christian.[23]

1. The dogma of transubstantiation.

4. An exhortation to the Greek Orthodox Christians to reunite with the Roman Catholic Church.

13. No new religious orders may be established, lest too great a diversity bring confusion into the church.

14-17. Irregularities of the clergy are named and forbidden, for example, incontinence, drunkenness, attendance at farces, and histrionic exhibitions.

18. Priests, deacons and subdeacons are forbidden to perform surgical operations.

21. "Omnis utriusque sexus," which commands every Christian who has reached the age of discretion [age seven] to confess all his, or her, sins at least once a year to his or her own priest.

78-79. Jews and Moslems shall wear a special dress to enable them to be distinguished from Christians.[24] Christians must take measures to prevent blasphemies against Jesus Christ.

The imperial church lasted politically until the Reformation of the sixteenth century, when Martin Luther attacked its abuses, beginning with the sale of indulgences, or paper certificates for the remission of sins granted by the pope in lieu of going to confession. King Henry VIII of England rejected papal authority in 1534 and made himself the "supreme head on earth of the Church of England." Roman Catholicism was abandoned under Elizabeth I in 1559 in favor of an independent "Anglican Church" (*ecclesia anglicana*). Formal recognition of Lutheran, Reformed (Calvinist), and Anglican churches was granted after the Thirty Years' War at the Peace of Westphalia in 1648; it rendered the medieval papal claims of universal supremacy impotent.

The papacy did try to reject scientific discoveries that threatened the existing climate of opinion. The now famous Italian physicist, astronomer, and mathematical philosopher Galileo Galilei was condemned by the Inquisition in 1616 for embracing the heretical view of the Renaissance astronomer Nicolas Copernicus (1473–1545) that the earth rotated around the sun. In 1637, Galileo was forced to recant his views in order to avoid life imprisonment. But he ignored the recantation and retired to Florence, where he taught his new astronomic insights until his death in 1642. The European Enlightenment "de-churched" culture, as it were, and began an enduring process of secularization, marked by the American and French Revolutions in the eighteenth century. The decline of papal power may be the reason why the dogma of papal infallibility of 1850 was employed only a century later when Pope Pius XII promulgated the assumption of Mary into heaven At that time, the Roman Catholic Church had become a minority church in the old, previously loyal superpowers of France, England, and Germany (and especially in Scandinavia). Gone was the age when a Roman Pontiff could dominate the politics of church and state.

Müntzer and Anabaptist Radicals

Protestant theocratic dominance began to appear sporadically in the early years of the Reformation. An early follower of Luther, Thomas Müntzer (1488?–1525), left the camp of the Wittenberg reformer because he felt Luther relied too much on the princes.[25] Müntzer wanted to create a militant movement that would remove the power of the nobility and establish an egalitarian rule. The movement would be led by a "Covenant of the Elect" from Müntzer's hometown of Allstedt, Saxony, combined with a revolutionary army of peasants.

While Luther was in voluntary exile at the Wartburg castle for almost a year (from May 1521 until March 1522) after his condemnation at Worms in 1521, Müntzer moved to Prague, where he hoped to gain the support of the Hussites, the followers of John Hus who had been martyred by the church in 1415 because of his rejection of papal authority. The Hussites had built a strong political following in Bohemia (formerly Czechoslovakia) and from Luther and his followers. In a "Manifesto," published on All Saints Day, November 1521, Müntzer claimed that he had received a special revelation from the Holy Spirit, negating the authority of the Bible and of the existing ecclesiastical authorities, be they Roman Catholic or Lutheran. True, living faith, he declared, comes through the inward mortification of earthly desires; it is a painful struggle

(*Anfechtung* in German, as Luther had called it). According to Müntzer, Luther never received a pure, inward illumination by the Holy Spirit and tried to combine the gospel with the law. Müntzer claimed to have experienced an illumination by which God appointed him to be the "new Daniel" who would prepare humankind for the imminent kingdom of God. That is why people should follow him rather than Luther, "Doctor Liar, the soft-living flesh in Wittenberg," more loyal to selfish worldly princes than to Christ. When Luther denounced Müntzer as an evil spirit inducing rebellion, Müntzer fumed in public.

The world will in two or three years realize what murderous and malicious harm he has done. He washes his hands of any guilt so that no one might notice that he is the persecutor of truth. For he insists that his preaching is the true word of God because it causes persecution. I am truly amazed that this shameless monk can claim to be persecuted when he drinks malmsey [wine] and eats the food of whores.[26]

Müntzer saw Luther as being in league with the nobility who abused the gospel to justify their lust for selfish political power, oppressing the common people. Müntzer urged others to unite with him as "a destroyer of unbelievers."[27] Here, Müntzer moved from an inward mysticism to a militant theocracy, contending that those who refused to accept the Holy Spirit in their hearts must be forced by the sword to do so. Moreover, Müntzer became convinced that not only the Saxon "Lutheran" princes were stubborn and needed a violent lesson, but that the whole world must experience a purification, since Christ's second coming was near (a notion quite popular at the time).

When Luther recommended that the Saxon Court call Müntzer to a hearing, Duke John ordered one for July 13, 1524 in Allstedt and asked Müntzer to prepare a sermon on his views. The sermon casts Müntzer in the role of a "new Daniel," based on an exposition of Daniel 2, in which Daniel interprets the dream of King Nebuchadnezzar. As the "new Daniel," Müntzer applied the prophetic judgment to his own time: The church had lost its original purity and had become an adulteress of the gospel; as a result, the Holy Spirit had withdrawn its support and called on special people to restitute the original loyalty to Christ as a preparation for his final coming. The princes are told:

Do not be seduced by your hypocritical priests who retain you with their false faith about God's goodness and patience. The rock torn from the mountain without the use of hands (Dan 2:34) has become large. The poor lay people and peasants have focused on it better than you . . . That is why a new Daniel must appear and interpret for you your revelation, and he must lead the way. He must placate the wrath of the princes and that of the furious people. . . . If you wish to be a true regent, you must begin your reign at the roots, as Jesus commanded; you must drive out his enemies from among the elect.[28]

When the princes rejected Müntzer's pleas and sided with Luther, Müntzer called them defenders of "the false faith of the unfaithful world," and he began signing his letters "Thomas Müntzer with the hammer." Denounced by Luther as "the satanic spirit of Allstedt," he fled from place to place, was seen in Switzerland, and finally joined the rebellious peasants in Mühlhausen, Saxony, in the spring of 1525. While the peasants took up defensive positions on a mountain near the town of Frankenhausen against an overwhelming force of princes, Müntzer urged them on through sermons depicting the imminent battle as the final event before the arrival of Christ's everlasting kingdom. A rainbow on May 15 signaled to him the victory of the "League of the Elect." But the "battle of Frankenhausen" was a bloodbath, yielding a total defeat of the peasants; about 5000 were killed and 600 were captured, among them Müntzer, who was tortured and beheaded. Luther's verdict made him the symbol of satanic power. "Whoever has seen Müntzer," Luther wrote three days after the execution, "may say that he has seen the devil himself in his great wrath."[29] Centuries later, Müntzer experienced the peculiar feat of being seen as a forerunner of Socialism and Communism in the East German Democratic Republic (1946–1989).[30]

In 1535, ten years after Müntzer's death, a group of "Anabaptists" established a theocratic reign of terror in the city of Münster, Westphalia (near the Dutch border).[31] They were a radical wing of the Brethren of Zürich, also known as Swiss Brethren, who, led by the Humanist Conrad Grebel, contended that Scripture does not teach infant baptism.[32] Moreover, one must first be converted before one is baptized, that is, one has to be an adult. But the reformer of Zürich, Ulrich Zwingli (1484–1531), had persuaded the city council to uphold the medieval practice of baptizing infants eight days after their birth. Refusal to do so would incur exile. Grebel responded by baptizing the most zealous "Anabaptist" (a nickname derived from the Greek *anabaptizein*, "rebaptize"), George Cajabob, a former priest known as "strong George" and "Bluecoat" (*Blaurock*, his favorite dress), at the home of Felix Manz in Zürich in 1525. Since it was a second baptism (after infant baptism), it was a heresy according to a tradition dating back to the fifth century, when Christianity had become a state religion. Such heresy would result in the death penalty. Since Swiss citizens do not like fighting each other, attempts were made to compromise. When they failed, Anabaptists were jailed. Some fled the country, and Felix Manz was drowned in Lake Zürich in 1527. A fanatic Dutch Anabaptist, Melchior Hoffmann, attracted followers through a vision concerning the end-time. Soon, "Melchiorites" roamed through the country, trying to establish a uniform, theocratic community as a link to the future kingdom of God. Two Dutch Melchiorites, John Beukels from Leiden and John Matthjis from Amsterdam, persuaded the Lutherans in Münster to transform the city into a model theocracy. Opponents were executed, polygamy was instituted, and Beukels began calling himself the "king of new Zion," presiding at "messianic banquets." For almost a year, the city was besieged by a military force of Lutheran and Catholic princes. When they invaded the city in 1535, they slaughtered most of the inhabitants. Three surviving leaders were tortured in public with red-hot tongs, then their seared bodies were placed in iron cages and suspended from the tower of the largest church. The cages can still be seen today in public.

Calvinism

Protestant theocratic dominance continued in less esoteric ways. Its political makeup changed. It was no longer conditioned by princes of church and state but by the power of a small group, an oligarchy (*oligarkes* in Greek, "a rule of few"), elected by majority vote. Oligarchic government became popular in Switzerland, the oldest European "democracy" since 1291 where citizens elected their leaders. Ulrich Zwingli, the city priest of Zürich, the German part of Switzerland, advocated the change from Roman Catholicism to independence based on modified "Lutheran" views. But in a military battle between the new Swiss Protestants and the old Catholics in 1531, Zwingli was killed. One year later, the Protestant cause also gained momentum in the capital of French Switzerland, Geneva, where the French preacher William Farel spread his Reformation views. In 1536, he persuaded the well-known Protestant Frenchman John Calvin to lead the reforms, even though Calvin was neither Swiss nor ordained.

Calvin had been drawn away from "popish" Catholicism to "Christian Humanism." He became fascinated by the biblical character of David, whom tradition praised as the author of the Old Testament Psalms.[33] Sometime in 1531–1532, Calvin felt "converted" to a peaceful faith and chosen by God, just as David had found inner peace and had felt divinely elected as king, despite being assailed by enemies. Like King David, he wanted to create a disciplined community in Geneva where the magistracy had adopted Protestant principles, replacing Catholic episcopacy. The new principles, derived from the Bible as "the Word of God," were strictly enforced, with rules for worship and morality. Priests were given a month to convert or face exile. All remnants of the old religion were removed and replaced in 1536 with "holy evangelical law."

Calvin's *Ecclesiastical Ordinances* of 1541 provided the oligarchic institutional structure for the new politics, "taken from the Gospel of Jesus Christ."[34] The Genevan *Ordinances* became the model for a move from oligarchy to theocracy in New England Puritanism in the seventeenth century. They proposed "four offices instituted by our Savior" for the government of the Church: pastors, doctors or teachers, elders (nominated and appointed by the government), and deacons. Pastors were to be carefully selected and trained; they must be a cooperating, disciplined team, and above reproach. Doctors or teachers were to teach children of all ages in an "academy," with separate schools for girls; the staff had to be approved by the pastors and the government. The elders were to form a "consistory" to supervise and enforce public morals. The deacons were to be in charge of stewardship, raising money and spending it for charity; they were to maintain a hospital and to care for the poor. Begging, the social curse of the Middle Ages, was to be abolished.

The Consistory of the elders, half laity, half clergy, functioned as an ecclesiastical court and became the strong arm of the government in Geneva. They held hearings, resulting in exclusion from the Lord's Supper and, in the worst cases, excommunication. Soon, life in Geneva became quite "puritan": no secular entertainment, not even secular music and art, and of course, obligatory Sunday worship. As an anti-Calvinist put it in 1553, "Before Calvin was in the city we drank good wine."[35] When local businessmen and other influential citizens refused to comply with the new puritanical laws against gambling and other "secular" entertainments, Calvin and the Consistory reacted with force. In 1546, the merchant Pierre Ameaux was compelled to do penance in public, barefoot and dressed only in a shirt. The citizen Jean Gruet was executed in 1547 for the crime of blasphemy.

Calvin was almost killed in the same year during a public commotion, organized against him by former friends and supporters. The most celebrated victim of Calvinism in Geneva was the Spanish physician Michael Servetus, who wrote passionate treatises against the dogma of the Trinity.[36] When he tried to discuss his views with Calvin in letters, Calvin denounced him and had him arrested in Geneva, where Servetus had stopped briefly to escape the Catholic Inquisition. On October 27, 1553, he was burned at the stake in Geneva. Because of his autocratic rule in Geneva, Calvin has been portrayed as an enigmatic theocrat, comparable with dictators like Napoleon Bonaparte, Vladimir Lenin, and Karl Marx.[37]

Calvin succeeded in his ambition to create an alternative to Catholicism, known as the Reformed Church in Europe, especially in France, the Netherlands, England, Scotland, and Poland, where he had many followers with whom he maintained a lively correspondence. They were trained at the Academy in Geneva. Calvin's successor, Theodore Beza, had added a strong theological faculty to the Academy in 1559, and many foreign students graduated from there. In France, a Calvinist elite, called "Huguenots," became involved in bloody military campaigns against Catholics, and gained equal rights with Catholics in 1598. When Dutch Calvinists, who were ruled by Catholic Spain, revolted, Spain reacted with a war of terror, executing about 18,000 "heretics." But the Dutch endured and gained independence as the Netherlands in 1579 (guaranteed by the Peace of Westphalia in 1648). These Calvinist uprisings were propelled by theocratic ideas resulting in religious uniformity. These ideas have theological roots in Calvin's doctrine of "double predestination."

> Scripture clearly proves that God, by his eternal and unchanging will, determined once and for all those whom he would one day

admit to salvation and those whom he would consign to destruction. His decision about the elect is based on his free mercy with no reference to human deserving.[38]

Those who were saved would rule. But questions arose concerning any sign or other concrete evidence that could reveal whether one was saved or damned. Signs of salvation became identified with the economic success of Calvinists, mirroring the well-known example of Job in the Old Testament: after his penance, God restored his fortunes by blessing his economic ventures, ranging from increased herds of animals to seven capable sons and three beautiful daughters (Job 42:10-17). Similarly, puritanical Christians felt blessed with economic success. "The devout Protestant lived a life of disciplined self-denial and hard work, counting God's approval in growing personal wealth. In turn, this created a new cultural norm of economic activity of the 'capitalist spirit.' "[39] The psychohistorical thesis is also warranted that Calvin might have arrived at his hard theological judgment through personal frustration about the unexpected opposition to his "puritan" rule in Geneva. Why, he could have asked himself, do some people not show up in church, or do not cooperate in a divinely willed organization, the Christian community in Geneva? Answer: Because God has "predested" them to be damned. The signs to indicate their lot are related to living a life involving few, if any, sacrifices. They do not want to give up gambling, drinking, dancing, and other "impure" ways of living. So there is no room for them in a puritanical society. There is no need for pastoral care for those who deviate from the establishment, and the doctrine of double predestination does not permit liberty of conscience or religious liberty.

Calvin viewed himself as the executor of the will of God in Geneva. When there was rioting in the streets in 1555 and hectic debates about excommunication from the Lord's Supper, Calvin vented his anger about decadent life in Geneva in a treatise *On the Scandals that Today Prevent Many People from Coming to the Pure Doctrine of the Gospel and Ruin Others*.[40] Echoing St. Paul (1 Cor 1:23), Calvin calls the Gospel a "scandal" (from the Greek *scandalon*), though not in the sense of "stumbling block," but as the decadence of those who, like the Greek Epicureans, reject faith in favor of earthly luxury and pleasure. One must do battle with those who violate the rules of the Gospel. That is why Jesus brings not only peace but also the sword (Matt 12:34), war, and discord.

Brothers, parents, and children will deliver each other up to death (Matt 10:21). Thus Calvin cites the Gospel of Matthew as the rationale for a crusade against decadence and heresy. People like Michael Servetus, who denounced the dogma of the Trinity, and the owners of gambling casinos in Geneva, are public enemies. They must be treated like "dogs" (a popular designation for blasphemers).

The sole purpose of Calvin's puritanical autocracy was to glorify God through spiritual formation in an evil world. When the seeds of such a formation sprout, there is total certainty, indeed a guarantee, of salvation. "It is impossible for the elect ever to be turned aside from the road to salvation."[41] This is the triumphalism of puritanism.

In England, Oliver Cromwell (1599–1658) embodied this triumphalism in his "Parliament of Saints" after his army of Psalm-singing puritan peasants defeated King Charles I and had him beheaded on January 30, 1649.[42] As "Lord Protector" during his last five years, Cromwell created a military dictatorship, convinced that he was an instrument of God called to create a pure theocracy. But after his death, England returned to parliamentary rule.

English Puritans revived the theocratic spirit of Calvinism when they rejected the union of church and state represented by kings and queens, as well as Anglican bishops. Since the 1630s, they had lobbied for independence, governed by four convictions: (1) "That humans are sinners who will not choose to be reconciled with God unless God initiates the processes of their salvation" through a conversion; (2) "that the Bible exerts a 'regulative' authority, which means that Christians, so far as possible, should do only what the Scriptures explicitly direct"; (3) "that God created society as a unified whole," that is, "church and state, the individual and the public, are not unrelated spheres of life but are complementary, intimately connected by God's act of creation and his continuing providence"; and (4) "that God always works with people through covenants, or solemn agreements."[43]

Puritanism in America

New England Puritans implemented these convictions in congregations that embodied a threefold covenant: (1) A Covenant of Grace, consisting of those who are invisibly tied together by faith in Christ, known in number only by God who elected them; (2) the Church Covenant, the visible communion of those who are converted and have joined a congregation, ruled by strict rules of faith and conduct; and (3) the Civil Covenant, guided by the counsel of the clergy whose rules were enforced by civil servants. Again the church dominated, as did the Roman Catholic Church in the Middle Ages, though in a different way. Members of government were elected and entrusted with the responsibility to enforce the rule of "the Word of God" as set forth in the Bible. "The Platform of Church Discipline," adopted by a synod of New England churches in Cambridge in 1648, describes the basic responsibilities of the Puritan theocratic government:

> The end of the Magistrate's office is not only the quiet and peaceful life of the subject in matters of righteousness and honesty, but also in matters of godliness, yea of all godliness. Idolatry, blasphemy, heresy, venting corrupt and pernicious opinions that destroy the foundation, open contempt of the Word preached, profanation of the Lord's Day, disturbing the holy things of God, and the like, are to be restrained and punished by civil authority. [44]

New England Puritans were convinced that their colony was destined to be the beginning of the kingdom of God on earth. As the Puritan leader Cotton Mather put it:

> Our Lord Jesus Christ carried some thousands of Reformers into the retirements of an American desert, on purpose, that with an opportunity granted unto many of his faithful servants, to enjoy the precious liberty of their ministry. . . . He might there, to them first, and then by them, give a specimen of many good things which he would have his churches elsewhere aspire and arise unto: and this being done, he knows not whether there be not all done, that New England was planted for.[45]

Cotton Mather (1662–1728) and Solomon Stoddard (1643–1729) embodied the Puritan theocracy in New England. "Pope" Stoddard (as he was called) was a minister in Northampton, Massachusetts, and Mather was a prolific theologian while serving as colleague-pastor to his father, Increase, at the North Church in Boston (not to be confused with the Episcopalian Old North Church linked to Paul Revere). "He was ostentatiously pious, shamelessly self-promoting, overbearingly moralistic, and his 469 separate books and pamphlets suggest that he never had a thought he felt was unworthy of publication."[46] He became fascinated by supernatural, invisible evidence of the divine. Such evidence seemed to him to present itself in the infamous witch trials in the village of Salem. They represent a very dangerous toxic spirituality.[47]

The trials began in 1692 when two young girls, Betty Parris, age nine, the daughter of the Reverend Samuel Parris, and Abigail Williams, age eleven, the cousin of Betty, exhibited an alarming pattern of behavior. They screamed and uttered strange sounds, they threw things about in the house, they crawled under furniture, and they contorted themselves into peculiar positions. They also felt pricked with pins and cut with knives, and they covered their ears when they heard Pastor Parrish preach. A physician diagnosed them as being bewitched, probably influenced by Cotton Mather's publication on the power of an Irish immigrant "witch" who imposed her craft on four Boston children.[48] Other females in the village showed similar symptoms. Rumor had it that the affected girls had been "entertained" by a slave of the Parrish family, Tituba, a woman described as "Indian." She was one of the first three women accused of witchcraft and arrested for allegedly having bewitched Ann Putnam, age twelve. The other two "witches" were described as anti-social: Sarah Good, a beggar who was known for uttering strange words under her breath when she walked away "cursing"; and Sarah Osburne, an irritable old woman who had married her indentured servant. Moreover, none of them went to church—a typical cause for suspicion.

The three women were jailed on March 1, 1692; three other women were also accused of witchcraft: Martha Corey, Rebecca Nurse, and Rachel Clinton, all of whom had doubted in public that the accused were witches. Even little Dorothy Good, age four, the daughter of Sarah Good, was accused of sharing her mother's witchcraft. Another twenty were rounded up a month later, mostly relatives of the accused; the Reverend George Burroughs was among them.

By the end of May, sixty-two residents were in custody, almost all of them girls and women, but also some boys and a few old men. The legal procedures disclosed the arbitrary and vengeful ways of the trials. Someone (usually a man) filed a complaint against an alleged witch because she had caused peculiar behavior, illness, or death in the family. When the complaint seemed credible, the witch was arrested, publicly examined, and pressed to confess her crime. A Superior Court dealt with the case, usually concluding that the accused had made a pact with the devil and should be executed by hanging, often on the day of the verdict. Occasionally, torture preceded the execution. Bodies were cut from the trees where they had been hanged and were buried in shallow ground nearby. Relatives often exhumed them secretly and buried them in unmarked graves on their property. The exact number of executions is not known, but they could have numbered twenty-two.

Hysteria and Puritan casuistry ruled in the trials. Pregnant "witches" would not be hanged until they had given birth. An eighty-year-old farmer refused to confess and was tortured to death: heavy stones were piled on a board that was laid on him until he was crushed to death after two days. The possessions of the accused were often confiscated before the trial. The church excommunicated them so that they could not have a proper burial. The executions were not recorded in the lists of deceased residents. Those who could escape found their property pillaged after their return. But Puritan self-righteousness can move quickly to penance. Guilt-ridden, the old pastor Increase Mather published a treatise in October of 1692 entitled "Cases of Conscience Concerning Evil Spirits." There, he stated that it would be better that ten thousand suspected witches should escape than that one innocent person should be condemned. Consequently, all those accused of witchcraft and jailed were set free in May of 1693. Twenty-two people received compensation in 1711 when the General Court reversed the judgment against the "witches" of 1692 and 1693. More than three centuries later, on October 31, 2001, the Massachusetts government, represented by Governor Jane Swift, finally proclaimed all the accused "witches" as innocent. It took three hundred years to purge the Salem church of such false devastating pride and prejudice! Today, the 38,000 residents of Salem attract countless visitors as "America's Bewitching Seaport with a little history at every step" (as listed in the tourist literature).

New England Puritan theocracy enforced a uniform faith in a "holy commonwealth" that did not tolerate any dissent. But the righteous immigrants from Europe knew that they, like the ancient Israelites, would encounter opposition to the kingdom of Christ—the devil, as it were. Cotton Mather pictured the "church militant" in New England as "a poor maid, sitting in the wilderness," threatened by wild animals and furious natives. In such circumstances, the "saints" were called to wage "the wars of the Lord."[49] Just as God put the Israelites to the test through famine and plague (1 Kgs 8:37), so were the Puritans tested by native Indians. Some disturbances and clashes with the native Americans quickly led to the judgment that Indians were instruments of the devil. The witches of Salem and the natives of the Massachusetts Bay had become the common enemies of the Puritan Holy Commonwealth; "holy war" was declared against them. Even moderate Puritans, like Thomas Shepherd, the first minister of Cambridge, spoke of the massacre of the Pequot Indians as a "divine slaughter"; several hundred were killed without any losses of the Puritans.[50] As a post-Puritan satirical adage puts it: "The Puritans first fell on their knees and then on all the aborigines."[51]

Puritan theocracy also had little, if any, interest in viewing arts and sciences as divine instruments. Cotton Mather and other academics spoke of a "Christian philosophy" that admired the brain for praising God through a scientific observation of the universe.

> The knowledge of nature is not an end in itself, it is valued for its religious improvements. It would have been as idle to ask the Puritans to experiment on the causes of lightning as it would have been to ask [Benjamin] Franklin to make religious improvements in his discoveries.[52]

Deviations from Puritanism were also viewed as a work of the devil. Typical is the case of Anne Hutchison (1591–1643), a devoted follower of her minister John Cotton.[53] An outspoken woman, she began discussing sermons in her home. Cotton and other ministers initially supported her, but soon accused her of "antinomianism" (a disregard for law) when she stressed the power of "free divine grace." Seemingly feeling crowded by persistent theological hearings, she called her views direct revelations of the Holy Spirit apart from the Bible. Such disregard for scriptural authority did her in. She was excommunicated in 1637 and banished from the colony. After a brief stay in Rhode Island, she moved to Pelham Bay, New York, where she was killed by Indians. Reports of the birth of a deformed child moved Cotton Mather to conclude that the pregnancy was the work of the devil. He gloried in describing the satanic details of Anne's motherhood: She delivered about thirty babies, "none in any human shape";

one was a monster without a head, the face appearing on the breast with ears like an ape and with three claws on each foot; the mid-wife was strongly suspected of witchcraft; and the little monster quickly died and was secretly buried. Exhumation proved that it was a monster.

Religious liberty, as preached and practiced by Roger Williams (c. 1603–1683) in Rhode Island, was condemned by Cotton Mather as a refuge for "religious misfits" (various sectarians) who had no true religion at all. Williams was viewed as someone who suffered from a "misguided conscience."[54] When Quakers attended Puritan worship services and interrupted them with their own testimony, or when they refused to remove their hats in court rooms, they were banished as anarchists. Three of them were hanged. Their belief in an "inner light" was interpreted as an attack against the light of Holy Scripture. Even though known as very pious, modest, and pacifist, to Mather they were the scum of the earth. He labeled them "beastly creatures" and felt attacked by them with foul language and sordid hostility. He could not and would not share any territory with them. His views prevailed.

Puritans worked hard to please God and not to enjoy themselves in the world. Since European rituals involved entertainment, whether feasts of food and drink, or dancing, they were abolished like the carnival season after Christmas and the celebration of Spring through a maypole. The celebration of Christmas Day was rejected as "popery." The Sabbath was a wedge against the sins of the flesh that included any sort of games or sport, and the elders even forbade children from playing in the street. As an older preacher put it,

> It must be spoken in the name of the Lord, O New England. Thy God expects better things from thee and thy children; not worldliness, not an itching after new things and ways; not a drawing loose in the yoke of God? Alas! How is New England in danger of being lost, even in New England?[55]

When some ministers broke away from the strict theocracy in favor of a church reflecting Presbyterian rules for doctrine and life, the Salem ministers accused them of compromising "the order of the Gospel" by being lax in spiritual discipline, exemplified by a "half-way covenant." Baptized second-generation Puritans, the children of the strict Puritans, could be members of the church; but they and their parents were not allowed to be partakers of the Lord's Supper unless there was a verified conversion. Desperate in the face of spiritual deformation in New England, Cotton Mather proposed to form "societies for the reformation of manners and for the suppression of vice." But it was all in vain. It seemed that God did not desire such a Puritan theocracy. "Increase Mather died in 1733, and Cotton Mather in 1728, both sour old men, persecuted persecutors, and with them died the last and most pompous incarnations of the political theocracy."[56]

Utopian Separatism

Now, because what is temporal doth not belong to us, but is foreign to our true nature, the law commandeth that none cleave to that which is temporal and alien . . . For if a man is to be renewed again in the likeness of God, he must put off all that leadeth him from him—that is, the grasping and drawing to himself of created things—for he cannot otherwise attain God's likeness.[57]

Fleeing from the world became popular in the second century when it seemed that the second coming of Christ was delayed. After all, he had promised to come soon, and the last book of the Bible ends with the plea "Come, Lord Jesus!" (Rev 22:20). Some apostolic injunctions advocated a retreat from a decadent, evil world.

Do not be conformed to the world (Rom 12:2).

Do not love the world or the things of this world. The love of the Father is not in those who love the world; for all that is in the world—the desire of the flesh, the desire of the eyes, the pride of riches—comes not from the Father but from the world. And the world and its desires are passing away, but those who do the will of God will live forever. (1 John 2:15-17)

Montanism

The issue of Christ's second coming began to dominate in some Christian circles. The apostle told his followers that "the day of the Lord will come like a thief in the night" to issue a final verdict over the fallen world

(1 Thess 5:2, 3-4). Rumors spread that the church's adoption of worldly customs was the major reason for the delay of the second coming; faith was institutionalized through secular structures, such as offices, policies, and other compromises.

Around 157 C.E., "prophetic" voices could be heard in Asia Minor (the western peninsula of Asia, now mostly Turkey) calling Christians to abandon worldliness in favor of a strict discipline consisting of fasting, the repudiation of sex (no marriage), and voluntary martyrdom. The principal prophet was Montanus who, together with two prophetesses, Priscilla and Maximilla, generated a movement of "Montanists" that quickly spread from Asia Minor to Greece, Italy, and parts of France.[58] Montanus claimed to be the "Paraclete" (from the Greek *parakletos*, "advocate"), the mediator of the Holy Spirit, promised by Jesus as the final sign before the end (John 14:16). He urged his followers to assemble in the village of Pepuza to meet the returning Jesus. They were to embody a radical separation from the world as the best preparation for the encounter with Jesus and the transition to his eternal kingdom. Priscilla left her husband in order to become committed to chastity. She proclaimed chastity to be the precondition for ecstasy, which was in turn the means by which the Holy Spirit was received as the source of prophecy. Some Christian leaders joined the Montanists, among them the well-known African church father Tertullian (c. 160–220). He issued a powerful call for voluntary martyrdom: "Do not desire to depart from this life in beds, in miscarriages, in soft fevers, but in martyrdom, that He who suffered for you may be glorified. . . . Those who receive the Paraclete know neither to flee persecution nor to bribe."[59] He summarized his approval of martyrdom in the saying, "The blood of martyrs is the seed of Christianity."[60] He left the church in 211 to become the leader of the Montanists in Carthage, although many Montanists were excommunicated, Tertullian was tolerated, probably because of his reputation as a productive, popular theologian.

Clearly driven by rigorist teachings—radical virginity, ecstasy as the means of prophecy, and the imminent end of the world—the Montanists also developed unusual spiritual habits. They ordained women as priests and bishops in honor of Eve who had eaten from the tree of knowledge (Gen 3:6).

After the church had excommunicated Montanists, the movement became more moderate and survived for a while in North Africa. Members constituted a tolerated special wing in congregations with a less rigorist discipline and without ecstatic prophecy. Tertullian defended Montanism as a model of proper penance over against the lax practice of the confession of sins in the church. He charged that the church substituted psychology for a true spiritual penance generated by the Holy Spirit.

Monasticism

Similar developments characterize the beginnings of monasticism (from the Greek *monazein*, "living alone"). "Alone" came to mean separated from the world. The first monks appeared in the Egyptian desert in the third century, driven there by three causes: to prepare for the second coming of Christ; to do battle with evil spirits on behalf of those who remained lax in the comforts of the world; and to become a spiritual elite, following special mandates of the gospel, or "evangelical counsels." The distinction between obeying the general laws of God (the Ten Commandments) and certain specific mandates for "perfection" is rooted in the biblical story of the rich young man who wanted to do more than just live by the Decalogue (Matt 19:16-30). Jesus told him: "If you wish to be perfect, go sell all your possessions, and give the money to the poor, and you will have treasure in heaven; then come and follow me." The young man could not do that, but it was assumed that the disciples of Jesus did (though none of them appeared to be rich). The distinction between general "precepts" and specific "counsels" was later justified (but abandoned by the Protestant Reformation and its descendants). "The counsels show the means by which that same end may be reached yet more certainly and expeditiously."[61] Young men flocked to the desert to live their lives in obedience to the "evangelical counsels." They were later called "desert fathers" and their writings were preserved as an exemplary Christian witness. Anthony of Egypt (c. 250–356) was the best known "desert father" because of his seemingly "miraculous" behavior:[62] He sold a rich family inheritance and lived in total isolation in a tomb near his native village; he recorded his fight with demons in the form of wild beasts; and toward the end of life he instructed others how to be "hermits" (from the Greek *eremos*, "solitary"). Often near death, he ate food left for him by strangers outside his abode, and he instructed his followers, who lived in nearby caves, to keep his grave secret in order to avoid its becoming an object of reverence.

Some of the hermits were known as "pillar saints" or "stylites" (from the Greek *stylos*, "pillar").[63] They wanted to be the most dedicated ascetics by standing (or sitting) on the tops of stone pillars until the mortification of their appetite ended their lives. Again, the statistics are mind-boggling and meant to be "miraculous." The prime example of such asceticism is Simon Stylites the Elder (c. 388–459) of Antioch (now Turkey), who allegedly sat on a pole for thirty-six years! But this time period seems quite impossible in the light of the contemporary world record for "pole sitting"—196 days, 13 hours, and 13 minutes by Daniel Baraniuk from Gdansk, Poland, on May 15, 2002. One "saint" is said to have stood upright for years, and when his feet could no longer support him, he lay on his side for some more years. Another was seen for years in a tub suspended in mid-air from poles! Yet many parishioners admired them as examples of exemplary penance in an age of pagan and Christian decadence and corruption. It is odd, indeed incredible, that such pathological behavior was admired and viewed as a source for spiritual renewal. But as in the case of Montanism, monasticism became more moderate over time as a movement of Christian idealists who abandoned a radical individualism and created cloistered communes in which the "evangelical counsels" were distilled into formal oaths of poverty, chastity, and obedience. There was also room for working in the world, as exemplified by the agricultural and educational work of the Benedictines and Dominicans.

Nevertheless, radical monastic asceticism did not die out. A French member of the Benedictine order, Robert of Molesme, became dissatisfied with the lax ways of his order and in 1098 organized his own rigorist group in Citeaux (meaning "cisterns"); they became known as "Cistercians." Though committed to the Benedictine vocation of farming, they preferred to live in isolated monasteries, each with its own independence, only linked with others through an annual conference. One of the abbots was an Italian mystic who founded an abbey in Fiore in the Calibri mountains and became known as "Joachim of Flora" (derived from "Fiore").[64] He undertook intensive Bible meditations and became convinced that he had uncovered the mystery of "the eternal gospel" (Rev 14:6) as a clue for predicting the second coming of Christ. His speculations are based on the biblical year-equals-day theory: "With the Lord one day is as a thousand years, and a thousand years as one day" (Ps 90:4; 2 Pet 3:8).

Daniel 7 and Revelation 13 were the biblical foundation for his scheme: After four empires, symbolized by four animals, the little horn that grew from the ten horns of the fourth animal would be the final ruler and would "wear out the holy ones of the Most High, and shall attempt to change the sacred seasons and the law" (Dan 7:25). The devil, a dragon-like beast with ten horns in Revelation 13, would be allowed to reign for forty-two months (13:5). Accordingly, the promised millennium, a final stage of purification, the "age of the Holy Spirit" following the ages of the Father and of the Son, would begin in 1260 c.e.

In Italy, the proclamation of the "age of the Holy Spirit" became linked to acts of public penance by self-flagellation.[65] Pious Italian lay people tried to prepare themselves for the advent of Christ as calculated by Joachim of Fiore and his disciples. They also wanted to follow the injunction of the apostle Paul for self-discipline, "I punish my body and enslave it, so that after proclaiming to others I myself should not be disqualified" (1 Cor 9:27). Led by an Italian hermit, Ranerio Fasani, they began in 1260 to roam the streets, stripped to the waist, scourging themselves with leather thongs till the blood flowed from open skin. They chanted hymns and canticles about the Passion of Christ, entering churches and prostrating themselves before the altars. The duration of such radical penance was thirty days, in honor of the thirty years of Christ's life on earth. The flagellants founded "lay brotherhoods" (known as *disciplinati*) and spread to Northern Italy, Southern Germany, and Bohemia (now the Czech Republic).

The devastating plague in 1348 revived the declining movement of flagellants, and it spread north as far as Poland. Eventually, all ages and classes joined flagellating processions, at times numbering 10,000. It was like a mental epidemic. One group became known as "Brothers and Sisters of the Free Spirit." In Germany they organized as the "Brotherhood of the Cross," so named because they wore a white habit and mantle, on each of which was a red cross. Members had to remain in the brotherhood for thirty years, swear obedience to "masters," have enough money to support themselves, and, if married, their membership had to be approved by their wives. Flagellation was linked to a specific discipline. Twice a day, they slowly processed to the public square or to the main church. They took off their shoes, stripped themselves to the waist and prostrated themselves in a large circle. Sins were revealed through body language: a murderer was lying on his back; an adulterer on his face, a perjurer on his side holding up three fingers, etc. First, they were beaten by the "master," then they rose and scourged themselves, crying out that they did penance for the whole sinful world, mixing their blood with that of Christ. After the scourging, the "master" read a letter from Christ, ostensibly delivered by an angel to the church of St. Peter's in Rome. It stated that Christ, angry at the world's sin, had threatened to destroy the world, but by the intervention of the Blessed Virgin, had decreed that anyone who joined the Brotherhood for thirty years would be saved. The public reading of the letter and the "show" of the Flagellants persuaded thousands of ordinary, uneducated people to enroll in the Brotherhood. They formed large processions, three or four abreast, walking slowly from town to town, bearing their whips, crosses, torches, and banners, and they chanted melancholy hymns. Their leaders used the successful revival event to increase rigorist demands: accidental contact with women was abhorred, Friday was a day of complete fasting, non-ordained brothers could absolve from sin, evil spirits were cast out, and miracles could be worked. "Masters" announced the suspension of ecclesiastical jurisdiction and extended membership in the order for another thirty-three years.

The flagellants began to disappear in the fourteenth century. But some of their practices reappeared now and then, attracting those who desired to do severe penance. The famous French Queen Catherine of Medici led a procession of Black Penitents in 1574 in Avignon, and in 1583, King Henry III organized a procession to the Church of Notre Dame, ordering all great dignitaries of the realm to participate. But when Parisians treated the event as a jest, the king withdrew his patronage.

Franciscans and Cathars

The Franciscans, like the Cistercians, generated a radical wing in response to the problem of laxity. Although their founder, Francis of Assisi (1182–1226), was committed to radical poverty, church leaders encouraged a compromise by declaring that Christ and his apostles did not renounce all private property, as the Franciscans had assumed, based on Peter's words in Matthew 19:27: "We have left everything and followed you." When the rigorist wing of the order, called "Spirituals," rejected the compromise,

Pope Gregory IX promulgated a bull in 1230 declaring the radical rule of St. Francis (his "testament") as null and void; the order could and should own private property and collect money for the church. Pope Nicholas III tried to persuade the dissatisfied Franciscans by way of another bull in 1279, declaring that the order would only be the *steward*, not the *owner* of papal property and finances. But Franciscan rigorists were not satisfied with such a compromise. They founded their own group, known as "Fraticelli" (a diminutive from the Italian *frate*, "little brother"), led by Brother Angelo de Clarena; they became quite numerous in various parts of Europe in the thirteenth and fourteenth centuries.[66]

Some Fraticelli viewed the crisis over poverty as a sign of the end. When they read the prophecies of Joachim of Fiore, they became convinced that their persecution by the church through the papacy was a sign of the end predicted by Joachim. In an enduring quarrel over poverty, also involving secular leaders who disliked papal power, some "Joachimites" spread the opinion that the pope was the antichrist portrayed in the dragon-like beast in Revelation 13:5. They felt strengthened in this conviction when, after decades of quarrels over the ideal of poverty, Pope John XXII declared in a bull of 1324 that Christ and his apostles had owned property; a denial of this "fact" was heresy. In response, one of the Fraticelli leaders, Brother Michele Berti from Calci near Pisa, publicly proclaimed that Pope John XXII was the real heretic by falsifying Holy Scripture; he and his successors had forfeited the papacy, and priests who supported them were false priests. It is an irony of history that Michele was arrested and condemned by the Franciscan archbishop of Florence to be burned at the stake in 1389.

Another example of separatism were the Cathars (from the Greek *katharos*, "pure"), also known as "Albigenses" (named after the town of Albi in Southern France), who appeared in the twelfth century in Asia Minor and the Balkans (a region in Southeastern Europe).[67] They were not influenced by the expectation of the imminent end of the world through the second advent of Christ, but by a strict theological dualism based on Manichaeism. Named after Mani, a Persian philosopher who was martyred in 277 in Persia (now Iran), Manichaeans believed that only reason, not faith, can explain the origin, composition, and future of the universe. This explanation was based on the speculation that there are two Principles, one Good and the other Evil, characterized by Light and

Darkness. An elaborate philosophical system of doctrine and discipline depicted Manichaeism as the one and only world religion that taught the truth about the origin and destiny of the universe. As in any philosophical or theological system, an attempt was made to explain the existence of evil. Manichaeans viewed evil as the intrusion of darkness into the light, creating a universal conflict between eternal, invisible, spiritual forces and mortal, material, visible power. The immortal human soul survives the conflict and enters eternity if the material human life is strictly disciplined. Believers were expected to give up property, sex, be vegetarians, drink no wine, and concentrate only on the spiritual world. Mani lived for some time in India and patterned his rules for spiritual formation after the strict discipline of Buddhist monks. Manichaeans organized their community as a kind of parallel to the Christian church by establishing five hierarchical classes as members: Masters (*magistri*), Bishops (*episcopi*), Elders (*presbyteri*), the Elect (*electi*), and Auditors (*auditors*). The Elect were the most faithful in pursuing "perfection," and the auditors were catechumens who remained lax. This hierarchy also imitated Christian practices such as the laying on of hands and anointing with consecrated oil. Mani, like Montanus, also claimed to be a "paraclete," but without any relation to the historical Jesus; he saw himself as the only anointed and appointed messenger of God, the source of Light.

The Cathars adopted essential Manichean teachings and discipline, marked by a dualistic worldview: a spiritual realm and a material one. The latter dominates and produces evil—whatever goes wrong in the world, ranging from natural disasters such as earthquakes, to human arrogance such as wars. The Old Testament reveals the problems of the material world that have imprisoned the immortal soul in a decadent, mortal body. The New Testament reveals how God sent Jesus as the redeemer of the soul and as the liberator from punishment. Faith in him requires abstention from earthly pleasures and full concentration on the way to perfection in a world without matter and evil. That is why one must be separate from the world in mind and body. The historical Jesus had already embodied a strictly spiritual, perfect way of life, free from the control of evil and matter. In his "celestial essence," he penetrated the ear of Mary, instructing her to present him as the Redeemer. He was never born of her, never suffered, and never died. He was not a human person, but a spiritual instruction preserved in the New Testament. This instruction continued in the "church" of the Cathars, who were led by bishops, priests, and deacons. But the church had no rituals, like sacraments. Instead, there was a ceremony called "consolation" (*consolamentum*) that purified the soul from evil and ensured its immediate return to heaven; there was no resurrection of the body because all flesh is evil.

The Cathars, or Albigenses, felt caught in the struggle between good and evil, darkness and light. The goal of life was the liberation of the soul from the evil body, even by suicide, which often occurred by starvation. There must be perpetual chastity, marked by a refusal to propagate through marriage or other physical relationships. Only vegetables and fish were to be eaten. War and capital punishment were condemned. In the community of the Cathars, as among the Manicheans, there were the "perfect" and the "hearers." When teachings and discipline relaxed after some time, penance was sufficient for restoring membership. Although the French Cathars left the Roman Catholic Church in 1165, the moderates continued until the fourteenth century without their being declared a heretics. However, the Inquisition put many to death during a crusade ordered by Pope Innocent III.

The Hutterites

The Protestant Reformation in its radical or "left-wing" expression also generated movements that advocated a separation from the evil world. The Mennonites, for example, taught a strict separation of church and state, best expressed in pacifism. But the Hutterites tried a radical, ambitious way of creating their own world, as it were, in their special communities based on economic communism.[68] They derived their name from the Tyrolian (Austrian) Anabaptist Jacob Hutter (d. 1536), who was a hatter by trade (*Hut* in German). As a young man, he traveled to Prague because some regional princes in Moravia and Bohemia (now the Czech Republic and Slovenia) tolerated, indeed supported, the Hussites—followers of John Hus, who was martyred in 1415 for opposing the papacy. They survived as "Brethren of Unity" (*unitas fratrum*), later known as the Moravian Church. Hutter and other dissidents seemed to experience the toleration granted to the Hussites. He eventually settled in the Austrian territory of Carinthia, near Tyrol, and was converted to Anabaptism sometime around 1529. An Austrian Anabaptist community had been founded by two of the original Swiss Brethren, George Bluecoat and Wilhelm Reublin.

But there was disagreement among Austrian and German Anabaptists about pacifism, a major assertion of the Schleitheim Confession. Some Anabaptists were influenced by Balthasar Hubmaier, who had found protection from Lord Leonard of Liechtenstein in Moravia. Hubmaier agreed with the prevalent tradition of a Christian "just war," justified as self-defense. Since he allowed self-defense by the sword, he and his followers were called "sword carriers" (*Schwertler* in German); a more moderate group of Anabaptists wanted to avoid bloodshed and carried only a staff, being called "stafflers" (*Stäbler*). After Bluecoat's execution in 1529, Hutter became the leader of the small Anabaptist group in Tyrol. He was immediately hunted by the Catholic Hapsburg authorities, who viewed all Anabaptists as violent revolutionaries who exhibited the "spirit of Müntzer and Münster." Hutter survived for a while, though his sister Agnes was executed. Many Hutterites escaped to Moravia where Hutter joined them after he had heard about a lack of unity among the Brethren. He claimed his right as an "apostle" and restored order. Part of the problem of spiritual division may have been material possessions. A follower of Thomas Müntzer, Hans Hut, had suggested that an ancient Christian custom be added to Anabaptist doctrine, namely, "having all things in common" (Acts 4:44). Private property can cause a schism between the rich and the poor, as the famous Humanist Erasmus of Rotterdam had written when he encountered the biblical custom. He regarded communal sharing of goods as "a true sense of 'brotherly love'" in a community where the normal tensions between rich and poor were nearly eliminated by intimate contact and at times desperate need."[69]

Hutter had heard that a group of "stafflers" had assembled in a small Moravian village and had begun the custom of sharing their goods. The Hutterite chronicles record the event that established an economic communism, as it were. These men laid a coat on the ground before the people and everyone placed his possessions on it, with a willing spirit and without coercion, for the support of the needy in accordance with the teachings of the prophets and apostles in Isaiah 23:18 and Acts 4:32-35.[70]

Constantly hunted by the Hapsburg authorities, Hutter was finally captured in 1535 and burned at the stake in Innsbruck in 1536. Moravian rulers, trying to become more independent, continued to tolerate Hutterites and employed them as farmers, craftsmen, and artisans.

Hutterites found a new leader in Peter Riedemann, who survived imprisonment and in 1540 drafted a defense of Hutterite beliefs entitled *An Account of our Religion, Doctrine, and Faith*. It contained twelve essentials of faith and seven special meditations. The essentials listed the traditional Christian teachings (faith, law, etc.), and they asserted the sharing of goods. They also suggested a compromise regarding secular politics in answer to the question of whether rulers could be Christians: they can, provided they divest themselves of worldly glory. But Hutterite utopian separatism prevailed. True Christian life meant to be sealed by the "covenant of freedom," manifested in "being grafted into Christ."[71]

Hutterites organized self-sufficient farms, called "Brethren farms" (*Bruderhof*). These farms were located away from the hustle and bustle of the world. While the adults worked, children were cared for in kindergartens (the first day care centers). Each community was led by a "domestic superior" (*Hausvorsteher*). New members were instructed about the rules before they were admitted for life, but wayward members were accepted again after new instructions. The Hutterite chronicles list thirty-nine distinct occupations, ranging from farming to the production of ceramics prized by the nobility.

Children were the center of attention. The Hutterite leader Peter Walpot composed a *School Discipline* in 1578 that predates modern child psychology: children should not be physically punished; they should be instructed with kindness and love based on the fear of God, without breaking their self-will; and teachers should always exercise diligent care so that they would retain a good conscience about their vocation.[72]

The Hutterite *Chronicle* begins with the creation of the world, contending that only the Hutterite way of life is the true Christian life; all other ways are dominated by evil. Private property is the result of "original sin." Utopian separation from the world is the goal: "God wished to have his own people, separated from all people . . . in the final age of this world."[73] That age began in Switzerland with the rise of the Brethren who organized the "believers' church." It should reflect life in Paradise, when Adam and Eve had everything in common. Hutterites identified the desire "to be like God" (Gen 3:5) as otherworldly economic communism, an interpretation of the Bible based on spiritual fear of living in the world.

They envisaged economic communism as the center of Christian life—a vision whose realization reminds one of Karl Marx, who viewed private property as criminal, as theft, robbing the community of its strength. But his Communist utopia was not Christian.

Pentecostalism

Separation from the world has also been manifested in movements known as "Pentecostal" (from the Greek *pentecoste*, "fifty"). They claim to have experienced the gift of the Holy Spirit granted to the apostles, fifty days after Easter, when they were able to communicate the gospel in foreign languages without having to learn them (Acts 2:1-13); the phenomenon is known as "xenolalia" (*xonos*, "strange," or "foreign" and *lalaein*, "to speak"). Some of the Pentecostals also claimed to speak "in tongues" (*glossa*, "tongue"), a phenomenon known as "glossolalia" (1 Cor 12:10), a childlike babbling in need of interpretation.

A Pentecostal movement began at Bethel College in Topeka, Kansas, during a vigil on December 31, 1900, when the evangelist leader Charles F. Parham laid hands on a student, Agnes N. Ozman, who reacted by speaking in tongues and in foreign languages, including Chinese.[74] Similar revival meetings were held in Kansas, Missouri, and Texas. One of Parham's followers organized meetings in Los Angeles in 1906. When the *Los Angeles Times* reported about the "holy rollers," they became a tourist attraction; they also claimed that the earthquake of April 18, 1906 was a sign of the end, calling for repentance and flight from the "secular" world. Large crowds attended the revival meetings. A visiting Norwegian tourist, the Methodist pastor T. B. Barratt, was converted and founded a Pentecostal center in Europe.

Three hundred delegates from various Pentecostal groups met in 1914 in Hot Springs, Arkansas, and founded a church known as the Assemblies of God. There was controversy about the dogma of the Trinity (whether or not one should only worship Jesus and "his" Holy Spirit). The first Pentecostal radio evangelist, Aimee Semple McPherson, known as "Sister Aimee," founded The International Church of the Foursquare Gospel, named in reference to the four creatures in Ezekiel 1:1-18, and maintained a vigorous revival schedule until her death in 1940.

The Pentecostal churches, often called the Church of God, taught spiritual "perfection" before the end-time, the experience of complete "sanctification" by the gift of the Holy Spirit. "Spirit baptism" was linked to millennial hope. When these experiences diminished, Pentecostal churches joined in ecumenical ventures led by the Pentecostal World Conference beginning in 1952. Some influential Pentecostals returned to the world, as it were, to establish a better morality in business, and the Full Gospel Business Men's Fellowship International was organized in 1953. But "speaking in tongues" was revived in 1959 when an Episcopal priest, Dennis Bennett, at St. Mark's Episcopal Church in Van Nuys, California, experienced glossolalia. Well-to-do members, employed by the Lockheed Aircraft Company, were baptized by the Holy Spirit and became missionaries, and a new charismatic movement spread within the mainline traditions of Episcopalianism, Roman Catholicism, and Lutheranism. The 1960s, with their turbulent events (the Civil Rights Movement and the war in Vietnam) seemed to provide a fertile soil, and Pentecostalism is still alive and well, advocating penance and separation from a sinful world.

An Unholy Alliance

The historical trajectory of triumphalism reveals a pattern modeled by the first generation of triumphalists in the Bible—Adam, Eve, and their children. Their son Cain killed his brother Abel, but remained in the care of God—and that was the beginning of civilization (Gen 4). The church, too, became a broken family, as it were. Politics and culture dominated the church when it formed an unholy alliance with the state. This alliance created an ideological uniformity that did not tolerate a reconciled diversity. After a millennium of struggle to stay united, Eastern and Western Christians went their separate ways. The latter, known as Roman Catholics, soon became entangled in a web of power struggles between emperors and popes. Popes claimed to have dominion over the world, based on the fraudulent doctrine that the church inherited the God-given leadership that had been granted to pre-Christian Greek and Roman emperors. The domination of the "Holy Roman Emperor," blessed by the Bishop of Rome, the pope, resulted in the evangelization of Europe, mostly by force, and in the "colonization" of other parts of the world by European superpowers such as Spain, France, Germany, and England.

After the discovery of America by Christopher Columbus in 1492, Spain eradicated the Aztec Indian culture in Mexico. In the seventeenth century, Dutch Protestants, together with French Huguenots, established a Christian colony in South Africa known as "Boers" (from the Dutch *boer*, "farmer") and as *Afrikaners*. They founded a Reformed (Calvinist) church and a government with a policy of strict apartheid based on the notion of "white supremacy." In the nineteenth century, England ruled South Africa until its independence in 1910. Apartheid dominated until 1994, when the first democratic elections eliminated racism and elected Nelson Mandela, a nonwhite activist, to be president. German missionaries began work in Tranquebar, India, in 1706, sponsored by the Danish government which had established a military and economic presence there.[75] Numerous German Protestant mission societies sent missionaries all over the world in tandem with efforts at colonization for economic gains. Roman Catholic foreign mission followed suit, with a concentration on China, until it became Communist in 1949. The frequent trend of linking the Christian mission to "national monopoly" had a serious impact on those national churches that had negotiated a place in the political sun, exemplified by German and Scandinavian "state churches." Some nineteenth-century German theologians, led by Adolf von Harless (1806–1879), taught a controversial doctrine of "orders of creation" (*Schöpfungsordnungen),* asserting that Christians, like all other human beings, must abide by specific, unchanging ways of life, ordered by God before, and independent of, the revelation and salvation in Christ proclaimed by the gospel.[76] Nation, state, race, marriage, and economics are principal orders that cannot be changed. Such assertions caused debate, especially regarding specific views on sexuality (no homosexuality), war (no pacifism), and race (no mixing).

American settlers, undisturbed by Christian consciences, devastated the culture of Native Americans, whose remnants were forced to live in ghettos known as "reservations." In addition, the subhuman treatment and killing of African Americans as slaves was spurred on by fanatic racist Christians such as the Ku Klux Klan. It is ironic that such a tradition of violence clashed with a tradition of nonviolence, exemplified by Mennonites and by the civil rights activists led by Martin Luther King.

Hindsight produced some penance after a long period of silence. When Pope Benedict XVI tried to play down the sins of Roman Catholic colonization in South America, he faced strong protests during his visit in Brazil in 2007. But his reaction was still more triumphalist than penitent when he acknowledged "various injustices and sufferings which accompanied colonization." Nevertheless, he described his trip as a "pilgrimage of praise to God for the faith which has shaped their (Latin American) cultures. . . . Certainly, the memory of a glorious past cannot ignore the shadows that accompanied the work of evangelizing the Latin American continent."[77]

The decades after World War II, marked by the brutal regime of Adolf Hitler and the holocaust of the Jews, generated a draft that could become a wind of change. Roman Catholic theologians have joined theologians from other traditions to present critical views of the ecclesiastical, papal hierarchy in their analysis of post-Vatican II official attempts to define Christian unity in terms of the New Testament concepts of "communion" (*communion* in Latin) and "fellowship" (*koinonioa* in Greek). These critics contend that "communion" and "hierarchy" are contradictory notions because, in the New Testament, the one church is seen as a series of "communions." Moreover, hindsight suggests that the notion of hierarchy has its roots in the sixth-century teaching about angels by Pseudo-Dionysius the Areopagite, and that his views were transferred to the teaching about offices in the church.[78] That is why these offices were interpreted as anchored in "divine law," representing a pyramid topped by the papacy.

New Perspectives

Given an emerging ecumenical consensus of experts in the study of the Bible and of the history of the church, the quest for Christian unity is combined with a critical study of church history, particularly the tradition of hierarchical and papal authority:

1. One can think of the unity of the church only as a communion of churches that are independent or autocephalous [a Greek Orthodox designation meaning "appointing their own heads"] but that share worship and are in "conciliar fellowship" [connected by councils] for advice and decision.

2. A jurisdictional primacy of the Roman bishop in terms of an unlimited and boundless holy rule over all other churches, which are then subordinated to this rule, is a guarantee for the enduring division of the church. Here the Roman Catholic Church must abjure its ecclesiological, primatial, and hierarchically constructed imperialism if it is serious in the effort to do and to further everything that serves the restitution of the koinonia of the churches in the unity of the church.[79]

Puritan theocracy, too, fell from its height of seeing and implementing its vision of a pure and righteous commonwealth in Massachusetts, based on John Calvin's reforms in Geneva. As one historian put it: "After the American Revolution [1775–1783] and certainly after the French Revolution [1789–1799] it was idle to build a theology in terms of sovereignty, vindictive justice and free grace. These concepts had become morally obsolete and therefore Calvinism had no moral basis to which it could appeal. . . . The righteous indignation of God had degenerated into a vindictive delight in punishing helpless sinners eternally. From this absurdly cruel conception Calvinism never recovered."[80]

Triumphalism perverts the original view of the church as a penultimate community, existing in the interim between Christ's ascension and second coming at the end of time. This is the basic understanding of the first Christian generation, as evidenced in the New Testament ("Now I know only in part, then I will know fully," 1 Cor 13:12). The Acts of the Apostles (authored by the apostle Paul's friend Luke), the letters of Paul, and the Gospel of John all view the church as anchored in the work of the Holy Spirit, who is the "advocate" (*paraclete* in Greek, "called to aid," John 14:16, 26, 16:7), helper, and counselor in the interim. The church *anticipates* the time when Christ will triumph. The Messiah is already exalted at the right hand of God, and he has already done the work of the Holy Spirit on earth (Acts 2:33). The Holy Spirit is the eschatological gift disclosing the royal rule of Christ in the church. In Paul's words:

> We know that the whole creation has been groaning in labor pain until now, and not only the creation, but we ourselves, who have the first fruits of the Spirit, groan inwardly while we wait for adoption, the redemption of our bodies. For in hope we were saved. (Rom 8:22-24)

Back to the Future

The Holy Spirit is the "pledge of our inheritance toward redemption as God's own people" (Eph 1:14); the church is the community of the adopted children of God (Gal 4:5). In this community there is much sharing, especially when there is a need to help others. To refuse such aid and/ or to lie about it for egotistical reasons is a sin against the Holy Spirit. Two members of the first church, Ananias and his wife, "fell down and died" after the apostle Peter chided them for withholding the profit from the sale of property (Acts 5:1-6). Life in the Spirit no longer permits moral casuistry. It is a new way of life. Christians are "strangers and foreigners on earth" who, like Abraham, trek to the final destination, no longer just a "promised land" but the "city of God" (Heb 11:13-16).

The first church already experienced the tensions generated by life in this world, ranging from the relationship between Jewish and Gentile Christians to problems about penultimate structures. That is why Paul spoke of the church as the "body of Christ."

> For as in one body we have many members, not all the members have the same function so we who are many, are one body in Christ, and individually we are members of one another (Rom 12:4-5). For in the one Spirit we were all baptized into the one body—Jews or Greeks, slaves or free—and we are all made to drink of one Spirit. (1 Cor 12:13)

This body is endowed with various gifts to be used for witness and mission, ranging from presiding at worship to speaking in tongues (1 Cor 12:1-11). But the greatest gift is love (1 Cor 13) and it is the best way to survive to the end when life in the Spirit will be perfected. On earth, the church exists in geographical dispersion (1 Pet 1:1) modeled in the Eucharistic bread.[81] Unity is given in baptism and in the Lord's Supper.

> As many of you as were baptized into Christ have clothed yourselves with Christ, there is no longer Jew or Greek, there is no slave or free, there is no longer male or female; for all of you are one in Christ Jesus (Gal 3:27-28). Because there is one bread, we who are many are one body, for we all partake of the one bread. (1 Cor 10:17)

Baptism also symbolizes life in the interim, between temporal and eternal existence. Being immersed and emerging from the water means "being buried with him [Christ] so that, just as Christ was raised from the dead by the glory of the Father, so we too might walk in newness of life" (Rom 6:4).

Organization, structure, and function are also seen in eschatological perspective. Leaders are, above all, "servants" (from the Greek *doulos*, "slave" and *diakonos*, "waiter,") who serve only Christ, not their own interest. There is no "Petrine" or "Pauline" denomination ("Was Paul crucified for you?" 1 Cor 1:13); there is only a "ministry of reconciliation" (2 Cor 5:18). The function of leadership is to "build up" the faith (1 Cor 14:26) and to do things "decently and in order" (1 Cor 14:40). There is no comprehensive view of ministry, such as a hierarchy of offices, but only a variety of services as works of the Holy Spirit, "charisms" (not to be confused with "charm" or "being attractive"). Eventually, a triad of offices came into being. "God has appointed in the church first *apostles*, second *prophets*, third *teachers*; then deeds of power, then gifts of healing, forms of assistance, forms of leadership, various kinds of tongues" (1 Cor 12:28). There is no basic difference between a "spiritual" ministry and "secular" activities.[82] Paul and his co-worker Barnabas did appoint "elders" in Antioch (Acts 14:23), but he does not list them together with other offices. He speaks of the qualifications of "bishops" and "deacons" in "the household of God," but without any references to "hierarchy" and "succession" (1 Tim 3:1-15).

Rethinking the Role of the Church

Christians *are* the church; they are not *in* the church. The gradual process of institutionalization is the usual human way to survive until the Last Day which, though delayed, will come "like a thief in the night" (1 Thess 5:2). That is why the term "church" in the New Testament (*ekklesia* in Matt 18:17) means an existing local community of Christians, compared to a local civic community. Its organization is secular, but it anticipates an eschatological future when all congregations will be united in the "perfect" church, triumphant over sin, evil, and death. So when the same term is used in the passage that, according to the controversial Roman Catholic interpretation, sanctions the rule of the papacy, it refers to the same future: "You are Peter [*petra* in Greek, "rock"] and on this rock I *will* build my church" (Matt 16:18, italics added). Jesus never founded a local congregation, and Peter never headed one. When Peter asked Jesus, "What then will we have?" (after the rich young man refused to give everything away), he was told that his power will be in the eschatological future—"At the renewal of all things, when the Son of Man is seated on the seat of his glory, you who have followed me will also sit on twelve thrones" (Matt 19:28). Peter will not have royal power and glory on earth, but only in heaven, and then only as "first among equals" as one of the twelve apostles. Any "Petrine function" on earth is fallible rather than infallible, as the papacy later saw itself; it did not see itself as a penultimate office in the light of the Last Day as the transition to an ultimate realm marked by a never-ending future with God in Christ.

The disciples were the first members and leaders of the church. They were told to be alert and to watch for the second coming of their Lord. "Keep awake, therefore, for you do not know on what day the Lord is coming" (Matt 24:42). They were not just loyal guardians and communicators of beliefs and morals, but were to be embodiments of the Holy Spirit who was leading them and their successors from the struggling "militant church" to the eternal "triumphant" one. Even under pressure, they were not to worry what they could do on their own, but were to rely on the Spirit. "When they bring you before synagogues, the rulers and the authorities, do not worry about how to defend yourselves or what you are to say, for the Holy Spirit will teach you at that very hour what you ought to say" (Luke 12:11-12).

The church of the first generation, described in the New Testament and in those other contemporary writings called "Apostolic Fathers," provided answers to what God did during and after the earthly life of Jesus. "At all events, they [the disciples, also known as "apostles"] did not understand the church as a solution for the dilemma of the delay of the Parousia [second coming]. For they were much too grateful and joyous about what they already now experienced in the church."[83]

The history of triumphalism reveals how the church ignored the reality of interim existence asserted in the New Testament. Instead of remaining vigilant in expectation of Christ's second coming, Christian leaders throughout history have devoted themselves to the desire to get the world ready for it through the use of political power, as exemplified in violent

crusades or in definitive hierarchical promulgations, in the forceful impo-
sition of Puritan morals, or in a gospel romanticism that withdrew from
the world. Ecclesiastical triumphalism claims to possess absolute spiritual
authority, equal to that of the Bible, indeed even a higher one, as exemplified by the fact that a solemn assembly of Catholic bishops, chaired by
the pope, determines the meaning of a biblical text. From this point of
view, tradition determines the authority of Scripture. Such a stance is not
ecumenical; Christian unity cannot be defined in only Roman Catholic
terms.

Puritan triumphalism is a toxic Christian tradition because it attempts,
in rhetoric and in action, to pursue a theocratic world view, marked by
an otherworldly spirituality that becomes self-righteous, judgmental, and
tyrannical when facing opposition. It views itself as the executor of God's
testament as it is revealed in the Bible.

Separatist triumphalism is the flip side of Puritan triumphalism;
it tries to accomplish the same end by being separate from the world.
Instead of using theocratic authority for establishing a pure society, it
attempts to attract people by exhibiting a proud, separatist humility. This
seems, at first glance, quite commendable in its abolition of violence and
financial greed (Hutterite economic communism). But such Christian
separatism also assumes that the price of discipleship should be paid by
involvement in an evil world, not through isolation from it. The separatist attitude puts the cart before the horse, so to speak, because the core
of the Christian tradition mandates that if suffering and persecution are
to be endured, they are to be experienced *in* the world of sin, death, and
evil, not *apart* from it. That is why such a separatism is truly utopian—
depicting "an imagined place or state of things in which everything is
perfect, idealistic."[84]

CHAPTER 4

Moralism

If the end is allowed, the means are also allowed [as in the case of escaping from prison]: It is allowed, at least before the bar of conscience, to deceive the guards, with the exclusion of force and injustice, by offering them, for example, food and drink so that they fall asleep; or by arranging that they are away; or by breaking into the prison.[1]

After the first generation of Christians, church leaders began to control Christian life by creating a common mindset. They did so by urging frequent use of auricular confession as the start of a penitent life immersed in mortal and venial sins. Gradually, a system of penance and forgiveness was established based on the sayings of Jesus that his disciples had the power to forgive or to retain sins. Peter was told that he would be given "the keys of the kingdom of heaven" (Matt 16:18), empowering him to forgive or to retain sins. The disciples were told that they should follow a process of visitation leading to penance: first, one disciple should "point out the fault" to the sinner without any witnesses; if that does not work, two or three should try to persuade the sinner to repent; finally, the entire congregation should be informed about the problem and, if the member remained impenitent, "let such a one be to you like a Gentile and a tax collector" (Matt 18:15-17). For the whole congregation, like Peter, has been given the power of the keys (Matt 18:18). This power is again confirmed by the resurrected Jesus when "he breathed on them [the disciples]" and told them that they received the Holy Spirit with the power of the keys (John 20:22-23). This power was also exercised by the apostle Paul, who banned a member of the Corinthian congregation because he had sexual relations with his father's wife. "You are to hand this man over to Satan for the destruction of the flesh, so that his spirit may be saved in the day of the Lord" (1 Cor 5:1-5).

Soon, there was talk about a "second penance" for sins committed after baptism. Adultery, murder, and fornication became sins that required life-long penance. By the sixth century, the western, Roman Catholic Church divided sins into "venial" or "minor" sins and "deadly" or "cardinal" sins. Their forgiveness was determined by a "Father Confessor," a parish priest, or an approved specialist. Since the deadly sins destroyed the life of grace and created the threat of eternal damnation, they became the focus of increased attention and increased fear among the parishioners. The fear factor motivated parishioners to follow uniform ecclesiastical moral rules leading to penance and forgiveness.

Uniformity

Pope Gregory I (c. 540–604) published an official list of seven "deadly sins," corresponding to seven "holy virtues": Lust (*luxuria*)—chastity; gluttony (*gula*)—abstinence; greed (*avaritia*)—liberality; sloth (*acedia*)—diligence; wrath (*ira*)—patience; envy (*invidia*)—kindness; and pride (*superbia*)—humility.[2] The Italian poet Dante Alighieri (1265–1321) popularized these sins in his famous work, *The Divine Comedy*, an entertaining guide to hell.[3] *Lust* involves a number of destructive elements, ranging from excessive thoughts to rape. In the "purgatory" (*purgatorio*) of Dante, the penitent has to walk within flames to be purged from lustful thoughts. *Gluttony* not only involves excessive eating and drinking but overindulgence in any one thing. Dante has the penitent stand between two trees, unable to reach or eat the fruit hanging from either, thus appearing starved. *Greed* leads to the excessive accumulation of wealth, but also involves robbery, manipulation of authority, and simony (the selling and buying of ecclesiastical offices). Dante sees the penitent bound and laid face down on the ground for having focused too much on earthly thoughts. *Sloth* is laziness leading to depression, apathy, and failure to love God and others. Dante depicts the penitent as being made to run continuously at top speed. *Wrath* is manifested in uncontrolled feelings and the desire to seek revenge, even through murder. According to Dante, the wrathful are enveloped in blinding smoke. *Envy* is the desire to have what others have and to fulfill this desire by trickery. In Dante's purgatory, the envious have their eyes sown shut with wire because of their sinful pleasure of seeing others brought down. *Pride* is the deadliest "original" sin, the desire to be like God (Gen 3:5), the ultimate self-love. Dante reports the penitents' being forced to walk with stone slabs on their backs in order to induce feelings of humility.

Church leaders encouraged special moral efforts known as "evangelical counsels," resulting in a commitment beyond simple obedience to the Decalogue or other general spiritual rules. These counsels were derived from the saying of Jesus, "If you wish to be perfect, go, sell your possessions and give the money to the poor and you will have treasure in heaven; then come, follow me" (Matt 19:21). The church made "perfection" attractive by promising absolute certainty about salvation if one was willing to be recruited into the uniform of monasticism, as it were—a life that exchanged the three main worldly features of life for the three main otherworldly features: wealth was exchanged for poverty, pleasure was exchanged for chastity, and the desire for worldly authority was exchanged for holy obedience. These three counsels led to the perfect life of faith, a disciplined discipleship visible in the uniform, the habit, of monks and nuns who were recruited and trained as the special forces of the "church militant." They also defended and protected the ordinary Christians, the civilians of the church, against the forces of evil. That is why monasticism, like a nation's military establishment, should be honored and supported as front-line fighters against the devil. Monks could also be called to be theologians and parish priests. Priests were mandated to provide advice and consent in the politics of everyday spirituality. That is why the auricular confession of sins (private hearing by a priest sworn to silence) made the Sacrament of Penance (now called the Sacrament of Reconciliation) the most popular of the seven Roman Catholic sacraments. Fear of damnation drove penitents to it.

The Institutionalization of Morality

Already in the fourth century, three specific ways of chastisement, related to public worship, appeared in Asia Minor. During the time of penance and before any absolution from sins, penitents received permission to hear the sermon and to join in prayer, but they could not participate in the Eucharist. Life in the world was regulated by moral standards applied to education, family, and vocations. Catechisms added moral rules to doctrines, based on the Decalogue. Marriage between Christians and non-Christians, as well as second marriages, were discouraged, and divorce was prohibited. After the first millennium, marriage was understood to be a sacrament, and the Roman Catholic Council of Trent (1545–1563) defined it as one of the seven sacraments.[4] Individual confession of sin was required beginning in 1215, when the Fourth Lateran Council mandated it before first communion at the age of discretion (seven years old). But some major moral flaws prevailed. While, for example, "pagan" entertainment (theater, circus, sports) was discouraged, ecclesiastical pomp and circumstance flourished. Moreover, slavery was accepted.

In contrast to Western Roman Catholicism, Eastern Orthodoxy became less rational and less legalistic in its development of moral uniformity. Eastern Christians felt a closer harmony between this world and the next, between the realm of God surrounded by angels and saints, and earthly life burdened by sin. Sin did not receive the kind of attention it did in the West. Meditation and the Eucharist, rather than confession and repentance, provided a mystical link with eternity. Monks and clergy tried to model such a life on an otherworldliness that reflected a harmony of the temporal and eternal realms. Theologians spoke of a "divinization" (*theosis* in Greek) of humanity, a gradual process of mystical fulfillment in anticipation of eternal life. In this context, the intellect was less valued in the East than in the West. This negligence of the mind nurtured a peculiar personal, ascetic piety found only in Eastern Orthodoxy, namely, being a "fool for God," or a "fool for Christ" (based on 1 Cor 4:10, "We are fools for the sake of Christ").[5] The two most famous "fools" (*salos* in Greek and *jurodivy* in Russian) were Symeon in sixth-century Constantinople and Andreas in tenth-century Russia. The cathedral on "Red Square" in Moscow is named after Andreas. He also found his way into world literature in the famous Russian novel, *The Idiot*, by Fyodor Dostoevsky (1821–1881). At times, such fools appeared in pulpits, throwing nuts at the worshippers and urging them not only to listen to sermons but also to pay more attention to the Eucharist as the true highlight of worship. The ritual of the celebration of the Mass was shrouded in mystery. After the priest(s) had experienced the eucharistic presence of Christ behind the icon-decorated walls that hid the altar from the view of the laity, the altar gates opened and worshippers were invited to commune. Christian life was to reflect the encounter with the glory of Christ in worship, and an otherworldly morality was part of the process of deification symbolized in the Eucharist.

In the West, morality was part of a rational, less mystical, theological system intended to care for people from cradle to grave. Its most accepted and popular form was developed by the Dominican theologian Thomas Aquinas, honored as the "angelic doctor," who used the seven virtues as a bridge from a faithful and principled life to its perfection of the afterlife. Using the scientific method of Aristotle, which taught a dualistic world view of "nature" and "supernature" (from the Latin *supra naturam*, "above nature," *physis* and *metaphysis* in Greek, "behind nature"), Aquinas presented a smooth arrangement of reality, both temporal and eternal, based on natural and divine laws as teachings bequeathed to the church by the Holy Spirit. "Thomism" became synonymous with "orthodoxy." Moreover, the canon law in the West was much more detailed than the canon law in the East. Church councils, popes, and universities continually refined and increased the collection of laws in the context of cultural climates of opinion. "Canonists" created detailed commentaries explicating innumerable rules as the foundation for a uniform morality aimed at pleasing God. Even at times of spiritual deformation, exemplified by three competing popes in the fourteenth century, the system prevailed in the midst of superstition linked to a belief in miracles and to the veneration of dead saints, relics, and the Virgin Mary. Fear of the devil and witches, as well as the threat of eternal damnation, kept the common folk loyal to the church.

The Protestant Reformation of the sixteenth century secularized morality by rejecting canon law and calling for moral discernment in a world where law and gospel were mixed. This change is exemplified by Martin Luther's advice to his friend Philip Melanchthon, who worried about the uncertainty of moral action. Given the reality of sin in the world, Luther told his friend, one can never do a perfect "good work," but can only do the best possible deed. It is, at best, a "bold sin", for "as long as we are here [in this world] we have to sin."[6] But the close relationship between secular and ecclesiastical power continued to impose many moral rules of medieval Christendom in new ways. It was no longer pope and emperor who mandated a uniform morality, but territorial princes and their clergy. Since Catholic bishops could no longer be trusted, Luther contended, the baptized lay territorial rulers should become "emergency bishops" (*Notbischöfe*) and be the guardians of faith and morals.[7] The secular princes soon became princes of the church with the title "highest bishops" (*summi epsicopi*) and were recognized as such by the Peace of Augsburg in 1555, which mandated that "whoever is in charge of a region is also in charge of its religion" (*cuius regio, eius religio*)—either Lutheran or Catholic. The emergency lasted for centuries, and ended when eighteenth-century democratic ideals changed the notion of a uniform Christendom. Luther still favored such a Christendom, identifying any opposition to established government as satanic. He condemned the uprising of enslaved peasants and condoned the illegal bigamy of his noble friend Philip of Hesse (though he admitted later that he had made a mistake).

Uniform morality was also the cornerstone of both Calvinism and Puritanism. Seventeenth-century theocratic puritans advocated a state dominated by the church, consisting of citizens who felt chosen by God to get the world ready for the transition from earthly to heavenly reality. Puritan discipline rejected worldly pleasure. Violations of Puritan laws were viewed as heresy, often punished by death.

Eighteenth-century Lutheranism was shaped by "Pietism," which stressed individual piety grounded in a conversion experience and driven by works of charity and mission.[8] A "religion of the heart" replaced the "religion of the mind" manifested in a focus on "pure doctrine" in seventeenth-century "orthodoxy." This was a move from creeds to deeds, from transforming rational belief into emotional spirituality. But Pietist communities, such as the one in Herrnhut, Germany founded by the Pietist Count Nicholas of Zinzendorf (1700–1760), tended to become quite odd in their spirituality. Baroque culture and style, with its emphasis on emotion and ornamentation, became the context of a piety which, at times, appeared eccentric, exaggerated, and indeed grotesque. Zinzendorf talked about his close relationship to Jesus with a love similar to marital love. His son, Christian Renatus (Latin for "born again Christian"), intensified such a spiritual emotionalism by transforming the usually bland Sunday service into a theater, as it were, consisting of instrumental music, erotic preaching, and exhibitions of pictures that were carried through the assembly to stimulate an intimate relationship with Jesus.

While Father Zinzendorf was away for a few years (1743–1749), the enthusiastic congregation founded the "order of fools" which, unlike the "fools" of Eastern Orthodoxy, generated a playful, silly sentimentality focused on the side wound of Jesus (John 19:34). Renatus encouraged childlike behavior, "sweet dallying," based on the saying of Jesus about infants ("Because you [Lord] have hidden these things [revelation of salvation] from the wise and the intelligent and have revealed them to infants," Matt 11:25). Some worshippers called the wound of Jesus "the little side-hole" (*Seitenhölchen*) where the faithful would nest like "little birds in the air of the cross" (*Kreuzluftvögelein*). Good Friday was celebrated as the birthday of the "little hole," and Jesus was addressed as the "little lamb" in the company of "Papa" (God) and "Mama" (the Holy Spirit)—an unsavory rephrasing of the Trinity. Though upset about the idiosyncrasies of his son, Father Zinzendorf explained these excesses as a time of sifting (from Luke 22:31, where Peter's denial of Jesus is depicted as the work of Satan, "Satan has demanded to sift all of you like wheat").

The Challenge of Reason and the Conscience

After the eighteenth-century European Enlightenment, it became customary to define Christian morality as loyalty to conscience when faced with moral choices. "Love of neighbor" became "duty to neighbor." This shift of paradigm was used by Protestant theologians and philosophers who became enamored of the ancient Stoic ethical notions that stressed the relationship between reason and nature. This relationship was viewed as embedded in the universe. Accordingly, reason and conscience have an innate tendency to create "happiness" by doing "natural" duties, such as seeking harmony with others, or letting "natural reason" find satisfaction in creating a uniform morality. The principal philosopher of the Enlightenment, Immanuel Kant (1724–1804), made this point of view popular among European intellectuals. Rejecting the medieval, scholastic metaphysics, he contended that true reality, "things in themselves" (*Dinge an sich*), cannot be known, but only experienced as "phenomena" (*phainomenon* in Greek, "something that is seen," or "appears"). Although God, freedom, and immortality may exist as assumptions, as "postulations" of the human mind they cannot be "proven" by sense experience. That is why reason is useful only as "practical reason," or moral consciousness as "oughtness" or "duty." Consequently, Kant spoke of a "categorical imperative" as the foundation for a universal moral uniformity, "a religion within the bounds of reason alone." The categorical imperative projects an ethics of individualism: "Act only according to those maxims through which you can simultaneously wish that they can become a common law" (or "can become a common law of nature").[9] This imperative is based on Kant's definition of "Enlightenment" (*Aufklärung*) as "the exit of man from his immaturity brought about by his own fault. Maturity (*Mündigkeit*) is the ability to use one's own mind without being led by another mind." This definition stands in stark contrast to the Christian view that defines a person as being with others in a relationship with Christ through faith. Spiritual survival is grounded in teamwork, in discipleship linked to Christ. "For where two or three are gathered in my name, I am there among them" (Matt 18:20).

Kantian moral uniformity is summed up in the term "duty" (*Pflicht*), namely, the mandate to lift oneself beyond egotistic drives, such as pleasure, ego power, and other self-righteous acts of the will, and to strive for a life of "pure reason." This reason is an innate universal phenomenon designed to detect and avoid any illusions about life in the universe. Enlightened minds have the duty to be responsible and thus make conscious ethical choices geared to preserve the "good" in the universe. Although there is always the danger that specific duties will collide and effect chaos, Kant assumes that the vigilance of "pure reason" would prevail.

The Reformed (Calvinist) theologian Friedrich Schleiermacher (1768–1834) created a theological system that reflected Kantian philosophy.[10] The system assumed that there is a divine "taste" of the infinite in all cultures and religions, a feeling of wonder and awe. Accordingly, humans have an innate sense of being dependent on a universal, divine power. The Christian religion is based on Jesus who had the highest and strongest sense of this power, the most powerful consciousness of "God," as illustrated in the Gospel of John. With Kant, Schleiermacher asserted that one lives with the stars above and with a moral consciousness within oneself. This sense and awe for what is "above" is beyond rational explanation. Religion and culture are combined in a uniform morality that tries to create harmony between personal and universal rules. Nineteenth-century "cultural Protestantism" identified patriotism, family values, and civility as Christian virtues. Schleiermacher's view of faith as " feeling" (*Gefühl*) and "moral attitude" (*Sitte*) is well demonstrated in his popular description of Christmas, *Christmas Eve*, a booklet that speaks of the *feeling* of the family under the Christmas tree without any reference to Christ. It is no surprise that German "cultural Protestantism" became an easy victim of National Socialism which, led by Adolf Hitler, advocated a German, Aryan, racist Christianity. That is why a majority of Protestants, led by influential bishops and theologians, agreed to and organized a national church known as "German Christians" (*deutsche Christen*). Their conscience and consciousness were shaped by Kantian philosophy and Schleiermacherian theology that made easy compromises between Christ and culture.

Fundamentalist and/or American evangelical Christians developed a primitive, naive moral uniformity based on the principle of biblical inerrancy. It is well illustrated in the selection of passages suited for the favorite fundamentalist sins, whether abortion, homosexuality, or other "evils" condemned in the Bible. If every word in the Bible were authoritative, the manger in which Jesus was born would be a divinely mandated place of birth! Is this uniformity at the price of liberty?

Casuistry

"Casuistry is the use of clever but unsound reasoning, especially in relation to moral questions, sophistry; the resolving of moral problems by the application of theoretical rules for particular instances."[11] Christian casuistry is a significant part of "moral theology." Its history "is a sensitive seismograph of changing forms of thought, of scientific ideals and of practical necessities."[12] It is a matter of "cases" against "principles." Example: Although lying is wrong in principle, a casuist would contend that, depending on the details of a case, lying might not be illegal or unethical. Lying might save a life. Such casuistry is based on "mental reservation"—"a qualification tacitly added in making a statement."[13] In the example, the qualification of saving a life is the "mental reservation," added without saying so.

Medieval scholastic theological systems, such as that of Thomas Aquinas in the thirteenth century, incorporated morality as the teaching of virtues rooted in the notion of natural law. Aquinas envisaged "blessedness" as the goal of Christian life, its final happiness. Private, or auricular, confession became the main instrument to achieve that end. The first generation of Jesuit theologians, guided by Anton Possevin (1533–1611), made moral theology a special part of speculative theology. At the beginning of the seventeenth century, the Jesuit Juan Azor provided the first influential textbook, entitled *Institute of Morals* (*Institutionum Moralium*). The Decalogue provided the basic scheme, leading to tracts on conscience, law, moral action, and sin, with great emphasis on the role of conscience. Virtues are nurtured by moral commandments, specified in rules on how to act. Soon, casuistic ecclesiastical teachings about sin began to dominate. There were mandates leading to a choice of many actions to obey them. Casuistic moral theology began to be transmitted through manuals offering detailed instructions for auricular confession and moral behavior.

The French theologian, philosopher, and mathematician, Blaise Pascal (1623–1662), attacked the Jesuit practice of casuistry.[14] He accused the Jesuits of using casuistry to favor the rich and noble while punishing the poor and lowly. Aristocratic penitents would confess their sins one day, re-commit them the next day, make a donation, and then return to re-confess their sins and receive only a very slight punishment (for example, reciting a prayer). Jesuits responded with the argument that only the abuse of casuistry deserves such criticism, not casuistry itself. Casuistry is to be used for utilitarian and pragmatic purposes as a way of rhetorical reasoning employed by utilitarian and pragmatic philosophers to persuade or impress opponents.[15]

The Roman Catholic manuals for private confession during the eighteenth-century European Enlightenment battled Deism (the belief in a deity not related to Christ) and a growing agnosticism. The increasing secularism led Roman Catholic moral theologians to a speculative analysis of life, the case of life without God—"as if there were no God" (*etsi Deus non daretur*), proposed by the Dutch theologian Hugo Grotius (1583–1645).[16] Using popular Deism, he contended that it is more reasonable to affirm the existence of God than to deny it, because the veneration of God is a natural human disposition (as Deism asserted), and it is best shown in Christianity. Accordingly, ecclesiastical moral theology identified the divine with natural law and the work of reason as the means to moral ends.

Manuals were used by "father confessors" to instruct the faithful how to make rational moral decisions. Christianity became coordinated with reasonableness and self-fulfillment. "The sacraments become means for the sanctification of the self."[17] In the middle of the nineteenth century, a renaissance of Thomism, sanctioned by the 1879 encyclical *Aeterni Patris* of Pope Leo XIII, promulgated a combination of natural law and moral casuistry. This stance was made popular by the Jesuit H. Noldin (1828–1922) in his textbook on moral theology, *Summa Theologiae Moralis*. He assumed that there was an innate human certainty about order and the human capacity to control thought processes, the ability to make logical deductions and to summarize them.[18] Moreover, casuistic moral rules were seen to be rooted in conscience which, combined with reason and an immortal soul, reflected the divine origin of natural law. Thus morality was still connected with metaphysics. The French theologian Jacques Maritain (1882–1973) retained the Thomistic dualism of a metaphysical and physical world, combining it with modern views on humanism and human rights in his 1936 work, *True Humanism*.[19] To assure the purity of a Christian humanism, Pope Pius XII rejected any non-metaphysical humanism, or "secular humanism," in 1952.

In the twentieth century, Protestant ethics did reject metaphysical speculations and flirted with secular humanism by the creation of a moral stance known as "situation ethics," "the doctrine of flexibility in the application of moral laws according to circumstances."[20] It was introduced in the 1960s by Episcopal priest Joseph Fletcher.[21] He argued the thesis that Christian love (*agape* in the New Testament), unlike love in general (often linked to desire, *eros* in Greek philosophy), is ultimate, absolute, and unchanging for all people, the true "love of neighbor."

Consequently, there are no other absolute laws, and if they are assumed and used in ethics, they must be broken and rejected. "Situation ethics" is concerned with the outcome of action, the end. Thus the end can justify the means. Fletcher contended that such a moral stance is better than legalistic and antinomian stances. The legalistic approach assumes unchanging moral mandates, such as the Ten Commandments and natural law. Example: If an unchanging law mandates that murder is wrong, one may have to make exceptions for killing in self-defense, killing in war, or killing unborn children, etc. This kind of casuistic ethics tried to achieve a balance between various situations without much regard for a proper distinction between law and gospel—the hallmark of Protestant ethics anchored in the theology of Augustine (354–430), who viewed Christian life as a conflict between evil, which must be contained by law, and the gospel, which is to be communicated as the promise of having a future in the eternal "city of God" (the title of Augustine's most famous work). Situation ethics is imbedded in existentialism, "a philosophical theory or approach that emphasizes the existence of the individual person as a free and responsible agent determining their own development through acts of the will."[22] This ethics has been traced to Søren Kierkegaard (1813–1855), and was expounded by the German philosopher Martin Heidegger (1889–1976) and the French playwright/novelist Jean-Paul Sartre (1905–1980). Protestant "situation ethics" could be called "existential casuistry" in contrast to the "ontological casuistry" espoused by Catholic neo-Thomists.

Probabilism

A radical and quite controversial version of moral theology is "Probabilism," a moral theory which holds that, in cases of doubt about the correct attitude, "one can remove the doubt by deciding in favor of an action for which there are good reasons, even though there may be better reasons for choosing the contrary."[23] Or more simply defined, it is "a theory of probability, subject to or involving chance variation."[24] This mind-boggling, rational gymnastics originated in medieval scholasticism and its treatment of the problem of moral uncertainty, based on a reflection on faith and morals by the apostle Paul when he dealt with the problem of judging others.

It is good not to eat meat or drink wine or do anything that makes your brother or sister stumble. The faith that you have, have as your own conviction before God. Blessed are those who have no reason to condemn themselves because of what they approve. But those who have doubts are condemned if they eat, because they do not act from faith; for whatever does not proceed from faith is sin. (Rom 14:21-23)

Medieval theologians proposed three rational procedures to remove doubt, especially when a divine mandate, a natural law, or canon law are at stake. The first procedure is to prefer the choice of a more certain (*tutior* in Latin) alternative which reduces the risk of sinning by obeying the law; this procedure was called "Tutiorism." The second procedure recommends a decision for that alternative which seems to be more probable (*probabilior* in Latin) or more plausible. This option was called "Probabiliorism." The third procedure permits the choice of two possibilities, provided that they are equally probable (*aeque probabiles*); this procedure was called "Equiprobabilism."

The Dominican moralist Bartholomew of Medina (1527–1581) proposed a fourth hair-splitting way. "It seems to me," he declared in 1577, "that, if an opinion is probable, one is allowed to follow it, even though the contrary might be more probable" (*sed mihi videtur, si est opinion probabilis, licitum est eam sequi, licet opposita probabilior sit*).[25] He followed a tradition that had distinguished between doubt or indecision, and an opinion that, out of fear or misgivings about the opposite, prefers one side of the alternative. In the face of rational confusion about all kinds of probable opinions, indeed errors, Medina recommended an opinion that is truly probable and worth discussing when held by wise minds and supported by good argumentation. One should follow such an opinion because it prevents searching for more probable opinions, which might lead to greater sinning. Pastoral care for the penitent quickly became attracted to Probabilism in order to find a way out of the moral embarrassment generated by the system of sins and virtues. Father confessors, especially in the Jesuit Order, often thought of ever more probable ways to detect sins and then provide ways of satisfaction. Confused by a hair-splitting casuistry, the repentance of sins and their forgiveness through the sacrament of penance often led to a moral laxity that ignored or denied the casuistry of a proper Probabilism. Such laxity became rampant in seventeenth-century France, where Catholicism had always been modified by a society that enjoyed more worldly pleasures than the church allowed. The liberal French attitude became known as "Gallicanism" (from the ancient Roman region known as "Gaul"); its counterpart was a conservative, pro-papal Italian "ultramontanism" (from the Latin *ultra mons*, "beyond the mountain," the Alps where Rome was located).

Moralistic hairsplitting and confusion about casuistic pastoral care ended with the wide use and ecclesiastical adoption of the moral theology of the Italian monk Alphonsus Liguori (1696–1787), the founder of the Redemptorists, also known as "The Most Holy Congregation of the Redeemer," who were dedicated to care for the common folk in the church.[26] Liguori opted for a simplified Equiprobabilism. It is guided by two presuppositions: first, that a doubtful law is not binding; and second, that a law is only doubtful if a position for or against it is kept in balance. Liguori tried to overcome scruples—"a feeling of doubt or hesitation with regard to the morality or propriety of a course of action"; being "scrupulous" means to be "very concerned to avoid doing wrong." That is why scrupulosity often creates a moral paralysis; fear of doing leads to doing nothing. So if I encounter a "doubtful law" (like the choice to turn right or left on my way to a specific destination), I am "right" to choose one direction because the cross road indicated a perfect balance. If I should end up on the wrong road, I should not feel guilty about my action because there was no indication that I could go wrong. Liguori would say that I followed the rule of "equal probability." Respect for this position and his authority as a moral theologian paved the way for a general acceptance of the validity of genuinely probable points of view. The church favored Liguori's stance and supported it by settling more and more probabilist issues through the power of the magisterium (the teaching authority of the church), especially after the promulgation of the dogma of infallibility in 1850. A popular test case was, and still is, contraception, which some Catholic moralists tried to view as "probable" since there had been a long period of silence about it on the part of the magisterium. But the papal encyclical *Humanae vitae* of 1968 ruled out any chance of viewing contraception as morally probable. It stuck to principle and ignored Equiprobabilism.

Probabilism has been, and still is, a controversial issue in moral theology because of its mind-boggling casuistry. It has been criticized even within Roman Catholic circles because it popularizes a "minimalist" and permissive morality. Some moral theologians also complained that probabilism burdens believers with a heavy legalism in order to prevent them from offending God. They cite the saying of Jesus, "Woe to you lawyers! For you load people with burdens hard to bear, and you yourselves do not lift a finger to ease them" (Luke 11:46).

Moral theology, too, has been criticized by ecumenical theologians. The critique centers on underlying theories of cognition, or epistemology. Morality cannot be established on the basis of an ahistorical view of reality, a rational structure of reality without the notion of time. Consequently, there is no objective rational moral truth, but only a subjective historical reality whose ethical value must be assessed by "practical," not "theoretical," reason (to use Kantian categories). Thus, not even the Bible is a source for normative ethics.

> Holy Scripture is insufficient, in content and method, as the source for normative ethics. Holy Scripture is no handbook of moral theology, neither does it elaborate an ethical system, nor does it represent a quarry of moral theological argumentation. Its statements are, above all in view of the arrangement of inner-worldly realms of life, frequently limited by contexts and thus need a differentiated hermeneutics.[27]

It is also questionable whether a divinely endowed sense of natural law, being created in "the image of God," is a sufficient foundation for assuming that all human beings have an equally powerful sense of knowing what is good. The rare biblical evidence for such a sense also includes the continual temptation of human creatures to pervert this sense. "For though they knew God, they did not honor him as God or give thanks to him, but they became futile in their thinking, and their senseless minds were darkened" (Rom 1:21). Moreover, the strength of any "natural" virtue is not preserved by a rational concentration on the inner self but by what has been "learned and received and heard and seen": "whatever is true, whatever is just, whatever is pure, whatever is pleasing, whatever is commendable, if there is anything worthy of praise, think about these things. Keep on doing the things that you have *learned and received and heard and seen* in me" (Phil 4:8-9; italics added). Faith is not synonymous with self-knowledge, and self-knowledge is limited by historical circumstances threatened by evil. That is why the "good" is known in a risky process of discovery which more often than not is handicapped by backsliding.

Confession and Clerical Conduct

The praxis of oral, or auricular, confession, the backbone of the sacrament of penance, exhibits the moral danger of casuistry. In 1547, the Council of Trent tried to remove the dangerous aspects of casuistry by putting the finishing touches on the rite of confession. Its basic function is defined as confession, absolution, and satisfaction. Confession is to be made with a sincere desire before a priest in an enclosed stall with a screen or curtain separating the priest and the penitent. There are, however, casuistic stipulations (using Aristotelian terminology) for a proper disposition of "contrition" and "attrition" as preparation for confession.

"Contrition" (from the Latin *contritio*, "a breaking of something hardened") is defined as "a sorrow of the soul and a hatred of sin committed, with a firm purpose of not sinning in the future."[28] There is a "perfect" and an "imperfect" contrition. Perfect contrition comes from the love of God who has been grievously offended; imperfect contrition arises from other motives, such as fear of hell and of punishment. The "qualities" of contrition are "interior," "supernatural," "universal," and "sovereign." *Interior* means a sincere sorrow of the heart, not merely an external manifestation of penance; *supernatural* means being prompted by the grace of God and aroused by faith, through the Holy Spirit, not merely by natural motives such as love of honor or of fortune; *universal* means a firm commitment to not sin in the future; and *sovereign* means that the commitment must dominate and cannot just be "intensive," because intensity does not constitute a true act (its "substance"). "Though contrition may sometimes be made perfect by charity and may reconcile men to God before the actual reception of this sacrament [of penance], still the reconciliation is not to be ascribed to the contrition apart from the desire for the sacrament which it includes." That is why the act of contrition must be strengthened by a firm disposition to the sacrament of penance.

"Attrition" (from the Latin *attero*, "to wear away by rubbing") is defined as "imperfect contrition," the fear of hell or punishment; it is not yet a gift, but an impulse of the Holy Spirit to denounce sin. "Although this attrition cannot of itself, without the Sacrament of Penance, conduct the sinner to justification, yet it does dispose him to receive the grace of God in the Sacrament of Penance."[29] This is a hairsplitting definition of the difference between contrition and attrition! Absolution from sins means reconciliation with the church and forgiveness of sins before God. Satisfaction consists of submission to God and of assigned actions reflecting distance from the world. Although the questions asked at private confessions are to be confidential, some priests make them known; they do so, it seems, for the purpose of making parishioners more comfortable, or to attract outsiders. A large American parish published a complete list of questions based on the Ten Commandments. The list of questions on sexuality and marriage seem to be longer than the lists pertaining to other commandments. Here is the list of questions on the Fifth Commandment ("You shall not kill"), focusing on the sanctity of life, and on the Sixth Commandment ("You shall not commit adultery").[30]

> *Fifth* (section on abortion): Did I have an abortion, or advise someone else to have an abortion? (One who procures an abortion is automatically excommunicated, as is anyone who is involved in an abortion, Canon 1398. The excommunication will be lifted in the sacrament of reconciliation [penance]). Did I use or cause my spouse to use birth control pills (whether or not realizing that birth control pills do abort the fetus if and when conceived?)

> *Sixth*: Did I willfully entertain impure thoughts or desires? Did I use impure or suggestive words? Tell impure stories? Listen to them? Did I deliberately look at impure TV, videos, plays, pictures or movies? Or deliberately read impure materials? Did I commit impure acts by myself (masturbation)? Did I commit impure acts with another—fornication (premarital sex), adultery (sex with a married person)? Did I practice artificial birth control (by pills, device, withdrawal)? Did I marry or advise anyone to marry outside the Church? Did I avoid occasions of impurity? Did I try to control my thoughts? Did I engage in homosexual activity? Did I respect all members of the opposite sex, or have I thought of other people as objects? Did I or my spouse have sterilization done? Did I abuse my marriage rights?

The proper definition of the sacrament of penance has been plagued by improper, indeed abusive, aspects, as illustrated by a businesslike attitude on the part of the penitent and a detectivelike probing on the part of priests. Medieval manuals have grown into massive tomes with a rich casuistry on how to hunt down and confess sins, especially in the realm of human sexuality. Rich families have "hired" their own father confessors in order to have a convenient way to do penance, often with an abusive sense of "guaranteed" absolution and satisfaction. Since the entire process of auricular confession is protected by a canon law of secrecy, abuses can remain undetected and legal verdicts are often puzzling. Case in point: one member of the famous Kennedy family in the United States, Sheila Rauch Kennedy, the spouse of Joseph P. Kennedy, objected to the annulment of her marriage in 1985 on the basis of Canon 1095. This canon allows a wide range of psychological factors to determine whether a marriage was "real." Since 57,000 annulments were granted in the year 2006, secular lawyers and Catholic theologians have questioned whether canon law truly protects the sacrament of marriage. Mrs. Kennedy was married for twelve years and had two children when a tribunal of the Archdiocese of Boston annulled the marriage, declaring that the marriage was never valid and that the children were not the offspring of a true Catholic marriage. A decade later, the Vatican agreed with Mrs. Kennedy and reversed the decision. In her editorial, "The Church's 'Loose Canon,'" she writes,

> There has to be a better way to protect the sanctity of marriage and show compassion to Catholics who wish to remarry after divorce. Invalidating marriages and dragging their defenders through psychological mud is hardly a Christian act.[31]

The epidemic of pedophilia among Roman Catholic priests has prompted casuistic rules. The Archdiocese of Cincinnati, for example, issued a list of "unacceptable acts" for priests, saying they should "not kiss, tickle, or wrestle children"; the latest version of the archdiocese's Decree on Child Protection prohibits "bear hugs, lap-sitting, and piggyback riding." But priests may "shake children's hands, pat them on the back, and give high-fives." The archdiocese declares that it updates the rules every five years.[32]

Some Protestant churches (like the Church of England) have laws derived from ecclesiastical ballots cast by bishops and, at times, by laypeople. But they have retained the non-sacramental custom of private confession (Anglican and Lutheran, for example), with its law of secrecy that is usually accepted by secular authorities and protects priests and confessors from legal prosecution in criminal cases.

Penultimate Christian Formation

The history of uniform and casuistic morality discloses a tradition which is theologically grounded in a pre-Christian metaphysical dualism. Fear of punishment on earth and idealistic promises of heaven have created more anxiety than serenity. People were tried by the special class of priests who, like prosecuting attorneys in court, exposed sins and offered forgiveness linked to satisfaction by way of a host of good works. Moral theology made a greater effort to cross-examine penitents than to lead them to the cross of Christ. It presupposed that lay people could not receive absolution from sins without a psychological analysis ranging from the power of intention to the desire for freedom from guilt. Unreliable proverbial wisdom seemed to guide the sacrament of penance, as exemplified by the sayings, "The road to hell is paved with good intentions," and "The devil is in the details."

When the Bible deals with promises, confessions, and oaths, it recommends a simple, moral clarity. "Let your word be 'Yes, Yes,' or 'No, No;' anything more than this comes from the evil one" (Matt 5:37). Jesus chides his first disciples for making untrustworthy confessions. "Why do you call me 'Lord, Lord,' and do not do what I tell you?" Such confessions are like a house without solid foundations that will not stand the tide of a flood (Luke 6:46-49).

The task of a moral theology or Christian ethics is not to develop casuistic rules linked to psychological analysis, but to provide catechetical instruction for a realistic spiritual formation. This formation, or building of Christian character, should be based on a Christ-centered faith that anticipates a transition from the world to a never-ending future with God through Christ. This faith, grounded in the gospel, makes spiritual formation penultimate and eschatological because Christians live in the interim between the first and second advents of Christ. The rational makeup of such a formation, its "system," or epistemology, is to be based on "historical reason," as it were, that is, on categories of time and space, rather than on metaphysical, timeless speculations. Its form should be a handbook or catechism, also known as "enchiridion" (from the Greek *encheiridion*, "something put into the hands") or a "dagger" for Christians as soldiers fighting evil—a promise made in the liturgy of baptism ("Do you renounce evil, the devil and all his empty promises?"). The basic purpose of spiritual formation is to anchor Christian life in the principal biblical ethical mandates: justice and love of neighbor (Mic 6:8; Matt 22:39).

These mandates remove self-love from the center of life. Using the paradigm of the cross, in contrast to the categories of ancient classical metaphysics, one can say that the human mind must bend sideways, as it were, from the center of the cross, from faith, to the sidebar, in the direction of love and service in the world. For without such a disciplined move, reason always tries to go upward, trying to storm heaven and use good works to merit salvation. That is why Christian life must endure the most elemental conflict between ego power and gospel power, between the desire to take God's place and the service of discipleship in Christ: "Let the same mind be in you that was in Christ Jesus" (Phil 2:5). The church as the pilgrim people of God on earth is the "church militant," or the "church in conflict" (to use traditional ecclesiological terms). It is not yet the "church triumphant" in "heaven."

Spiritual formation, healing, and salvation must begin with a realistic recognition of evil, including its power of illusion, seduction, and terror. But healing and salvation do not occur without a precise, correct, and cold-blooded diagnosis of an illness. One must be "wise as a serpent" in addition to being "innocent as a dove" (Matt 10:16).[33] To be wise as a serpent means to use the mind for a proper diagnosis in order to move to a realistic prognosis. "Serpenthood," as it were, is the sharp discernment of evil and disease. This is an essential feature of spiritual formation, sorely missed in the history of the church, which more often than not has "played God," ranging from ruthless crusades to the use of tyrannical power. Sometimes a "second opinion" is needed to clarify confusing data and to make them as reliable as possible. The best possible reality check is needed in order to assure the best treatment for survival.

Church history reveals that there is toxic spirituality, often manifested in a spiritual lethargy that leaves no room for vigilance in an evil world, and transforms "the church militant" into a lethargic church without a struggle and without freedom. Moreover, global communication today has made it possible for evil to become organized as global terror, be it in the guise of international terrorism or under the mask of a rampant religious fanaticism. In addition, poverty, disease, war, and apathy may remind us of another team of contemporary images: the four horsemen of the apocalypse (Rev 6). In such a world, Christians need more than the traditional catechisms still used in many denominations. They need a program of formation which takes into account the drastic changes during the last century—a revised catechesis for spiritual formation in the twenty-first century. What follows is a summary of a catechism or handbook for Christian formation in the mean meantime between the first and second advent of Christ.[34]

A Catechism

Preface

Modern Christians must become once again a pilgrim people, living between Christ's ascension and his return at the end-time. "Remember," he said, "I am with you always, to the end of the age" (Matt 28:20). Christians are people "on the way" to a future with "new heavens and a new earth, where righteousness is at home" (2 Pet 3:13). They are "ambassadors for Christ" (2 Cor 5:20) in a strange land. Pilgrims must travel with few comforts, face unforeseen obstacles, and remain alert in order to stay on track in an evil world; they need to be moving targets, constantly fighting evil and trying to contain it. In this mean meantime, there are scheduled occasions to gather for worship and education as the sources for new strength. In worship, the faithful are like "innocent doves" who praise God in childlike faith and give thanks for the promise of salvation from evil, sin, and death through Christ. In education, the faithful become "wise as serpents," trained for survival through effective spiritual formation.

Evil

God-talk, or theology, must begin by directing the mind to expose evil. Evil works by way of illusion, deception, fear, and terror. The human mind cannot detect or destroy its full power. Like a clever motion picture made for escapists, evil creates artificial realities, lulling the audience into illusions. Escapists love the veiling of reality on a screen through optical illusions. But they, like the realists, have to face the harsh reality of the outside world. In a similar way, Christians must continually redirect their minds to face evil.

The domination of evil is complete in idolatry. Its religious form is the disregard for the First Commandment of the Decalogue, "You shall have no other gods." Playing God is the dangerous pastime of tyrants who terrorize any opponents. But Christians are empowered to diagnose evil, just as physicians are authorized to detect disease through skillful examination that leads to a diagnosis. The diagnosis in turn is the basis for a prognosis that issues in a verdict of healing or death. This is done through the use of reason. The diagnosis of evil is the first step in Christian formation.

Justice

Once evil has been diagnosed as the most dangerous reality in the world, Christians can cooperate with non-Christians in creating laws for the restraint of evil. There must be law and order through the power of government, ranging from rules for small communities to complicated juridical configurations. Thus, the first aim of spiritual formation is justice, symbolized by the scale with the best possible balance of weight. The quest and work for justice through laws and their enforcement is the basis for human cooperation on all levels of society.

Baptism

Baptism is the initiation into the Christian community, the church, at any stage of life, whether right after birth (infant baptism) or later (adult baptism). It is a "sacrament," a consecratory act, or rite, consisting of words and actions based on the mandate of Jesus, "All authority in heaven and on earth has been given to me. Go therefore and make disciples of all nations, baptizing them in the name of the Father and of the Son and of the Holy Spirit" (Matt 28:18-19). The ritual of baptism includes a pledge to fight evil ("Do you renounce all the forces of evil?"), to adhere to the apostolic faith (confessed in the words of the Apostles' Creed) and to be alert to the gift of the Holy Spirit and to anticipate a cruciform life ("you have been sealed by the Holy Spirit and marked with the cross of Christ forever"). Thus the liturgy begins with attention to "serpenthood" and ends with a reminder of "dovehood." The baptismal certificate is proof of a new identity; it is also a passport for safe spiritual travel through this earthly life, indeed through death, to the city of God. The water bath is a symbol of the daily drowning of what is evil and the emergence of what is pure in the sight of God. In this sense, evil is exorcized, and faith is cleansed from toxic waste, though never fully before the Last Day. But baptism is the constant reminder that God is in charge. Otherwise, spiritual formation will just be a generic discipline, similar to, if not identical with, self-centered exercises of minds and bodies.

Church

The church is the gathering of those who are baptized. Members help and support each other in their daily struggle to remain faithful. If one member becomes weak, indeed is in danger of losing his or her faith, that person lives on another member's faith, just as is the case in financial survival when money is borrowed on credit and is paid back later. For faith is a shared commodity rather than the exclusive possession of an individual. The church is like a human body in which all members are to function for the good of the whole. But the head of the body is the resurrected Christ. As a visible institution, the church is always tempted by evil to become idolatrous, to be like God. That is why the church needs elected leaders, such as pastors and bishops (from the Greek *episcopos*, "overseer"), who pledge to serve and to preserve the gospel. Other designations may be used to describe such leadership. Juridical serpentine wisdom is needed to keep the church faithful.

The Lord's Supper

The Lord's Supper is the center of public worship because of Christ's special presence in the meal. It sustains and strengthens Christian life in the midst of evil in the world. That is why the celebration ought to be frequent—at least every Sunday, when Christians gather to recall the day of Christ's resurrection. In this sense, the Lord's Supper is also a celebration signaling a future life without end, "a foretaste of the feast to come."

Prayer

Prayer is the direct communication with God through the mediation of Christ and the Holy Spirit. That is why prayer should end with the phrase "in the name of Christ." Prayer encompasses all aspects of life and can consist of petitions mirroring many situations. Good prayer begins with gratitude for the gifts of God and ends with intercessions for others in need of help. Model petitions are offered in The Lord's Prayer: (1) For food from the earth to remain physically strong and healthy ("give us this day our daily bread"); (2) for mutual reconciliation so that the trek through life is not endangered by unforgiven sins ("forgive us our debts as we have forgiven our debtors"); and (3) for rescue from paralyzing suffering through the trials of evil ("do not bring us to the time of trial"). Some prayers ask for something God wisely never grants, or perhaps something is granted without any petition. But prayer is the lifeline to God.

Music

Music transcends the problem of language through words. It expresses the whole scale of human emotions, and, if played for the glory of God, it provides relief from the evils of anxiety, depression, and fear. Christians are significantly poorer without musical communication. It is the kind of dovehood needed for the pilgrimage through time into the "promised land." It cheers on through songs, hymns, and the power of compositions provided by classical and modern giants of music.

Conclusion

The catechism, with its stress on the interim life, provides education for living and dying. Death is a reminder of quality time in the world and beyond it. Christians should be known by a special freedom and doxological joy because they "have tasted the goodness of the Word of God and the powers of the age to come" (Heb 6:5). Their reality check of *evil* and *justice* shows them the abyss that separates them from God. But they receive the Holy Spirit in *baptism* as the initiation into a *church* where Christ is present in the *Lord's Supper*. They know how powerful *prayer* can be when they read in the Bible how the first disciples of Jesus proclaimed the good news about the future with Christ, healed the sick, and even resurrected the dead (Acts 9:36-41). That is why Christians oftentimes say that *music* transports them into another realm.

Only the quintessential features for contemporary spiritual formation are offered in the catechism. It starts from scratch, as it were, positioning the mind for the best possible start in the brief run of life (as did the short-distance runners in the ancient Olympic games, by using one foot to scratch for solid ground to start). But whoever is ready for spiritual formation by way of this catechism should do it with a well-developed and constantly refined sense of serpenthood and dovehood: a diagnosis of obstacles, a spiritual conditioning, and an enduring stamina of faith with a sense of childlike joy in everyday life.

This catechism is ecumenical with a common sense, sharpened by life in the twenty-first century for the ancient apostolic call to become "servants of Christ and stewards of God's mysteries" (1 Cor 4:1).

Pelagianism Revived

Moralism discloses the ancient heresy of Pelagianism, named after the fifth-century British (or Irish) monk Pelagius (d. c. 419), who taught that there is no original sin, that the human will is free to accept or reject the divine offer of salvation, and that moral deeds earn it. The church father Augustine opposed these teachings, and the North African Synod of Carthage condemned them in 418. Casuistic interrogations of penitents in the confessional, based on a Pelagian or semi-Pelagian moral theology, transform the spiritual freedom granted in baptism into a psychological dependency on fear, continually instilled by a proclamation of punishment for more sins than can be confessed. Moralism is an unholy, wayward Christian tradition because it uses honest and dishonest intentions as fear factors to control consciences. When fear is temporarily removed through absolution and satisfaction with good works, penitents tend to leave the confessional with a sense of individualistic piety that has little, if any, room for a spirited communal life. They assume that assigned "good works" will make them secure from eternal damnation. But this kind of moralism only creates a false sense of spiritual security; the fear factor returns like an unavoidable poison. It endangers the spiritual health of the church.

CHAPTER 5

Concluding Reflections

In his treatise on the proper definition and use of an ecumenical council, Martin Luther offered a witty explanation of why there is a toxic spirituality.

> Now when the devil saw that God built such a holy church, he was not idle, and erected his chapel beside it, larger than God's temple. This is how he did it: he noticed that God utilized outward things, like baptism, etc., whereby he sanctified his church. And since the devil is always God's ape, trying to imitate all God's things, he also tries his luck with external things purported *to make man holy*—just as he tries with rain-makers, sorcerers, exorcists of devils, etc.[1]

The quotation highlights the means and the end of the devil's work: to use "outward things," externals, such as religious rites, for deifying human nature ("to make man holy"). Externals can be used for good and evil purposes. Water, used in baptism, represents the change from sin to sanctification; but water can also be used to execute heretics by drowning, a punitive, not sanctifying use. Or, wine, used in the Lord's Supper, represents an "element" of Christ's "real presence"; but wine can also be used as a drug to create an artificial reality, a mind-altering, not edifying, use. Or, the Bible, as "the good book," contains the Word of God mixed with various accounts of religious history; but the Bible can also be used as a mediator of all earthly truths, guaranteed by divine inspiration. Or, an ecclesiastical overseer, titled "bishop," can be used to protect the integrity of Christian doctrine and life; but this temporal office can also be used as an untouchable, infallible guarantor and enforcer of absolutist institutional interests. Or, the ritual of the Mass celebrates the saving power of Christ; but it can also be used as a "black Mass" to glorify the devil as a substitute for Christ. Such use of the external structure of the Mass does not invalidate it. Similarly, the idolatrous abuse of sacraments, Scripture, tradition, and office does not destroy their power as mediators of the gospel. Abuse and use need to be carefully distinguished.

"Abuse does not eliminate proper use" (*abusus no tollit usum*). The baby should not be thrown out with the water. But there is the enduring temptation to empty the whole tub—symbolizing the "natural" human tendency to overkill.

Sixteenth-century Lutheran reformers used the term "adiaphora" (from the Greek *adiaphoros,* "indifferent") for "ceremonies and ecclesiastical practices that are neither commanded nor forbidden in God's word [*Mitteldinge* in German, "things in the middle"] but have been introduced into the church with good intentions for the sake of good order and decorum or to maintain Christian discipline."[2] Using the classic metaphor of the church as a ship,[3] one could speak of maritime externals as ecclesiastical "adiaphora": sails—theologians who are trained to tame the confusing "winds of doctrine" ("people's trickery, craftiness, and deceitful scheming," Eph 4:14); crew—bishops, pastors, and deacons to make sure the ship remains on course ("varieties of services, but the same Lord," 1 Cor 12:5); passengers—parishioners transported to their destination ("bringing many children to glory," Heb 2:10); lifeboats and other safety equipment—sacraments and spiritual formation to move through dangerous waters ("so that we may receive mercy and find grace to help in time of need," Heb 4:16). But there is no guaranteed prevention of accidents; shipwrecks happen because the sea is always more powerful than the ship. Similarly, the church must be built to sail well and safely in the interim between the departure from the home port (Pentecost) and the promised destination (the eternal city of God). Many calls are made at many ports; lives may be lost because of toxic food or storms; drills for discipline and safety must be scheduled often. But there is the joy of service and the anticipation of landing at a most desired spot. It is the earthly "church militant" on its way to become the heavenly "church triumphant."

There is nothing wrong with a church being well equipped for witness in a penultimate world. Although all members are spiritually equal in baptism, there is need for specific structures to bring the divine promise of salvation to a troubled world, a hierarchy, as it were, which, as in medical emergencies, needs to get into quick action from the top, the expert physicians—theologians and bishops—to the bottom, nurses and other assistants—pastors and parishioners. There may be room even for a papal office, as long as it is a position of honor which, like that of the Surgeon General of the United States, represents the saving power of global Christianity, with the advice and consent of the whole church on earth; it cannot be an infallible office promulgating inerrant truths.

But adiaphora should only serve the gospel, not replace it. The Bible as a book is not the Word of God, but contains it. An ecclesiastical office cannot guarantee salvation; it oversees its communication. Political government cannot establish "a holy commonwealth" without tyranny; its realm should be properly separated from the church rather than fused with it in a theocracy. On the other hand, a separatist seclusion from the outside world does not create immunity from sin; toxic spirituality pervades life in its totality. Moral deeds do not earn eternal life, but provide discipline to survive to the Last Day. Egotistic minds, however, pretend that the means, adiaphora, are the end. Using the paradigm of music, the four toxic Christian traditions echo the popular song of Frank Sinatra (1915–1998), "My Way," rather than the words of Jesus, "I am the way" (John 14:6).

A careful reform can be compared to the medical steps in the treatment of poisoning. First, there must be meticulous detection, leading to the identification of a particular poison and to an assessment of the gravity of the situation. Then, an antidote must be found and, if death appears imminent, a blood transfusion may have to be performed in order to purify the toxic blood. Recovery can be enhanced by a discipline of mind and body (exercise, diet, emotional balance) to strengthen the process of purification. Similarly, Christian scholarship should be scrutinized to develop enlightening programs of Christian education for pastors and parishioners, and catechetical formation should enable church members to become aware of enduring temptations and to develop a healthy resistance to any toxic spirituality. These therapeutic steps could generate enough healthy, spiritual power to isolate, or even fend off, the four toxic traditions from everyday Christian life.

A critical comparison of Christian roots and life threatening fruits in the history of the church can pinpoint the difference between true faith and unfaithful aberrations. Moreover, the roots can also be used to grow healing herbs to combat toxic spirituality. Here, the analogy with stem cell research and therapy comes to mind. A stem cell is "an undifferentiated cell of a multi-cellular organism that is capable of giving rise to indefinitely more cells of the same type, and from which certain other kinds of cells arise by differentiation."[4] In other words, a stem cell can impart its power to other cells and thus help vulnerable or damaged cells survive. Likewise, research into, and the use of, the roots of Christianity, its stem cells, can make it possible to develop an immunity to certain substances of toxic spirituality. This root tradition is powered by the Holy Spirit, which works through the earthly church and its members, if they are alert and vigilant in protecting faith from the serious threats of toxic spiritual traditions. That is why "dovehood," child-like, innocent faith, is to be combined with "serpenthood," sharp, wise discernment of evil.

Anti-Semitism, Fundamentalism, Triumphalism, and Moralism embody sin in their direct, or indirect, rejection of Christian life as penultimate, and they fall victim to a realized eschatology—as if the hope for the ultimate, eternal life with God in Christ had already been fulfilled. *This historical perversion is the most visible symptom of spiritual poisoning.* It also exhibits the human folly revealed in the story of the Fall: just as Adam and Eve ended up covering their nudity with loincloths of fig leaves, so they try to boost their ego with a "comedy of errors," ranging from exaggerations to pious lies and forgeries. Many aspects of their historical trajectories deserve to be labeled "mondo cane"[5] because of their bizarre character—the "pillar monks," the "fools for Christ," the claim of popes to be successors of Roman emperors, not to mention Fundamentalists, Millenarians, and Pentecostals who freeze, as it were, in time. Some of God's chosen people become frozen and toxic. Many contemporary Christians just dismiss such odd phenomena of church history with a smile signaling disbelief; others are saddened, and even become angered, when they encounter some horrendous claims made in the past or present and experience the pollution of toxic spiritual waste. When prejudice, ignorance, violence, and fear rule over faith, demanding guaranteed security, the church is tempted to build protective walls, comparable to a contemporary "gated community—a residential area with roads that have gates to control the movement of traffic and people into and out of the area."[6] The proponents of toxic Christian traditions have tried to organize such a community, a poisonous snake pit, as it were, with gates of "isms" trying to control the traffic of faith. But the church as "the body of Christ" on earth is not a "gated community," but a "gifted community" in the double sense of "gifted"—namely, being equipped with an extraordinary creaturely ability to brainstorm for God in its mission to the world, and, having received the Holy Spirit as "the Advocate," being sent by God in the name of Christ (John 14:26) to be sustained in its mission.

Alert and vigilant Christians have their ears burning with the final injunction of Jesus, recorded before his ascension: "Remember, I am with you always, to the end of the age" (Matt 28:20). They know that Christ is the head of the church in the present "age" and in the future "kingdom." He is experienced in the historical process of the Christian tradition, in the handing on from one believer to another. He is not experienced as a mystical resident in the human mind, or as a "truth" captured in an impressive theological formula, or as a "holy man" with miraculous power. He is the Jewish Jesus who fully embodies the unconditional love of God for earthly creatures who are trapped in the inexplicable network of evil. They cannot save themselves, but depend on outside help because they have forfeited their original power as creatures of God through the Fall. Thus, salvation from sin, evil, and death comes only from the man Jesus who died on a Roman cross and was resurrected as Christ and savior. He alone is truly inspired, eternal, and infallible. No one on earth can "own" him, "box him in," or "reserve" him as the holy host of the church.

This Christ-centered, cruciform insight is the leitmotif, the "red line," the "rubric," that guides, unites, and equips Christians to be "ambassadors for Christ" in the world (2 Cor 5:20). Such faith is best summarized in doxological terms, as the apostle Paul did in the letter to his congregation in Rome.

Who will separate us from the love of Christ? Will hardship, or distress, or persecution, or famine, or nakedness, or peril, or sword? . . . No, in all these things we are more than conquerors through him who loved us. For I am convinced that neither death, nor life, nor angels, nor rulers, nor things present, nor things to come, nor powers, nor height, nor depth, nor anything else in all creation, will be able to separate us from the love of God in Christ Jesus our Lord. (Rom 8:35, 37-39)

Abbreviations

BC   *The Book of Concord: The Confessions of the Evangelical Lutheran Church*, ed. Robert Kolb and Timothy J. Wengert. Minneapolis: Fortress Press, 2000.

CE   *The Catholic Encyclopedia.* 17 vols. New York: Encyclopedia Press, 1917. Updated edition available on internet.

DS   *Enchiridion Symbolorum:* Definitionum et Declarationum de Rebus Fidei et Morum, 29th ed. Edited by Heinrich Denzinger and A. Schönmetzer. New York: Herder/Crossroads, 1953.

JBL   *Journal of Biblical Literature.* Atlanta: Society for Biblical Literature.

NOAD   *The New Oxford American Dictionary*, 2nd ed. Edited by Erin McKean. Oxford: Oxford University Press, 2005.

RGG III *Die Religion in Geschichte und Gegenwart: Handwörterbuch für Theologie und Kirche*, 3rd ed. 7 vols. Tübingen: Mohr, 1957–65.

——IV.   4th ed. Tübingen: Mohr, 1968–2006.

TRE   *Theologische Realenzyklopädie.* Edited by G. Krause and G. Müller. 31 vols. Berlin: de Gruyter, 1977–2005.

Notes

Epigraphs

1. Quotation from Bernard of Chartres (d. c. 1130), a French Platonic philosopher. The quotation is found in the treatise *Metalogicon* III, 4 (1150), written by John Salisbury, an English philosopher, historian, and churchman. The work has been edited by C. C. J. Webb (Oxford, 1909).
2. George Santayana (1863–1952) was a Spanish philosopher. The quotation is found in his book *Reason and Common Sense* (New York: Scribners, 1906), 284.
3. Jaroslav Pelikan (1923–2006)) was an American church historian. The quotation is found in *The Vindication of Tradition* (New Haven: Yale University Press, 1984), 65.

Introduction

1. "Neuralgia," in NOAD.
2. "Anti-Semitism," ibid.
3. "Fundamentalism," ibid.
4. "Traditionalism," ibid.
5. "Triumphalism," ibid.
6. "Moralism," ibid.

1. Anti-Semitism

1. Martin Luther, *Luther's Works*, ed. Jaroslav Pelikan and Helmut Lehmann. (Philadelphia: Fortress Press; St. Louis: Concordia, 1955–1986), 47:157.
2. Wilhelm Marr, *The Way to Victory of Germanicism over Judaism* (*Der Weg zum Sieg des Germanentums über das Judentum*, Bern, 1879).
3. Arthur A. Gobineau, *The Inequality of the Human Races*, trans. Josiah C. Nott (Torrance, Cal: Noontide Press, 1983). The translation is doctored in favor of racism and polygamy.
4. Bernard Lewis ("Semites and Anti-Semites," in *Islam in History: Ideas, Men and Events in the Middle East*, [London: Alcove, 1973]) points out that "Antisemitism has never anywhere been concerned with anyone but Jews." This explains the confusion between anti-Semitism and anti-Judaism in so much of the literature. The topic of Christianity's relation to Jews and Judaism has been a source of concern at least since Karl Barth's 1949 essay "The Jewish Problem and the Christian Answer" (in *Against the Stream: Shorter Post-War Writings, 1946–1952*, London: SCM Press, 1954). In this essay, Barth argued forcefully for Christian responsibility in defending Jews against the anti-Jewish heritage within Christian theology and Biblical exegesis: "Without any doubt the Jews are to this very day the chosen people of God in the same sense they have been so from the beginning . . . They have the promise of God; and if we Christians from among the Gentiles have it too, then it is only as those chosen with them, as guests in their house, as new wood grafted on to their old tree" (p. 200). Major Christian theological writings which defend Jews and Judaism, and descry the history of Christian anti-Semitism and anti-Judaism include Malcolm Hay, *The Roots of Christian Anti-Semitism* and Rosemary Radford Ruether, *Faith and Fratricide: The Theological Roots of Anti-Semitism*.
5. So argued in one of the best introductions to the history of anti-Judaism, by Albert S. Lindemann, *Anti-Semitism before the Holocaust* (New York: Pearson, 2000).
6. Ibid., 15.
7. Ibid.
8. Ibid.
9. Ibid.
10. For a challenge to the traditional understanding of the role of the crowd, see John Dominic Crossan, "Jewish Crowd and Roman Governor," in *Mel Gibson's Bible: Religion, Popular Culture, and* The Passion of Christ, ed. Timothy K. Beal and Tod Linafelt (Chicago: University of Chicago Press, 2006).
11. Frederick M. Schweitzer, "Medieval Perceptions of Jews and Judaism," in *Jewish-Christian Encounters over the Centuries: Symbiosis, Prejudice,*

Holocaust, Dialogue, ed. Marvin Perry and Frederick M. Schweitzer (New York: Lang, 1994), 147. This book is the best source for the history of Jewish-Christian relations.

12. This is an interpretation that was probably added after Paul's death, perhaps by Roman zealots. Besides linguistic evidence through text criticism, there is also evidence that early Christian writers transferred the responsibility for the death of Jesus from Romans to the Jews. See Daryl Schmidt, "1 Thessalonians 2:13: Linguistic Evidence for an Interpolation," *JBL* 102 (1983): 269–79; and Helmut Koester, "Jesus the Victim," *JBL* 111 (1992): 10.

13. Robert Michael, "Anti-Semitism and the Church Fathers," in *Jewish-Christian Encounters over the Centuries: Symbiosis, Prejudice, Holocaust, Dialogue,* ed. Marvin Perry and Frederick M. Schweitzer (New York: Lang, 1994), 115 on Chrysostom. 115 on Augustine.

14. Frederick M. Schweitzer, "Medieval Perceptions," 133–38.

15. Ibid., 136.

16. Ibid., 144.

17. Scarlett Freund and Teofilio Ruiz, "Jews, Conversos, and the Inquisition in Spain," in Perry and Schweitzer, *Jewish-Christian Encounters,* 169–95.

18. Lindemann, *Anti-Semitism,* 23.

19. Schweitzer, "Medieval Perceptions," 160.

20. Muslims had to wear a blue patch. In some regions, Jews were required to wear a cone-shaped pointed hat, and on high Christian festivals they were not permitted to leave their ghettos. Detailed study of these and other anti-Ghetto measures in Solomon Grayzel, *The Church and the Jews in the XIIIth Century: A Study of their Relations during the Years 1198–1254,* 2nd rev. ed. (New York: Hermon Press, 1966); see also Schweitzer, "Medieval Perceptions."

21. Schweitzer, "Medieval Perceptions," 146.

22. Ibid., 142.

23. Heiko A. Oberman, *The Roots of Anti-Semitism in the Age of Renaissance and Reformation,* trans. James I. Porter (Philadelphia: Fortress Press, 1984), 64.

24. Ibid., 84.

25. Luther, *Luther's Works,* 45:201.

26. Ibid., 229.

27. Ibid., 47:96; italics added.

28. Ibid., 267. On the impact of the treatise, see Johannes Wallmann, "The Reception of Luther's Writings on the Jews from the Reformation to the End of the Nineteenth Century," in *Stepping Stones to Further Jewish-Christian Relations: Key Lutheran Statements,* ed. Harold H. (Minneapolis: Fortress Press, 1990), 120–44; see also Eric W. Gritsch, "Luther and the Jews: Toward a Judgment in History" in Ditmanson, *Stepping Stones,* 104–119; and "The

Jews in Reformation History," in Perry and Schweitzer, *Jewish-Christian Encounters*, 197–212.

29. John Calvin, *The Institutes of the Christian Religion* (1559), III.19.17, quoted in *John Calvin: The Institutes of the Christian Religion*, ed. Tony Lane and Hilary Osborne (Grand Rapids: Baker, 1987), 195.

30. Quoted in Bernard Cottret, *Calvin: A Biography*, trans. Wallace McDonald (Grand Rapids: Eerdmans, 1995), 315.

31. See Gritsch, "The Jews in Reformation, 202–4.

32. Ibid., 203.

33. See Susannah Heschel, "The Image of Judaism in Nineteenth-Century Christian New Testament Scholarship in Germany," in Perry and Schweitzer, *Jewish-Christian Encounters*, 215–40.

34. Lindemann, *Anti-Semitism*, 42.

35. Ibid., 43, 46, 47.

36. Ibid., 77–79.

37. See Celia S. Heiler, "Philosemites Counter Anti-Semitism in Catholic Poland during the Nineteenth and Twentieth Centuries," in Perry and Schweitzer, *Jewish-Christian Encounters*, 269–91. See also: *The Whitewashing of the Yellow Badge: Antisemitism and Philosemitism in Postwar Germany* by Frank Stern, or *Philosemitism: Admiration and Support in the English-Speaking World for Jews, 1840–1939* by Hilary L. Rubinstein & William D. Rubinstein.

38. See Marvin Perry, "Racial Nationalism and the Rise of Modern Anti-Semitism," in Perry and Schweitzer, *Jewish-Christian Encounters*, 257–59.

39. The Nazis called the Holy Roman Empire "The First Empire," counting the time from about 800–1800 C.E. They called the German Empire "The Second Empire," counting the years of Prussian power from 1870–1918. See Robert Wilde, "The Three Reichs," *European History*, E-mail Newsletter.

40. Quoted in Marvin Perry, "Racial Nationalism," 261.

41. See Ernst C. Helmreich, *The German Churches under Hitler: Background, Struggle, and Epilogue* (Detroit: Wayne State University Press, 1979), chs. 12–14. See also the critical evaluation by Robert E. Krieg, "The Vatican Concordat with Hitler's Reich," *America* 189 (September 1, 2003): 5.

42. Article 30 of the Concordat, quoted in Helmreich, *The German Churches*, 245; italics added.

43. Guenther Lewy, *The Catholic Church and Nazi Germany* (New York: McGraw-Hill, 1964), 93.

44. The phrase appears in the Encyclical "With Burning Sorrow" (the first words become the title). But the words "spiritual Semites" were omitted from the text in all Italian newspapers including the papal *L'Osservatore Romano*. See Guenther Lewy, "Pius XII, the Jews and the German Catholic Church," in *Betrayal: German Churches and the Holocaust*, ed. Robert P. Erickson and Susannah Heschel (Minneapolis: Fortress Press, 1999), 143.

45. On Pius XII, see Michael Phayer, *The Catholic Church and the Holocaust, 1930–1966* (Bloomington: Indiana University Press, 2000), 41–66. The stance of Pius XII was severely criticized in 1963 in the sensational play by the German writer Rudolf Hochhut, *The Deputy (der Stellvertreter)*. On the reason for papal silence, see Phayer, 49, 52, 61–62.
46. See Eric W. Gritsch, *A History of Lutheranism* (Minneapolis: Fortress Press, 2002), 223–24.
47. See Ruth Zerner, "Martin Niemoeller, Activist as Bystander," in Perry and Schweitzer, *Jewish-Christian Encounters*, 327–40. See also Helmreich, *The German Churches*, chs. 6–11.
48. Original text in Arnold Dannenmann, *Die Geschichte der Glaubensbewegung Deutsche Christen* (Dresden: Günther Verlag, 1933), 37–40; English text in Franklin Littell, *The German Phoenix: Men and Movements in the Church in Germany* (Garden City: Doubleday, 1960), 189.
49. See Robert P. Erickson, "Assessing the Heritage: German Protestant Theologians, Nazis and the Jewish Question," in Erickson and Heschel, *Betrayal*, 23–33.
50. Original text in Joachim Beckmann (ed.), *Kirchliches Jahrbuch 1933–1944* (Gütersloh: Bertelsmann Verlag, 1948), 63–65; English text in Littell, *The German Phoenix*, 184–88.
51. Quoted in Kenneth C. Barnes, "Dietrich Bonhoeffer and Hitler's Persecution of the Jews," in Erickson and Heschel, *Betrayal*, 128. Bonhoeffer's assistance in smuggling Jews to Switzerland was known as "Operation 7." See Eberhard Bethge, *Dietrich Bonhoeffer: A Biography*, 2nd rev. ed. (Minneapolis: Fortress Press, 2000), 817–18.
52. Original text in Joachim Beckmann (ed.), *Kirchliches Jahrbuch 1945–1948*, 26–27; English text in Littell, *The German Phoenix*, 189.
53. For Denmark, see Martin Schwarz Lausten, *Jodesympati og Jodehad I Folkekirken* (Copenhagen: Anis, 2007), ch. 5.
54. For Norway, see Bjarne Höye and Trygve M. Ager, *The Fight of the Norwegian Church against Nazism* (New York: Macmillan, 1943).
55. Quoted in Micha Brumlik, "Post-Holocaust Theology: German Theological Responses since 1945," in *Betrayal: German Churches and the Holocaust*, ed. Robert P. Erickson and Susannah Heschel (Minneapolis: Fortress Press, 1999), 175.
56. *Nostra Aetate*, in Austin Flannery, ed., *Vatican Council II: The Conciliar and Post-Conciliar Documents* (Newport: Costello, 1981), 742; italics added.
57. Quoted in Phayer, *The Catholic Church and the Holocaust*, 213.
58. Latin-English text in *Daily Missal* (Charlotte, NC: Catholic Co., 1962); italics added. Introduced at the Council of Trent (1545–1563) and restituted by the pope in a "Personal Declaration" in July 2007. In February 2008, he ordered the reformulation. See the Vatican newspaper *L'Osservatore*

Romano of July 7, 2007 and February 5, 2008. Vatican II had introduced a missal without such a prayer. Protestant versions of the Mass have a prayer about the "glory" of Israel. See below, n. 59.

59. It may have been just an informal meeting, elevated by Luke to a council issuing a decree. The text of Acts 15:6–29 varies in its transmission. For the best version see Bruce M. Metzger and Bart D. Ehrmann, *The Text of the New Testament: Its Transmission, Corruption, and Restoration* (New York: Oxford University Press, 2006). Details also in TRE 34:425–27.

60. On the mandate to circumcise, see "Circumcision" in *The Oxford Dictionary of the Jewish Religion*, ed. R. J. Zwi Werblowsky and Geoffrey Wigoder (Oxford: Oxford University Press, 1997).

61. This prophecy has become part of the celebration of the Lord's Supper as the "post-communion canticle": "My eyes have seen the salvation which you have prepared in the sight of all people, *a light to reveal you to the nations* ["Gentiles" in some versions] *and the glory of your people Israel.*" See, for example, *Lutheran Book of Worship* (Minneapolis: Augsburg Publishing House, 1978), 73; italics added.

62. I worked with the excellent commentary by Leander E. Keck, *The Letter of Paul to the Romans*, Abingdon New Testament Commentaries, ed. Victor Paul Furnish (Nashville: Abingdon, 2005). For the historical context, see 29–30. This commentary reflects a new, albeit controversial, perspective on Paul, offered by a number of scholars, led by E. P. Sanders, *Paul, the Law, and the Jewish People* (Minneapolis: Fortress Press, 1983). Accordingly, Paul does not support the old, negative perspective on Jewish law (the Torah) as a self-righteous effort to please God through "good works" (the classical Lutheran and Reformed interpretation). According to the new perspective, the law is part of the divine covenant fully realized in Jesus Christ. Why Israel does not "convert" to Christ is a mystery: only at the end of time will the mystery be revealed.

63. This is the persuasive interpretation of Keck, *Romans*, 245–46, over against the later popular view of Christ as the "stumbling block" (1 Cor 1:23). This view encourages anti-Semitism.

64. Ibid., 278–81.

65. Ibid., 286.

66. See RGG III, 6:1575–1577.

67. Keck, *Romans*, 288.

68. This formula echoes a well-known Stoic rhetorical formula, used, for example, in the *Meditations* of the Roman emperor Marcus Aurelius (161–80 C.E.) quoted in Keck, *Romans*, 288; "All things come *from* you, all things exist *in* you, all things are destined *for* you." Stoicism was founded by Zeno of Citium (d. 284 B.C.E.) and taught that there is a "divine seed" (*logos spermatikos*) in every human being, a sense, but not a real knowledge, of what is divine.

69. Jules Isaac, *The Teaching of Contempt: Christian Roots of Anti-Semitism*, trans. Helen Weaver (New York: Holt, Rinehart, & Winston, 1983), 39, 74, 109.
70. Ibid., 71. What follows is based on my essay, "The Jews in Reformation History," 204–8.
71. Isaac, *Teaching of Contempt*, 70.
72. Luke T. Johnson, "Christians and Jews: Starting over—Why the Real Dialogue Has Just Begun," *Commonweal* (January 11, 2003): 1–2.
73. Gerald C. Treacy (ed.), *The Mystical Body of Christ, Mystici Corporis Christi: Encyclical Letter of Pope Pius XII* (Costa Mesa, 1951), par. 29.
74. See above, p. 25.
75. "Declaration on the Relation of the Church to Non-Christian Religions," *Nostra Aetate*, par. 4 in Flannery, *Vatican Council II*, 740.
76. Johnson, "Christians and Jews," 2.
77. See Kendell Soulen, *The God of Israel and Christian Theology* (Minneapolis: Fortress Press, 1996). The author emphasizes the need for viewing Jewish-Christian relations in an eschatological context, as Paul argued (Rom 9–11).
78. Text in Franklin H. Littell, *The Crucifixion of the Jews* (New York: Harper & Row, 1975), Appendix A, 134–38.
79. See the Nicene Creed.
80. "Declaration on the Relationship of the Church to Non-Christian Religions," par. 4, in Flannery, *Vatican Council II*, 741.
81. There are some good primers for the Christian-Jewish dialogue; see, for example, Lily Edelman, *Face to Face*, Jewish Heritage Series (New York: Anti-Defamation League of B'nai B'rith, 1967). See also *The Sunflower: On the Possibilities and Limits of Forgiveness* by Simon Wiesenthal (New York: Schocken, 1998). On the dialogue between Lutherans and Jews, see *Christian Witness and the Jewish People*, Report of the Consultation held under the auspices of the Lutheran World Federation in 1975 in Oslo, ed. Arne Sovik (Geneva: Lutheran World Federation, 1976).
82. See Alan Davies, "The Holocaust and Christian Thought," in Perry and Schweitzer, *Jewish-Christian Encounters*, 343. The essay summarizes the work of a number of theologians and contends that theological reflection must move beyond Paul. See the initial steps proposed by Edward H. Flannery, "Israel Reborn: Some Theological Perspectives," in *Jewish-Christian Encounters over the Centuries: Symbiosis, Prejudice, Holocaust, Dialogue*, ed. Marvin Perry and Frederick M. Schweitzer (New York: Lang, 1994), 368–87.
83. How biblical justice can work today in the United States after the terrorist attack of 9/11/2001 has been well demonstrated by Dan O. Via, *Divine Justice, Divine Judgment: Rethinking the Judgment of a Nation* (Minneapolis: Fortress Press, 2007). Some scholars have challenged the assumption that

Christians and Jews have had a parting of their ways. They contend that there was an ongoing relationship in various ways, especially documented in the first centuries of the Common Era. See the collection of essays in Adam H. Becker and Annette Yoshiko Reed (eds.), *The Way that Never Parted* (Minneapolis: Fortress Press, 2007).

2. Fundamentalism

1. Quoted from Gray, "Inspiration of the Bible" 3:17.
2. "Bibliolatry," in NOAD. On Fundamentalism, see Ernest R. Sandeen, *The Origins of Fundamentalism: Toward a Historical Interpretation* (Philadelphia: Fortress Press, 1968), and Eric W. Gritsch, *Born Againism: Perspectives on a Movement*, 2nd ed. (Minneapolis: Fortress Press, 2007), 39–41. A helpful summary can be found in RGG III 2:1178–79, and detailed research in TRE 11:732–38;
3. See "Inspiration," in RGG III 3:775–76.
4. Thomas Aquinas, *Summa Theologiae*, Pt. 1, q. 1; 10, ad. 1, quoted ibid., 775.
5. *Luther's Works*, 31:25.
6. Ibid., 35:123.
7. See Robert D. Preuss, *The Theology of Post-Reformation Lutheranism: A Study of Theological Prolegomena*, 2 vols. (St. Louis: Concordia, 1970–1972). Original texts cited in footnotes. Subsequent quotations are transferred from Preus to Gritsch, *A History of Lutheranism*, 123–26, 129.
8. Text in Sandeen, Appendix A, 275–77.
9. John Wesley, *A Plain Account of Perfection*, ed. Mark K. Olson (Philadelphia: Epworth, 2007), 109.
10. Quoted in Sidney E. Ahlstrom, *A Religious History of the American People* (New Haven: Yale University Press, 1958), 818, n. 8.
11. So argued by Hodge in his *Systematic Theology* of 1874; see Sandeen, *The Origins of Fundamentalism*, 118–19.
12. Quoted from Gray, "The Inspiration of the Bible," 3:17
13. See the detailed account in Norman F. Furness, *The Fundamentalist Controversy, 1918–1931* (New Haven: Yale University Press, 1954), ch. 5.
14. Sidney E. Ahlstrom, "From Puritanism to Evangelicalism: A Critical Perspective," in *The Evangelicals: What They Believe, Who They Are, Where They Are Changing*, ed. David F. Wells and John D. Woodbridge (Nashville: Abingdon, 1975), 270–71. In Germany, "evangelical" (*evangelisch*) is the legal definition for "Protestant." How "Evangelicalism" has shaped American Christianity is analyzed in Garry Wills, *Head and Heart: American Christianities* (New York: Penguin, 2007). It is one of two "Christianities"— "mindlessly enthusiastic, all heat and no light." The other is the religion of the European Enlightenment (linked to the "founding fathers") which is

"desiccated and cerebral, all light and no heat." Both exist in "an absolute or sterile stultifying division."

15. This and subsequent quotations are from *The New Bible Dictionary* and *The New Bible Commentary of the Inter-Varsity Fellowship*, in James Barr, *Fundamentalism* (London: SCM, 1977), 41, 57.

16. C. Rene Padilla, ed., *The New Face of Evangelicalism*, International Symposium on the Lausanne Covenant (London: Hodder & Stoughton, 1976), 53; italics added.

17. Billy Graham, *How to be Born Again* (Waco: Word Books, 1977), 39–40.

18. Gritsch, *Born Againism*, 48.

19. In its widely distributed "Statement of Faith," 2008.

20. See David E. Harrell, Jr., *Oral Roberts: An American Life* (Bloomington: Indiana University Press, 1985).

21. See Susan F. Harding, *The Rev. Jerry Falwell: Fundamentalist Language in Politics* (Princeton: Princeton University Press, 2000).

22. See Mark Noll and George Rawlyk, *Amazing Grace: Evangelicalism in Australia, Canada, Britain, and the United States* (Montreal: McGill-Queen University Press, 1994). In the other English-speaking countries, the religious right advocates a separation of church and state.

23. E. Clifford Nelson, ed., *The Lutherans in North America*, 2nd rev. ed. (Philadelphia: Fortress Press, 1980), 534.

24. Vatican II on "Divine Revelation", par. 9. See Austin Flannery, ed., *Vatican Council II*, (Newport: Costello, 1981), 755.

25. Quoted from Vincent's *Commonitorium*, 2, 3 in Migne, *Patrologia, Series Latina*, 221 vols., ed. J. P. Migne (Paris, 1844–1904), 50:637; English text in "St. Vincent of Lerins," CE.

26. CE contends that the "Roman Catholic" meaning of the texts had not been challenged before the rise of certain sixteenth-century heresies. It also claims that the slanted meaning of the texts is supported by works of early "church fathers." But CE did not include the findings of the ecumenical dialogues that refute such claims. See "The Pope" in CE.

27. This is the conclusion of the Lutheran-Catholic Dialogue, based on an ecumenical study by Catholic and Protestant New Testament scholars; see Raymond E. Brown, Karl P. Donfried, and John Reumann, eds., *Peter in the New Testament*, (Minneapolis: Augsburg Publishing House, 1973). The quotation can be found in *Papal Primacy and the Universal Church: Lutherans and Catholics in Dialogue*, V, ed. Paul G. Empie and T. Austin Murphy (Minneapolis: Augsburg Publishing House, 1974), 16.

28. See "Wycliffe, John," in RGG III 6:1850.

29. See Eric W. Gritsch, "Luther's View of Tradition," in *The Quadrilog: Tradition and the Future of Ecumenism: Essays in Honor of George T. Tavard*, ed. Kenneth Hagen (Collegeville: Liturgical Press, 1994), 72.

30. The Tridentine declaration is quoted in Norman P. Tanner, ed., *The Decrees of the Ecumenical Councils*, 2 vols. (Washington: Georgetown University Press, 1990), 2:663.

31. Ibid.

32. Ibid; italics added.

33. The original text of the dogma can be found in DS 3074, and the English text in Infallibility CE; italics added. See also TRE 34:539.

34. The encyclical can be found in Benedictine Monks of Solesmes, *Papal Teachings: Our Lady*, trans. Daughters of St. Paul (Boston: St. Paul Editions, 1961), no. 62. A popular critique of the dogma was offered by the Swiss Catholic theologian, Hans Küng, *Infallibility? An Unresolved Inquiry* (New York: Doubleday, 1971). Küng was censured by the removal of his license to teach as a theologian of the church, but he continued to teach at the German state university in Tübingen. His colleague on the faculty, J. Ratzinger, now Pope Benedict XVI, invited him to a meeting in Rome; he let it be known that Küng was still a member in good standing in the Roman Catholic church.

35. The original text can be found in DS 2015, and the English text in W. J. Doherty and J. P. Kelly, eds., *Papal Documents on Mary* (Milwaukee: Bruce, 1954), 299–320. Text here is quoted from "Immaculate Conception" in CE. The defense of the one-sentence dogma consists of thirteen pages!

36. Ibid., 1.

37. "Other texts," ibid., 2.

38. Ibid., 9.

39. The original text can be found in DS 3903, and the English text under "Assumption of Mary" in CE.

40. *Evangelisches Gutachten zur Dogmatisierung der leiblichen Himmelfahrt Marias* (Munich: Kaiser, 1950), 21.

41. Gerhard Ebeling, "Zur Frage nach dem Sinn des mariologischen Dogmas," *Zeitschrift für Theologie und Kirche* 47 (1950), 391.

42. "Dogmatic Constitution on Divine Revelation" (*Dei Verbum*), 10 in *Vatican II*, ed. Austin Flannery, 755, 756 in BC; italics added.

43. See "Transubstantiation" in Hillerbrand, Hans. J., ed., *The Oxford Encyclopedia of the Reformation* (Oxford: Oxford University Press, 1996), 4:169–70, and TRE 1:92-93. See also *Vatican II*, ed. Austin Flannery, "On the Worship of the Eucharistic Mystery," 3f, 104.

44. An Archbishop of Canterbury, John Tillotson, who held office from 1691–1694, has been credited with this explanation. But he may have been influenced by anti-Roman Catholic polemics.

45. "Hocus pocus," in NOAD.

46. *Service Book and Hymnal of the Lutheran Church in America* (Philadelphia: Board of Publication, 1968), 1: "The Confession of Sins." Later hymnals substitute the phrase, "We confess that we are in bondage to sin and cannot

free ourselves." See *Lutheran Book of Worship* (Minneapolis: Augsburg Publishing House, 1978), 56.

47. See Kolb and Wengert, BC, 541:57.

48. See Gritsch, *A History of Lutheranism*, chap. 4, esp. 123.

49. "Abomination," in NOAD.

50. See Shira Lander, "The Formation of the Biblical Canon," in Michael J. Gorman, ed., *Scripture: An Ecumenical Introduction to the Bible and its Interpretation* (Peabody: Hendrickson, 2005), 114.

51. The texts can be found in J. K. Elliott, ed., *The Apocryphal New Testament: A Collection of Apocryphal Christian Literature in an English Translation* (Oxford: Clarendon Press, 1993), covering 747 pages!

52. Elliott, 76:4.

53. Michael W. Holmes, ed., *The Apostolic Fathers* (Grand Rapids: Baker, 1999).

54. See the evidence for such a possibility in "Korintherbriefe," RGG III: 4, 18:1.

55. See Lander, "The Formation of the Biblical Canon," 113.

56. See Jaroslav Pelikan, *Whose Bible Is It? A History of the Scriptures through the Ages* (New York: Viking Press, 2005).

57. See Martin Marty and Scott Appleby, eds., *The Fundamentalism Project*, 5 vols. (Chicago: University of Chicago Press, 1991–1995).

58. Jeffry K. Hadden and Anson Shupe, eds., *Secularization and Fundamentalism Reconsidered* (New York: Paragon, 1989), 109–22.

3. Triumphalism

1. Assertion of the Bull *Unam Sanctam* of 1303, promulgated by Pope Boniface VIII. Original text in DS 870; English text in "Unam Sanctam" in CE. Its authority is questioned in Roman Catholicism. See George H. Tavard, "The Bull *Unam Sanctam* of Boniface VIII," in *Lutherans and Roman Catholics in Dialogue V: Papal Primacy and the Universal Church*, ed. Paul C. Empie and T. Austin Murphy (Minneapolis: Augsburg, 1974), 112–19 (English text, 106–107). On the overestimated power of Boniface VIII, see TRE 7:68. The zenith of papal power is represented by Innocent III (1198–1216), who was elected at age thirty-seven!

2. Captain Edward Johnson, *A History of New England, or Wonder-Working Providence of Sion's Saviour* (London, 1654), quoted in Herbert W. Schneider, *The Puritan Mind* (Ann Arbor: University of Michigan Press, 1958), 8, n. 1.

3. Account of the miraculous conversion of Constantine in *The Library of the Nicene and Post-Nicene Fathers*, 14 vols., second series (New York: Christian Literature Co., 1990), 1:489–491. Both the first chapter ("Anti-Semitism") and this chapter have much in common with the massive, masterly,

written study of James Carroll, *Constantine's Sword: The Church and the Jews—A History* (New York: Houghton Mifflin, 2001). His film *Constantine's Sword* (2008) also includes a persuasive critique of Fundamentalism and Moralism.

4. See "The First Council of Nicaea," in CE, based on a summary from various accounts. The origin of phrase "of one being with the Father" (*homoousios*) is unknown. See TRE 24:34.

5. See *Nicäa, Konzile von 325 und 787* in RGG III 4:1453.

6. See "The Donation of Constantine," in CE, and the critical summary in TRE 8:196–202.

7. Oliver J. Thatcher (ed.), *The Library of Original Sources*, 5 vols. (Milwaukee: University Research Extension, 1971), 4:69–71; italics added.

8. See "Justinian I," in CE. He was not an innovator, but made existing traditions into law; see also TRE 17:481–82.

9. See "Pope Leo III," in CE.

10. See "False Decretals," in CE and *Pseudoisidorische Dekretalen* in RGG III 5:664–65.

11. "False Decretals," in CE.

12. See *Blondel, David* in RGG III 2:1321.

13. See *Johanna* in RGG III 3:803.

14. See "False Decretals," in CE. The theses are known as *Dictatus Papae*. Latin text in Karl Hoffmann (ed.), *Der "dictatus papae" Gregors VII* (Paderborn: Schöningh, 1933), 101–08.

15. Quotation from Caesar Baronius in "Pope St. Gregory VII," in CE

16. Ibid.

17. Ibid.

18. Decrees of the Lenten Synod of 1074.

19. Catholic legal enforcement of clerical marriage is generally traced to the Council of Trent, 1563. See *Zölibat*, in RGG III 6:1925.

20. "Pope Gregory VII," in CE; see also TRE 14:145–52.

21. See "Pope Innocent III," in CE; see also TRE 16:175-82.

22. "Fourth Lateran Council (1215)," in CE; see also TRE 16:180-81.

23. Ibid.

24. Ibid., 19.

25. See Eric W. Gritsch, *Thomas Müntzer. A Tragedy of Errors*, 2nd ed. (Minneapolis: Fortress Press, 2006); see also "Müntzer, Thomas" in Hillerbrand, *Oxford Encyclopedia*, 3:99–102.

26. Quoted in Gritsch, *Thomas Müntzer*, 89. Apostate nuns were labeled "whores," in this case Luther's spouse, Catherina von Bora.

27. Ibid., 55.

28. German text in Günther Franz (ed.), *Thomas Müntzer's Schriften und Briefe*, Kritische Gesamtausgabe, Quellen und Forschungen zur Reformationsgeschichte

33 (Gütersloh: Mohr, 1968), 222–63; English text in Gritsch, *Thomas Müntzer*, 68–70.

29. Ibid., Gritsch, 119.

30. Ibid., Gritsch, 128–129.

31. See George H. Williams, *The Radical Reformation*, 3rd rev. ed., Sixteenth Century Studies 15 (Kirkville: Sixteenth Century Journal, 1992), 553–58. See also "Münster" in Hillerbrand (ed.), *The Oxford Encyclopedia of the Reformation*, 3:97–98.

32. There is no clear evidence for or against infant baptism in the New Testament. It came into use in the third century when church and state began to merge. See *Taufe* in RGG III 6: 637:8; 638:1.

33. See Bernard Cottret, *Calvin: A Biography*, trans. M. Wallace McDonald (Grand Rapids: Eerdmans, 2000), 65–70. Calvin's major work is *The Institutes of the Christian Religion*, ed. Tony Lane and Hilary Osborne (Grand Rapids: Baker, 1987).

34. English text in G. R. Potter and M. Greengrass, *Jean Calvin* (London: Edward Arnold, 1983), 71–76.

35. Cottret, *Calvin*, 107.

36. See Roland H. Bainton, *Hunted Heretic: The Life and Death of Michael Servetus, 1511-1553* (Boston: Beacon, 1960).

37. Cottret, *Calvin*, xiii.

38. Calvin, *Institutes*, Book III, Part 22, ch. 21, quoted from Lane and Osborne (eds.), *John Calvin*, 216.

39. See "Capitalism" in Hillerbrandt (ed.), *The Oxford Encyclopedia of the Reformation* 1:258–59, summarizing the controversial argument of the German sociologist Max Weber (*The Protestant Ethic and the Spirit of Calvinism*, 1905) and his interpreter R. H. Tawney (*Religion and the Rise of Capitalism*, 1925).

40. A treatise published in French and in Latin in 1550; see the summary and analysis in Cottret, *Calvin*, 200–204.

41. Quoted from a sermon in Cottret, 307.

42. See Peter Gaunt, *Oliver Cromwell* (Oxford: Blackwell, 1996).

43. See Mark A. Noll, *A History of Christianity in the United States and Canada*. (Grand Rapids: Eerdmans, 1992), 32–34.

44. *The Cambridge Platform* of 1648, ch. XVII, sec. 6-8, quoted in Schneider, *The Puritan Mind*, 24.

45. Cotton Mather, *Magnalia Christi Americana* (1702), Introduction, par. 3, quoted in Schneider, *The Puritan Mind*, 32.

46. Noll, *Christianity in the United States*, 87.

47. Amazing details of the "trial" are found in Francis Hill, *A Delusion of Satan: The Full Story of the Salem Witchcraft Trials* (Cambridge: da Capo Press, 2002).

48. Cotton Mather, *Memorable Providences Relating to Witchcraft and Possessions*, 1689.
49. Cotton Mather, *Magnalia*, ch. 1, Part 1, quoted in Schneider, *The Puritan Mind*, 36.
50. Ibid., 40–41.
51. See Alden T. Vaughan, *New England Frontiers: Puritans and Indians, 1620–1675*, 2nd rev. ed. (Norman: University of Oklahoma Press, 1965), vii.
52. Quoted in Schneider, *The Puritan Mind*, 47.
53. Described by Cotton Mather in *Magnalia*, quoted in Schneider, *The Puritan Mind*, 49–50.
54. Ibid., 57.
55. Ibid., 85–86.
56. Ibid., 94.
57. Peter Riedemann, *Account* [of the Hutterites], 1540, quoted in George H. Williams, *The Radical Reformation*, 3rd. rev. ed. Sixteenth Century Essays and Studies 15 (Kirksville: Sixteenth Century Journal, 1992), 656.
58. Montanism generated all kinds of rumors about strange cults, such as child sacrifice and the mutilation of bodies; see "Montanism" in CE. Separation from the world in expectation of the end created and maintained the movement for a while in the second century. Luke 10:42 ("There is need of only one thing") seems to have motivated the Montanists. See *Montanismus* in RGG III 4: 1117–18, and TRE 23:271–79.
59. Quoted in "Montanism," in CE.
60. Quoted ibid. from his work, "On Running Away from Persecution" (*de fuga in persecutione*). On Tertullian, see TRE 33:93-107.
61. This is the apologetic Roman Catholic interpretation of the "counsels"; see "Evangelical Counsels," in CE.
62. See "St. Anthony," in CE. It is difficult to discern between legends and facts. The best attempt is in TRE 23:150–62.
63. See "Stylites," in CE. They did exist but the details of their lives are mostly based on hearsay.
64. See *Joachim von Fiore* in RGG III 3:799.
65. See the detailed, somewhat legendary, account of "Flagellants," in CE. There is a good, critical summary in RGG III 2:971-972.
66. See "Fraticelli," in CE, and *Spiritualen* in RGG III 6:253–54.
67. See Malcolm Lambert, *The Cathars* (Oxford; Blackwell, 1998), *Katharer* in RGG III 3:1192–93, and *Albigenser* in RGG III 1:217.
68. On the Hutterites, see Williams, *The Radical Reformation*, 637–57, and "Hutter" and "Hutterites" in Hillerbrand (ed.), *The Oxford Encyclopedia of the Reformation*, 2:282–87.
69. *Oxford Encyclopedia*, 283.

70. *Oxford Encyclopedia,* Quoted from the Hutterite Chronik; English text in the *Chronicle of the Hutterian Brethren* (Rifton: Hutterite Brethren, 1987).

71. Quoted in Williams, *The Radical Reformation,* 649.

72. See Harold S. Bender, "A Hutterite School Discipline of 1576 and Peter Scherer's Address to the Schoolmasters," *The Mennonite Quarterly Review* 6 (1931): 231–41.

73. Quoted in Williams, *The Radical Reformation,* 1077.

74. Historical summary of "the charismatic movement" and literature in Eric W. Gritsch, *Born Againism: Perspectives on a Movement,* 2nd ed. (Minneapolis: Fortress Press, 2007), 71–88.

75. The mission originated through Lutheran Pietism; see Eric W. Gritsch, *A History of Lutheranism* (Minneapolis: Fortress Press, 2002), 166–69.

76. See *Schöpfungsordnung* in RGG III 5:1492–94.

77. Quotation from various news services. I read the one in *The Baltimore Sun,* May 23, 2007.

78. See *Dionysius Areopagita* in RGG III 2:201–202, and *Engel* in RGG III 2:466. See also Johannes Brosseder, "Koinonia: Ökumenische Anfragen an die römisch-katholische Ekklesiologie," in Johannes Brosseder and Markus Wriedt (eds.), *"Kein Anlass zur Verwerfung": Studien zur Hermeneneutik des ökumenischen Gesprächs: Festschrift für Otto Hermann Pesch* (Frankfurt am Main: Otto Lembeck, 2007), 316, and see below, n. 80.

79. This is the conclusion of a Roman Catholic theologian, based on a detailed survey of ecumenical work on the *communio-koinonia* notions by Catholic, Protestant, and Eastern Orthodox scholars. See Johannes Brosseder, "Koinonia," in Johannes Brosseder and Markus Wriedt (eds), "Kein Anlass zur Verwerfung." Studien zur Hermeneutik des ökumenischen Gresprächs. Festschrift für Otto Hermann Pesch (Frankfurt am Main: Otto Lembeck, 2007), 332–33; italics added. See also the critique of ecclesiastical "imperial rhetoric," part of triumphalism, by the Roman Catholic biblical scholar Elizabeth Schüssler-Fiorenza, *The Power of the Word: Scripture and the Rhetoric of the Empire* (Minneapolis: Fortress Press, 2007).

80. Schneider, *The Puritan Mind,* 231, 232.

81. According to the *Didache,* a manual of church discipline composed in the second half of the second century; see *Kirche* in RGG III 3:1301.

82. See *Amt* in RGG III 1:337:3.

83. Quotation from *Kirche* in RGG III 3:1303.

84. "Utopia," in NOAD.

4. Moralism

1. The quotation is from the German Jesuit Hermann Busenbaum, *The Heart of Moral Theology* (*Medulia theologiae moralis*, Münster, 1650), IV, cap. 3, dub. 7, art. 2, quoted in "Busenbaum, Hermann," in *Biographisch-Bibliographisches Kirchenlexikon*, Internet Publication (Nordhausen: Traugott Bautz, 2007), 1:829-830.

2. The list is derived from the work of a Spanish Christian poet, Clemens Prudentius (348—c. 405), *Contest of the Soul* (*Psychomachia*), describing the battle between good virtues and evil vices; see "Prudentius, Clemens," in RGG III 5:671.

3. Dante Alighieri, *The Divine Comedy*, ed. John Ciardi (London: Penguin, 2003).

4. See "Marriage," in CE.

5. See "Orthodoxe Kirche," in RGG III 4:1714:8.

6. See *Luther's Works*, 48:282.

7. Ibid., 44:129: The Protestant secularization of Canon Law has been elaborated by John Witte, Jr., *Law and Protestantism. The Legal Teachings of the Lutheran Reformation* (New York: Cambridge University Press, 2002).

8. See Eric W. Gritsch, *A History of Lutheranism* (Minneapolis: Fortress Press, 2002), 151–56.

9. Immanuel Kant, *Was ist Aufklärung?* (*What is Enlightenment?*), ed. Norbert Kinsky (Darmstadt: Wissenschaftliche Buchgesellschaft, 1973), 7:53.

10. See Gritsch, *A History of Lutheranism*, 199.

11. "Casuistry," in NOAD.

12. So described in "Moraltheologie," in TRE 23: 295.

13. "Mental reservation," in NOAD. The practice was introduced by the Spanish Jesuit Father Confessor and Professor of Canon Law in Granada, Thomas Sanchez (1550–1610). See RGG III 5:1361.

14. Blaise Pascal, *The Provincial Letters of Blaise Pascal*, tr. Thomas M'Creie (London: Chatto & Windus, 1808).

15. Albert Jonson and Stephen Toulmin, *The Abuse of Casuistry: A History of Moral Reasoning* (Berkeley: University of California Press, 1990).

16. TRE 23:296.

17. Ibid.

18. Ibid., 296-307.

19. See the edition of 1938 (Santa Clarita: Books for Libraries).

20. "Situation ethics," in NOAD.

21. Joseph Fletcher and John W. Montgomery, *Situation Ethics* (Minneapolis: Dimension Books, 1972).

22. "Existentialism," in NOAD.

23. "Probabilismus," in TRE 27:465.

24. "Probabilism," in NOAD.

25. TRE 27:465.
26. See "St. Alphonsus Liguori," in CE.
27. A critical assessment can be found in TRE 27:299.
28. "Contrition," in CE.
29. "Attrition," in CE.
30. Posted on the Internet. See "St. Charles Borromeo Catholic Church: Guide for Examination of Conscience for Confession of Sins." The parish is located in Picayune, Mississippi.
31. Her editorial appeared in various newspapers. I read it in *The Baltimore Sun*, July 19, 2007.
32. Reported in *The Baltimore Sun*, August 12, 2008, 2A.
33. See the interpretation of this passage in the Introduction, 7.
34. A summary of Eric W. Gritsch, *A Handbook for Christian Life in the 21st Century* (Delhi: American Lutheran Publicity Bureau, 2005).

Concluding Reflections

1. "On the Councils and the Church," 1539, in *Luther's Works*, 41:167–68.
2. See Formula of Concord 10:1–2, in Kolb and Wengert, BC 635.
3. In early Christian art found in catacombs and churches. See in particular the famous painting of a ship by Giotto di Bondone in 1298 in the Church of St. Peter in Rome. See also "Schiff" in RGG III 5: 1410–11.
4. See "Stem cell," in NOAD.
5. See "Mondo cane," in NOAD, meaning "dog-world" in Italian, depicting bizarre behavior. It was the title of an Italian film in 1962.
6. See "Gated community," in NOAD.

Bibliography

Ahlstrom, Sidney. 1958. *A Religious History of the American People*. New Haven: Yale University Press.

_____. 1975. "From Puritanism to Evangelicalism: A Critical Perspective." In *The Evangelicals: What They Believe, Who They Are, Where They Are Changing*, ed. David F. Wells and John D. Woodbridge, 269–288. Nashville: Abingdon Press.

Bainton, Roland H. 1960. *Hunted Heretic: The Life and Death of Michael Servetus, 1511–1553*. Boston: Beacon.

The Baltimore Sun. Staff editorial. July 19, 2007.

_____. May 23, 2007.

_____. August 12, 2008.

Barnes, Kenneth C. 1999. "Dietrich Bonhoeffer and Hitler's Persecution of the Jews." In *Betrayal: German Churches and the Holocaust*, ed. Robert P. Erickson and Susannah Heschel, 110–28. Minneapolis: Fortress Press.

Barr, James. 1977. *Fundamentalism*. London: SCM.

Barth, Karl. 1954. "The Jewish Problem and the Christian Answer." zin *Against the Stream: Shorter Post-War Writings: 1946–1952*. London: SCM.

Becker, Adam H., and Annette Yoshiko Reed, eds. 2007. *The Ways That Never Parted*. Minneapolis: Fortress Press.

Beckmann, Joachim, ed. 1948. *Kirchliches Jahrbuch 1933–1944.* Gütersloh: Bertelsmann Verlag.
———. 1950. *Kirchliches Jahrbuch 1945–1948.* Gütersloh: Bertelsmann Verlag.
Bender, Harold S. 1931. "A Hutterite School Discipline of 1576 and Peter Scherer's Address to the Schoolmasters." *Mennonite Historical Review* 6:231–41.
Benedictine Monks of Solesmes. 1961. *Papal Teachings: Our Lady.* Trans. Daughters of St. Paul. Boston: St. Paul Editions.
Bethge, Eberhard. 2000. *Dietrich Bonhoeffer: A Biography.* 2nd rev. ed. Minneapolis: Fortress Press.
Biographisch-Bibliographisches Kirchenlexikon. 2007. Internet Publication. Nordhausen: Traugott Bautz. (http://www.bautz@bautz.de)
Brosseder, Johannes. 2007. "Koinonia: Ökumenische Anfragen an die Römisch-katholische Ekklesiologie." In *"Kein Anlass zur Verwerfung": Studien zur Hermeneutik des ökumenischen Gesprächs: Festschrift für Otto Hermann Pesch*, ed. Johannes Brosseder and Markus Wriedt, 312–34. Frankfurt am Main: Otto Lembeck.
Brown, Raymond E., Karl P. Donfried, and John Reumann, eds. 1973. *Peter in the New Testament: A Collaborative Assessment by Protestant and Roman Catholic Scholars.* Minneapolis: Augsburg.
Brumlik, Micha. 1999. "Post-Holocaust Theology: German Theological Responses since 1945." In *Betrayal: German Churches and the Holocaust*, ed. Robert P. Erickson and Susannah Heschel, 169–88. Minneapolis: Fortress Press.
Busenbaum, Hermann. 1650. *Medulia theologiae moralis.* Münster.
Calvin, John. 1987. *Institutes of the Christian Religion.* Edited by Tony Lane and Hilary Osborne. Grand Rapids: Baker, 1987.
Carroll, James. 2001. *Constantine's Sword: The Church and the Jews—A History.* New York: Houghton Mifflin.
———. 2008. *Constantine's Sword.* A film directed by Oren Jacobi. Vista, Cal.: Storyville Films.
Chronicle of the Hutterian Brethren. 1987. Rifton: Hutterite Brethren.
Cottret, Bernard. 2000. *Calvin: A Biography.* Trans. M. Wallace McDonald. Grand Rapids: Eerdmans.
Crossan, John Dominic. 2006. "Jewish Crowd and Roman Governor." In *Mel Gibson's Bible: Religion, Popular Culture, and* The Passion

of Christ, ed. Timothy K. Beal and Tod Linafelt, 59–67. Chicago: University of Chicago Press.

Dannenmann, Arnold. 1933. *Die Geschichte der Glaubensbewegung Deutsche Christen.* Dresden: Günther Verlag.

Dante Alighieri. 2003. *The Divine Comedy.* Edited by John Ciardi. London: Penguin.

Davies, Alan. 1994. "The Holocaust and Christian Thought." In *Jewish-Christian Encounters over the Centuries: Symbiosis, Prejudice, Holocaust, Dialogue,* ed. Marvin Perry and Frederick M. Schweitzer, 341–67. New York: Peter Lang.

Ditmanson, Harold H., ed. 1990. *Stepping Stones to Further Jewish-Christian Relations: Key Lutheran Statements.* Minneapolis: Fortress Press.

Dixon, A. C., ed. 1910–15. *The Fundamentals: A Testimony to the Truth.* 12 vols. Chicago: Testimony Publishing Company.

Doheny, William J., and J. P. Kelly, eds. 1954. *Papal Documents on Mary.* Milwaukee: Bruce.

Ebeling, Gerhard. 1950. "Zur Frage nach dem Sinn des mariologischen Dogmas." *Zeitschrift für Theologie und Kirche* 47:391, 383–91.

Edelman, Lily, ed. 1967. *Face to Face: A Primer in Dialogue.* Jewish Heritage Series. New York: Anti-Defamation League of B'nai B'rith.

Elliott, J. K., ed. 1993. *The Apocryphal New Testament: A Collection of Apocryphal Christian Literature in English Translation.* Oxford: Clarendon.

Empie, Paul C., and T. Austin Murphy, eds. 1974. *Papal Primacy and the Universal Church: Lutherans and Catholics in Dialogue, V.* Minneapolis: Augsburg Publishing House.

Erickson, Robert P., and Susannah Heschel, eds. 1999. *Betrayal: German Churches and the Holocaust.* Minneapolis: Fortress Press.

————. 1999. "Assessing the Heritage: German Protestant Theologians, Nazis, and the Jewish Question." In *Betrayal: German Churches and the Holocaust,* ed. Robert P. Erickson and Susannah Heschel, 23–33. Minneapolis: Fortress Press.

Evangelisches Gutachten zur Dogmatisierung der leiblichen Himmelfahrt Marias. 1950. Munich: Kaiser.

Flannery, Austin, ed. 1981. *Vatican Council II: The Conciliar and Post-Conciliar Documents.* Newport: Costello.

Flannery, Edward H. 1994. "Israel Reborn: Some Theological Perspectives." In *Jewish-Christian Encounters over the Centuries: Symbiosis, Prejudice, Holocaust, Dialogue*, ed. Marvin Perry and Frederick M. Schweitzer, 369–87. New York: Peter Lang.

Fletcher, Joseph, and John W. Montgomery. 1972. *Situation Ethics: True or False*. Minneapolis: Dimension.

Franz, Günther, ed. 1968. *Thomas Müntzers Schriften und Briefe*. Kritische Gesamtausgabe. Quellen und Forschungen zur Reformationsgeschichte 33. Gütersloh: Mohr.

Freund, Scarlet, and Teofilio Ruiz. 1994. "Jews, Conversos and the Inquisition in Spain." In *Jewish-Christian Encounters over the Centuries: Symbiosis, Prejudice, Holocaust, Dialogue*, ed. Marvin Perry and Frederick M. Schweitzer, 169–95. New York: Peter Lang.

Furness, Norman F. 1954. *The Fundamentalist Controversy, 1918–1931*. New Haven: Yale University Press.

Gaunt, Peter. 1966. *Oliver Cromwell*. Oxford: Blackwell.

Gobineau, Joseph Arthur. 1983. *The Inequality of the Human Races*. Trans. Josiah C. Nott. Torrance, Cal.: Noontide.

Graham, Billy. 1977. *How to be Born Again*. Waco: Word.

Gray, James M. 1910–1915. "The Inspiration of the Bible—Definition, Extent, and Proof." In *The Fundamentals: A Testimony to the Truth*, ed. A. C. Dixon, 3:17. Chicago: Testimony Publishing Company.

Grayzel, Solomon. 1968. *The Church and the Jews in the XIIIth Century: A Study of their Relations during the Years 1198–1264*, 2nd rev. ed. New York: Hermon.

Gritsch, Eric W. 1990. "Luther and the Jews: Toward a Judgment in History." In *Stepping Stones to Further Jewish-Christian Relations: Key Lutheran Statements*, ed. Harold H. Ditmanson, 104–19. Minneapolis: Fortress Press.

―――. 1994. "The Jews in Reformation History." In *Jewish-Christian Encounters over the Centuries: Symbiosis, Prejudice, Holocaust, Dialogue*, ed. Marvin Perry and Frederick M. Schweitzer, 197–212. New York: Peter Lang.

―――. 1994. "Luther's View of Tradition." In *The Quadrilog: Tradition and the Future of Ecumenism: Essays in Honor of George H. Tavard*, ed. Kenneth Hagen, 61–75. Collegeville: Liturgical Press.

―――. 2002. *A History of Lutheranism*. Minneapolis: Fortress Press.

_____. 2005. *A Handbook for Christian Life in the 21st Century*. Delhi: American Lutheran Publicity Bureau.

_____.2006. *Thomas Müntzer: A Tragedy of Errors*, 2nd ed. Minneapolis: Fortress Press.

_____. 2007. *Born Againism: Perspectives on a Movement*. 2nd ed. Minneapolis: Fortress Press.

Hadden, Jeffrey K., and Anson Shupe, eds. 1989. *Secularization and Fundamentalism Reconsidered*. New York: Paragon.

Harding, Susan F. 2000. *The Rev. Jerry Falwell: Fundamentalist Language in Politics*. Princeton: Princeton University Press.

Harrell, David E., Jr. 1988. *Oral Roberts: An American Life*. Bloomington: Indiana University Press.

Hay, Malcolm. 1984. *The Roots of Christian Anti-Semitism*. New York: Anti-Defamation League of B'nai B'rith.

Heiler, Celia S. 1994. "Philosemites Counter Antisemitism in Catholic Poland during the Nineteenth and Twentieth Centuries." In *Jewish-Christian Encounters over the Centuries: Symbiosis, Prejudice, Holocaust, Dialogue*, ed. Marvin Perry and Frederick M. Schweitzer, 269–91. New York: Peter Lang.

Helmreich, Ernst C. 1979. *The German Churches under Hitler: Background, Struggle, and Epilogue*. Detroit: Wayne State University Press.

Heschel, Susannah. 1994. "The Image of Judaism in 19th Century Christian New Testament Scholarship in Germany." In *Jewish-Christian Encounters over the Centuries: Symbiosis, Prejudice, Holocaust, Dialogue*, ed. Marvin Perry and Frederick M. Schweitzer, 215–40. New York: Peter Lang.

Hill, Francis. 2002. *A Delusion of Satan: The Full Story of the Salem Witchcraft Trials*. Cambridge: da Capo Press.

Hillerbrand, Hans. J., ed. 1996. *The Oxford Encyclopedia of the Reformation*. 4 vols. Oxford: Oxford University Press.

Hoffmann, Karl, ed. 1933. *Der "dictatus papae" Gregors VII*. Paderborn: Schöningh.

Holmes, Michael W., ed. 1999. *The Apostolic Fathers: Greek Text and English Translation*. Grand Rapids: Baker.

Höye, Bjarne, and Trygve M. Ager. 1943. *The Fight of the Norwegian Church against Nazism*. New York: Macmillan.

Isaac, Jules. 1983. *The Teaching of Contempt: Christian Roots of Anti-Semitism*, trans. Helen Weaver. New York: Rinehart & Winston.

Johnson, Luke T. 2003. "Christians and Jews: Starting over—Why the Real Dialogue Has Just Begun." *Commonweal*, January 11:1–2.

Jonsen, Albert, and Stephen Toulmin. 1990. *The Abuse of Casuistry: A History of Moral Reasoning*. Berkeley: University of California Press.

Kant, Immanuel. 1973. *Was ist Aufklärung?* Edited by Norbert Kinsky. Darmstadt: Wissenschaftliche Buchgesellschaft.

Keck, Leander E. 2005. *The Letter of Paul to the Romans*. Edited by Victor Paul Furnish. Abingdon New Testament Commentaries. Nashville: Abingdon.

Koester, Helmut. 1992. "Jesus the Victim." *Journal of Biblical Literature* 111:10.

Kolb, Robert, and Timothy J. Wengert, eds. 2000. *The Book of Concord: The Confessions of the Evangelical Lutheran Church*. Minneapolis: Fortress Press.

Krieg, Robert E. 2003. "The Vatican Concordat with Hitler's Reich." *America* 189, September 1:5.

Küng, Hans. 1971. *Infallbility? An Unresolved Inquiry*. New York: Doubleday.

Lambert, Malcolm. 1998. *The Cathars*. Oxford: Blackwell.

Lander, Shira. 2005. "The Formation of the Biblical Canon." In *Scripture: An Ecumenical Introduction to the Bible and its Interpretation*, ed. Michael J. Gorman, 103–17. Peabody: Hendrickson.

Lewis, Bernard. 1973. "Semites and Anti-Semites." In *Islam in History: Ideas, Men, and Events in the Middle East*. London: Alcove.

Lewy, Guenther. 1964. *The Catholic Church and Nazi Germany*. New York: McGraw-Hill.

———. 1999. "Pius XII, the Jews and the German Catholic Church." In *Betrayal: German Churches and the Holocaust*, ed. Robert P. Erickson and Susannah Heschel, 129–48. Minneapolis: Fortress Press.

Lindemann, Albert S. 2000. *Anti-Semitism before the Holocaust*. New York: Pearson.

Littell, Franklin. 1960. *The German Phoenix: Men and Movements in the Church in Germany*. Garden City: Doubleday.

———. 1975. *The Crucifixion of the Jews*. New York: Harper & Row.

Lutheran Book of Worship. 1978. Minneapolis: Augsburg.

Luther, Martin. *D. Martin Luthers Werke, Kritische Gesamtausgabe*. 70 vols. Weimar: Verlag Hermann Böhlaus Nachfolger, 1883–.

———. 1955–86. *Luther's Works*. Edited by Jaroslav Pelikan and Helmut Lehmann. 55 vols. Philadelphia: Fortress Press.

Maritain, Jacques. 1938. *True Humanism*. Santa Clarita, Cal.: Books for Libraries.

Marr, Wilhelm. 1879. *Der Weg zum Sieg des Germanentums über das Judentum*. Bern.

Marty, Martin, and Scott Appleby, eds. 1991–95. *Fundamentalism*. 5 vols. Chicago: Chicago University Press,

Metzger, Bruce M., and Bart D. Ehrman. 2006. *The Text of the New Testament: Its Transmission, Corruption, and Restoration*, 4th ed. New York: Oxford University Press.

Michael, Robert. 1994. "Anti-Semitism and the Church Fathers." In *Jewish-Christian Encounters over the Centuries: Symbiosis, Prejudice, Holocaust, Dialogue*, ed. Marvin Perry and Frederick M. Schweitzer, 101–29. New York: Peter Lang.

Migne, J. P., ed. 1844–1904. *Patrologia: Series Latina*. 221 vols. Paris.

Nelson, Clifford E., ed. 1980. *The Lutherans in North America*. Second rev. ed. Philadelphia: Fortress Press.

Noll, Mark A. 1992. *A History of Christianity in the United States and Canada*. Grand Rapids: Eerdmans.

———, and George A. Rawlyk. 1994. *Amazing Grace: Evangelicalism in Australia, Canada, Britain, and the United States*. Montreal: McGill-Queen University Press.

Oberman, Heiko A. 1984. *The Roots of Anti-Semitism in the Age of Renaissance and Reformation*. Trans. James I. Porter. Philadelphia: Fortress Press.

Padilla, Rene, C., ed. 1976. *The New Face of Evangelicalism: An International Symposium on the Lausanne Covenant*. London: Hodder & Stoughton.

Pascal, Blaise. 1808. *The Provincial Letters of Blaise Pascal*. Trans. Thomas M'Crie. London: Chatto & Windus.

Pelikan, Jaroslav. 1984. *The Vindication of Tradition*. New Haven: Yale University Press.

———. 2005. *Whose Bible Is It? A History of the Scriptures through the Ages*. New York: Viking Press.

Perry, Marvin, and Frederick M. Schweitzer, eds. 1994. *Jewish-Christian Encounters over the Centuries: Symbiosis, Prejudice, Holocaust, Dialogue.* New York: Peter Lang.

————. 1994. "Racial Nationalism and the Rise of Modern Anti-Semitism." In *Jewish-Christian Encounters over the Centuries: Symbiosis, Prejudice, Holocaust, Dialogue,* ed. Marvin Perry and Frederick M. Schweitzer, 231–67. New York: Peter Lang.

Phayer, Michael. 2000. *The Catholic Church and the Holocaust, 1930–1966.* Bloomington: Indiana University Press.

Potter, G. R., and M. Greengrass. 1983. *Jean Calvin.* London: Edward Arnold.

Preuss, Robert D. 1972. *The Theology of Post-Reformation Lutheranism: A Study of Theological Prolegomena.* 2 vols. St. Louis: Concordia.

Ruether, Rosemary Radford. 1996. *Faith and Fratricide: The Theological Roots of Anti-Semitism.* Eugene, Ore.: Wipf & Stock.

Salisbury, John. 1906. *Metalogicon.* Edited by C. C. J. Webb. Oxford.

Sandeen, Ernest R. 1968. *The Origins of Fundamentalism: Toward a Historical Interpretation.* Philadelphia: Fortress Press.

Santayana, George. 1906. *Reason and Common Sense.* New York: Scribner's.

Schaff, Philip, and Henry Wace, eds. 1990. *Nicene and Post-Nicene Fathers.* Second Series, 14 vols. New York: Christian Literature Co.

Schmidt, Daryl. 1983. "1 Thessalonians 2:13: Linguistic Evidence for an Interpolation." *Journal of Biblical Literature* 102: 269–79.

Schneider, Herbert W. 1958. *The Puritan Mind.* Ann Arbor: University of Michigan Press.

Schüssler Fiorenza, Elisabeth. 2007. *The Power of the Word: Scripture and the Rhetoric of the Empire.* Minneapolis: Fortress Press.

Schwarz Lausten, Martin. 2007. *Jodesympati og Jodehad I Folkekirken.* Copenhagen: Anis, 2007.

Schweitzer, Frederick M. 1994. "Medieval Perceptions of Jews and Judaism." In *Jewish-Christian Encounters over the Centuries: Symbiosis, Prejudice, Holocaust, Dialogue,* ed. Marvin Perry and Frederick M. Schweitzer, 131–68. New York: Peter Lang.

Scofield, Cyrus Ingerson, ed. 2007. *The Scofield Reference Bible.* Oxford: Oxford University Press.

Service Book and Hymnal of the Lutheran Church in America. 1968. Philadelphia: Board of Publication.

Soulen, Kendall. 1996. *The God of Israel and Christian Theology.* Minneapolis: Fortress Press.

Sovik, Arne, ed. 1976. *Christian Witness and the Jewish People.* Report of the Consultation Held under the Auspices of the Lutheran World Federation in 1975 in Oslo. Geneva: Lutheran World Federation.

Stern, Frank. 1992. *The Whitewashing of the Yellow Badge: Antisemitism and Philosemitism in Postwar Germany.* Trans. William Templer. Oxford: Pergamon.

Tanner, Norman P., ed. 1990. *The Decrees of the Ecumenical Councils.* 2 vols. Washington: Georgetown University Press.

Tavard, George H. 1974. "The Bull Unam Sanctam of Boniface VIII." In *Papal Primacy and the Universal Church: Lutherans and Catholics in Dialogue,* ed. Paul C. Empie and T. Austin Murphy, 112–19. Minneapolis: Augsburg.

Thatcher, Oliver J., ed. 1971. *The Library of Original Sources: Ideas That Have Influenced Civilization, in the Original Documents, Translated.* 5 vols. Milwaukee: University Research Extension.

Treacy, Gerald C., ed. 1951. *The Mystical Body of Christ, Mystici Corporis Christi: Encyclical Letter of Pope Pius XII.* Costa Mesa.

Vaughan, Alden, T. 1965. *New England Frontiers: Puritans and Indians, 1620–1676.* 2nd rev. ed. Norman: University of Oklahoma Press.

Via, Dan O. 2007. *Divine Justice, Divine Judgment: Rethinking the Judgment of a Nation.* Minneapolis: Fortress Press.

Wallmann, Johannes. 1990. "The Reception of Luther's Writings on the Jews from the Reformation to the End of the 19th Century." In *Stepping Stones to Further Jewish-Christian Relations: Key Lutheran Statements,* ed. Harold H. Ditmanson, 120–44. Minneapolis: Fortress Press.

Werblowsky, R. J. Zwi, and Geoffrey Wigoder, eds. 1997. *The Oxford Dictionary of the Jewish Religion.* Oxford: Oxford University Press.

Wesley, John. 2007. *A Plain Account of Perfection.* Edited by K. Olson. Philadelphia: Epworth.

Wilde, Robert. "Three Reichs," European History, E-Mail Newsletter.

Williams, George H. 1992. *The Radical Reformation*. 3rd. rev. ed. Sixteenth Century Essays and Studies 15. Kirksville, Mo.: Sixteenth Century Journal.

Wills, Gary. 2007. *Head and Heart: American Christianities*. New York: Penguin.

Witte, John Jr. 2002. *Law and Protestantism: The Legal Teachings of the Lutheran Reformation*. New York: Cambridge University Press.

Zerner, Ruth. 1994. "Martin Niemoeller, Activist and Bystander." In *Jewish-Christian Encounters over the Centuries: Symbiosis, Prejudice, Holocaust, Dialogue*, ed. Marvin Perry and Frederick M. Schweitzer, 327–40. New York: Peter Lang.

Index